# EDUCATION AND DEVELOPMENT IN AFRICA

An introduction to the study of the role education may play in national development intended primarily for teachers in training and in service.

## A. R. Thompson

First published 1981 by
**THE MACMILLAN PRESS LTD**
London and Basingstoke
Associated companies throughout the world.

*Printed in Hong Kong*

ISBN 0—333—30018—1
ISBN 0—333—30020—3 (paperback)

*This book is dedicated to the teachers of Africa in sympathy and faith.*

# Contents

# Part I

# Social Change, Development and Education in Africa

# I

# Social Change and Development

This study of the relationships which exist or are often thought to exist, between systems of education and the societies they are intended to serve must begin with a cautionary note. The African countries south of the Sahara with which we are mainly concerned are often studied from a pan-African point of view, and this book will be no exception. But this approach has severe limitations. In particular, it is often difficult to avoid the tendency to treat these more than forty countries as if they were a homogeneous group, to assume too readily that they share a common heritage and a common experience, and to pay too little regard to the very considerable differences between them. These differences range from the obvious considerations of size and population, wealth and economic resources, governmental systems, political ideologies and international outlook, to even more fundamental distinctions of culture and social organisation. These latter factors are deeply rooted in a long history in which, as we are at last coming to understand, the colonial experience was a relatively short-lived, if profoundly disturbing, episode. Consequently the ideas advanced in this book must be regarded as broad generalisations and tentative hypotheses to be studied critically by the reader in the light of personal knowledge as he or she seeks to relate them to particular countries. The purpose of the study is to advance questions and considerations which will assist the reader to set out in pursuit of fuller understanding of his or her own country, of its development, and of the place of education in that process. It cannot take the reader to the end of this journey.

Having said this however, it may be argued that there are indeed a number of characteristics which are common to most of our countries, sufficient to justify the breadth of this approach.

Four characteristics in particular are important to the study. The first is that, by any set of criteria in common use, all our countries may be classified as among the less-developed countries of the world. Using the common criterion of average per capita income, the great majority of African states are among the poorest countries, with only one or two (including South Africa, with which this study is not concerned) having any claim to be ranked alongside the richer of those countries commonly regarded as 'developing'.

The second common characteristic is that of cultural diversity. With the possible exception of Somalia, Malagasy, Swaziland and Lesotho, our countries embrace, within artificial and fortuitously determined frontiers, a wide range of culturally-differing groups. Each group is likely to possess its own vernacular language, its own pattern of religious beliefs, its own moral and aesthetic values, and its own distinctive clusters of social institutions, customs and codes of behaviour. There may also be significant differences in the modes of production, in the kinds and levels of technology in use by neighbouring groups for the exploitation of the natural resources available to them. Some groups are strong numerically and possess considerable capacity to secure their own interests. Other groups are much weaker, though often no less conscious of their own cultural identity. The strength of these identities has been amply demonstrated in internal conflicts within our countries in recent years and we are therefore acutely concerned with reconciling and harmonising these cultures, with generating feelings of belonging and loyalty to our new nations so that through cooperation we may seek to mobilise and maximise the development capacity of the whole people.

The third common characteristic stems in part from this. All our countries are committed to the notion of national development and are therefore seeking consciously to bring about often quite fundamental change in the lives of our peoples, change which will extend into the political and social as well as the economic spheres. Commonly, too, we are seeking to achieve this change whilst at the same time seeking to preserve as much as possible of the distinctive local cultures which, in spite of the problems they may present, we believe may also enrich our national life and contribute towards the evolution of our national cultural identity. In order that we may seek change but at the same time seek to preserve valued traditional elements, all our countries have adopted the principle of planned development whereby change is to be initiated and sustained largely by our central political authorities and whereby the energies and abilities of individuals and groups may be liberated and productively channelled within an agreed framework of national development. It may be added that all our countries possess a firm belief in the power of education to assist in this process.

Fourthly all our countries are undergoing far-reaching processes of social change. This is sometimes a consequence of conscious planning but is also to a very considerable extent independent of (and indeed in spite of) planning. These processes, through their incoherence and the variable nature and speed of their impact upon various sections of the national population, are tending to create new conditions of tension and strain between them. In certain respects change is occurring which may be damaging the capacity of our countries to develop and which may run counter to national development policy. Some would argue that rapid rates of population growth and migration from the rural areas to the towns are among such changes. But there are of course many views as to which changes are desirable and beneficial since what benefits one may be harmful to another. The point is that change is taking place and, whether we like it or not, will continue to take place; that much of this change is unplanned and uncontrolled; and that no change is likely to be equally acceptable to all sections of the population.

We shall be returning to the consideration of these various characteristics. But first we need to examine further the nature of social change and of planned development so that we may begin to consider the roles which are being played by educational systems. These are matters of which we have as yet very inadequate understanding and which are so complex as to defy simple explanation.

The origins of social change are many. It is highly unlikely that any human society has ever been completely static though some have experienced substantially less or different kinds of change from others. Every society is forced to contend with problems and strains. Some of these may derive from external forces, from the impact of contact with other peoples and other cultures, which takes many forms, and others from internal forces such as population growth or decline, natural disasters (famine, flood, pestilence), conflict between individual members of the society, and the like. Whilst it is probably true that in smaller, more simply structured and vulnerable societies more emphasis was naturally placed upon maintaining the security and stability of the society than on seeking to improve and develop it, we need perhaps to remind ourselves that changes were sometimes deliberately engineered by influential individuals and groups, and these, as Schapera has pointed out, may include persons such as chiefs who were more generally responsible for the maintenance of custom.[1] Mair has suggested that 'the social pressures which operate in a rapidly changing society are those which are to be found in any society',[2] though their strength and direction will vary and their effects will be moderated by the capacity and desire of the society to resist them. These pressures have their own origin in other factors and we can rarely trace a particular change back to a single originating factor or event, or even to a particular combination of such factors and events. The changes to which these factors give rise themselves become the sources of pressure for further change. Change is thus a continuous process without discernible beginning or end. It might be argued that for African countries colonialism was the origin of many current changes and an important distinguishing feature of the nature of social change in these countries when compared with others which have not shared this experience. Some particular changes may be attributed to colonialism, notably the establishment of larger political units within clearly defined boundaries, but even here it may be questioned whether the basic process of establishing political units from previously separate groups and communities and of drawing lines to demarcate their geographical limits was significantly different in basic essentials from the process which had been going on in Africa since the beginning of time. The same reasons that impelled colonial powers to draw lines on maps had always impelled African peoples to demarcate boundaries on the ground. Indeed it may be that the colonial experience should be regarded more as a catalyst, speeding up the process, rather than as the originating force for change.

Mair and others have viewed the changes in material culture and technology as those which have had the most potent impact upon our societies and which have been largely responsible for political and social change. Man's increasing mastery of his environment has been achieved partly through the use of new and inanimate sources of power, partly through the use of new tools (often utilising this power to multiply the effect of human effort), and partly through the extension of the range of human co-operation through new patterns of organisation. Though the impact of these developments has been patchy and uneven in our countries, on the whole production has been increased and diversified, and it has been complemented by our increasing dependence upon the exchange of goods and services, facilitated by the growth of a money economy which reduces our dependence upon subsistence production.

There has consequently occurred a trend away from living in communities which are relatively culturally homogeneous and the well being of which depends largely upon the acceptance of communal responsibility by interdependent individuals and groups, towards a pattern of living which provides new and greater scope for individual talents and initiatives and new patterns of human interdependence which are wider in scale and more complex. The growing separation of many kinds of production activities from the family and descent group has produced the change from an economy based upon primary production to one in which secondary industry – processing, manufacture and exchange – is of increasing importance. The wider availability of paid employment has left the individual with greater freedom from communal constraints, freedom to determine how he will earn his livelihood and how he will dispose of his income, whilst the development of employment opportunities outside his community, together with the availability of efficient transport and communications, has encouraged him to move physically away from his community with a further consequent slackening of communal constraints upon the way he chooses to live his life.

Instead of a limited number of employment possibilities which may in practice predetermine the way of life and status to be enjoyed by an individual, a far larger number of possibilities may now be available at least to some individuals through the growing complexity and increasing specialisation of economic and governmental activity. The same trends offer greater opportunities for individual self-advancement, with status as well as financial rewards for those who can apply their energy and ability more successfully. Whereas upward social mobility was previously largely constrained by age and parentage, roles being allocated by ascription, personal achievement is now increasingly regulated by educational attainment. These new possibilities may be enjoyed within a growing, new modern sector of national life which in many respects tends to be added to and distinct from the traditional sector, the links between the sectors being often limited (and sometimes tenuous in the extreme).

The modern sector is characterised by competition between individuals for employment and advancement, encouraging an individual to behave in the light of self-interest as he or she perceives it rather than in the traditional terms of custom and mutual obligation. Whilst many individuals who take up new roles in the modern sector will retain their loyalties to the families and communities they may have left behind, and will often continue to accept and to exercise their responsibilities to their kinfolk and communities, they will at the same time have entered into new relationships and new responsibilities of a somewhat different character. In a more traditional context a man might relate to another man in a variety of ways – as relative, neighbour, leader or follower, teacher or learner, and so on – with his overall status determined by the sum total of these relationships. These relationships would be subtle and quite complex, tending to bind members of the community closely together. In the modern sector, with its greater structural complexity, a man is more likely to enter into a set of relationships in which his relationship to another is of a single kind, confined to only one part of his life. He will also enter into a wider range of relationships and often these will be based upon formal contracts, such as a contract of employment within new economic institutions like the firm, or membership of an organisation like a trade union or a welfare club. To a considerable extent he may choose what relationships he will enter into and will have greater ability to change and vary his pattern of relationships in a way not easily possible in a more traditional and simply-structured community. Interdependence remains, and indeed is likely to be far greater and more complex in the modern sector, but is far more impersonal: a man's life may be radically changed by decisions made by others whom he does not know and with whom he may not be aware he has any relationship. This matter of relationships between people is central to our concern since social change is fundamentally a question of changes in relationships between individuals. The greater complexity of a modern society makes it more subject to change and, despite the impressive array of new institutions to regulate its life, less able to control and direct change. Not only does the growth of a modern sector tend in the ways we have suggested to weaken the pattern of relationships which has enabled communities in the traditional sector to preserve their own way of living but the differences in the patterns of relationship between the two sectors makes it all the more difficult to integrate the two within a single national society.

The creation of a national political framework with its panoply of decision making and administrative institutions has complemented the growth of larger-scale economic activities and relationships in opening up new fields in which individuals may play new roles and offering new opportunities for geographical and social mobility. But it has also introduced new relationships between government and governed. Because of its greater scale and in spite of the commonly declared democratic principle of extending opportunities for participation in public affairs to all citizens, government has tended to become increasingly remote and impersonal. Because of its commitment to planning and initiating change and its acceptance of new responsibilities for ensuring the well being of the people, government has become more directive, more concerned with intervening in the day-to-day lives of individuals and communities. Because of the greater social complexity associated with modernisation, relatively simple bodies of custom and convention have been overlaid by ever-mounting quantities of laws and regulations, the operation of which is less based upon consensus acceptance than upon compulsion. In these ways, and perhaps inevitably, the individual is diminished and systems, structures and institutions are overvalued. In recent years there has been growing recognition of the importance of people as individuals rather than as masses and sections of society which has been demonstrated in political philosophies such as Zambian 'Humanism' and in concern elsewhere for the restoration of participatory forms of government, often through decentralisation.

The trends we have described emanating from economic and political stimuli have been accompanied by normative change, changes in the patterns of beliefs and values which in the past have served to cement societies together through their common acceptance by all members. The need to find technological solutions to our material problems has encouraged a move away from traditional explanations of the nature of natural phenomena and of cause and effect towards more scientific explanations. Passive and sometimes fatalistic attitudes derived from the apparent powerlessness of human beings to deal with the forces of nature and associated with animistic patterns of belief in the supernatural have tended to give way in face of new belief in the capacity of man to solve his own problems, demonstrated in the application of new technologies. New patterns of religious belief placing man in a new and personal relationship with his God, relationships in which God is thought of as benign but allowing the individual liberty to mould his own fate, have been accompanied by the growth of secular opinion which permits the individual to reject religious ideas and to live his life according to secular criteria. Whilst these trends have liberated the minds and energies of man and reinforced other modernising factors, there have been less productive consequences also. Many of the old certainties have disappeared. Man finds himself adrift at the mercy of contending currents without a compass to tell him where he has come from and where he should be going, without reference points by which he may measure his progress. National leaders and other groups concerned with the design and reconstruction of society may possess or believe themselves to possess these things but many individuals find themselves lost in the management of their daily lives, disoriented and bewildered by change, and saddened by the gradual disappearance of many things by which they were accustomed to regulate their lives. A new generation is growing up which is more at home in the new circumstances, which tends to accept change and flux as a normal condition of life but which finds itself often unable to understand and relate to older generations or others of their own generation who stand largely outside the modern sector. The process of arriving at the national cultural synthesis to which we are sometimes told we should aspire is by no means an easy or painless one.

The trends of change which we have been discussing, which in many ways are welcomed and sought after, are therefore also extremely worrying to many of us. In the period between the world wars in particular the literature about social change in the then colonies and dependencies of European nations was much concerned about the apparently imminent breakdown of indigenous cultures, a concern stimulated by the relatively recent recognition of the quality and value of many of these cultures. There was much controversy at that time as to whether change should be brought about as speedily as possible, or more gradually in order to minimise the disruptive effects it was likely to involve. Opinion generally was that steady evolutionary change was desirable in order that cultures might adapt and absorb change as it occurred and retain their integrity. It was recognised that cultures did not consist of collections of beliefs and customs which existed independently of each other, parts of which might be changed without affecting other parts; rather, it was agreed, a culture was an indivisible whole in which the various parts were interdependent. Systems of land holding and of production, kinship ties, religious beliefs and modes of decision making were all bound up with each other. Too sudden a change in any respect might, it was thought, bring down the fabric of the society. In the event of course, changes proceeded at a pace which rendered all these discussions largely academic and thrust aside the gradualistic policies which had been evolved. However in the course of the last half century a number of things have become a little clearer.

The impact of social change has been extremely uneven. It has gone furthest and fastest where new communities have formed, in the urban centres where industrialisation has taken place and where the newer institutions of government and other forms of social organisation have been set up. It has proceeded much less far and much more slowly in those areas which have remained rural, based upon the age-old occupations of farming and animal husbandry. One man may be operating a computer whilst his father follows a way of life little different from that of his ancestors. A dual society has come into being and the problem of development is often thought of as being one of seeking to stimulate desirable change in the rural sector, amongst people who still live according to customs and beliefs which so many years ago were thought to be in grave danger of being destroyed. This may lead us to the conclusion that traditional cultures are by no means the fragile structures which they have sometimes been thought to be, that often they are robust with considerable capacity to resist and to absorb change, to assimilate and indigenise those elements of change which they have been forced to accommodate. As recently as 1974 a distinguished African historian thought it necessary to inform fellow Africanists that 'there is little ground for suggesting that there has been a sweeping wholesale collapse of African culture and values as a result of European contact'[3] and that the impact of this contact was more likely to be more far-reaching in areas of science and technology such as medical practice than in terms of general culture, life styles, ideas and attitudes. Whilst we have suggested that no clear distinction can be made between such areas, a point which will further be illustrated later in this chapter, Professor Ajayi's statement makes a point which we sometimes are inclined to overlook. We should further ask ourselves how far Myrdal's argument, based upon extensive and deeply penetrating study of Asian societies, can be applied to Africa:

> The great bulk of historical, anthropological, and sociological evidence and thought suggests that social stability and equilibrium is the norm and that all societies, and underdeveloped societies in particular, possess institutions of a strongly stabilizing character. In view of these findings the real mystery is how they can escape from equilibrium and can develop. The Western experience of scientific, technological, and economic advance may well be unique: a series of extraordinary circumstances.[4]

Even so, our concern about the harmful aspects and consequences of change, and at the same time our desire to retain our cultural individuality and identity, is justifiably strong. It has become commonplace for statements of national goals to include reference to the need to protect and revitalise national cultures in order that they may remain viable and contributing elements in the modernising process. Consequently, whether our main concern is with conserving our traditions, with stimulating desirable change or, as is true of most of us, with a selective combination of preservation and innovation, we all have one thing in common – the wish to direct and control the processes of change to create the kind of society which we wish to see. In a word we are concerned with development.

Development is not an easy term to define more specifically than this. We all can list some of the more obvious characteristics of an underdeveloped society and we can all compare such a society with a more developed one in terms of these characteristics. But we find it extremely difficult to define, except in the most general terms, what our society should look like in a more highly developed form. Consequently we are bound to be unclear about how we can best bring it about. There are many of us who have fallen into the trap of assuming that a more developed society must be patterned on the model of the modern industrial societies which we can observe elsewhere in the world and that the path we must follow should be the same as that followed by these societies before us. Of course there have always been those who have argued that the industrial societies are far from appropriate models for African countries and who have demanded that Africa should follow its own development path towards the creation of a modern society which will be authentically African. We have applauded such people but when called upon to take action in support of development we have often been disappointed that they have not given us concrete practical guidance as to how these principles should be applied. As often as not we have been in a great hurry to get something done and have been impatient with those who suggest we should hurry more slowly and should conduct careful research about the probable effects of alternative courses of action before taking our decision. The Western world offers us short cuts, technological and organisational practices which we may readily be able to adopt and then adapt. Indeed in all our discussions of the individuality of African culture, we may have been guilty of neglecting and undervaluing those features which all mankind holds in common. Many African thinkers would argue that much of what has been brought to Africa from outside, the ideas, tools, institutions and organisational procedures, should not be regarded as belonging to one culture (and therefore as being alien to others) but as being part of the common heritage of all mankind. The problem may rather be in the use we make of this common heritage. As Nyerere has argued, 'The first problem we have not solved is that of building sufficient self-confidence to refuse what we regard as the world's best . . . and to choose instead the most appropriate for our conditions'.[5]

Wherever we personally stand in this debate, we owe it to ourselves as educationists to consider more carefully what we mean by development and not to confuse the issue by vague reference to national models. Since poverty is seen to be at the root of underdevelopment in Africa, as well as elsewhere, it is not surprising that development has been thought of principally in economic terms. The United Nations has classified as under-developed countries those with an average per capita income below the equivalent of 500 US dollars, and commonly we establish our objectives and measure our progress in terms of such criteria. Since we shall be referring to some of these indices later in this book we should perhaps at this point look at some of the terms we shall be using.

We may refer to gross domestic product (GDP) which is the value of all the goods and services produced within a country in the course of a year, leaving out of account the effect on market prices of indirect taxes and subsidies. We may also refer to gross national product (GNP) which is the GDP plus any income such as interest and dividends received from outside the country and less any such payments we make to other countries. Sometimes we use the term national income to refer to GNP minus the cost of depreciation, that is the cost of maintaining the capital equipment which our country possesses; this should tell us better than either GDP or GNP what resources are actually available for further development. It must be pointed out that whilst all of these measures are extremely difficult to calculate, national income presents particular problems and consequently is less often used in practice (though the term national income may be used more loosely).

The inaccuracy of these measures, the fact that they often under-value subsistence production and are inflated by the inclusion of non-essential and non-productive economic activities, and their liability to distortion by artificially set rates of exchange for international comparisons, means that they should be used with extreme caution. However they suffer from one further deficiency of considerable importance for our purposes in this study – the averaging of national wealth per head of population conceals the great discrepancies of income which actually exist between individuals and groups. It is of little comfort to the farmer whose income level has risen only slightly at best to be informed that the country as a whole had achieved a substantial increase in its GDP during a particular period and we ourselves should not allow complacency to conceal from us the fact that such an increase may well mean that some sections of the population are gaining the lion's share of the benefit.

We should further recognise that the apparent simplicity and all embracing quality of these measures tends to reinforce the economic bias of our concepts of development. How can we seriously believe that real development has taken place if during a period when average per capita incomes have risen we know that inequalities between groups have increased; when we see massive expenditure upon luxury goods by a minority at a time when the majority are barely able to survive; when new hospitals and schools are being built in our towns which already have far more such facilities than exist in the countryside; when even within the towns unemployment is rife, law and order is not being maintained, and corruption in public life goes unchecked? Development cannot be thought of simply as an accumulation of wealth but must be concerned with the distribution and use made of that wealth, with the impact both of the way in which it has been created and the way in which it is used upon the quality of the lives people lead. One of the most acceptable definitions of development is that given by Curle – the creation of a form of society in which certain conditions prevail for human beings:

Safety, in that the society is generally non-violent, and that individuals are protected from victimisation by the state, or the police or each other; Sufficiency, in that they have enough food, clothing and other material things so that they are not prevented from making the full use of their potential; Satisfaction, in that their lives are generally pleasant and that sufficiency is not achieved at the cost of psychological and cultural disruption and disturbance; Stimulus, in that the people are kept aware of their intellectual, emotional, social or spiritual potentiality, and encouraged to fulfil it.[6]

These things cannot be achieved without economic growth, but economic growth is not an end in itself but a means (and not the only one) of achieving development. There is clearly also a parallel political dimension to development which involves the establishment of a framework of declared principles, according to which a society is to be developed, and machinery whereby decisions may be taken in accordance with these principles or action be measured against them. However since we must recognise that individuals and groups within the national society are likely to have their own views as to the form which development should take and not all are likely to be satisfied at once, it is the task of the political machinery to seek to harmonise and reconcile as far as possible these divergent interests. In this book we shall be very much concerned with the ways in which this may be done and with the impact which different views of development may have upon centrally initiated strategies and measures. But the outcome of political development, like that of economic development, must be to serve the kinds of goals outlined by Curle if real development is to take place and not mere illusions of progress and some empty mockery of modernisation.

At this point we must take up again the question of how change may be initiated, controlled and directed. The task of promoting real planned development is one of far greater difficulty than we are sometimes led to believe by the jargon of development plans. We must beware of assuming too readily that we have the basic understanding of the processes of change and the techniques to control them, for experience is teaching us that this is by no means the case. As Brookfield argues: 'to pretend that we have yet understood the process of change so well as to be able to predict it . . . is the most arrogant conceit. The task remains before us, and what any of us has yet achieved is no more than a beginning.'[7] It may be helpful to the reader in understanding this argument to refer to Figure 1. It may be argued that a national society embraces three broad dimensions – its material culture and technology, its social institutions, and its underlying complex

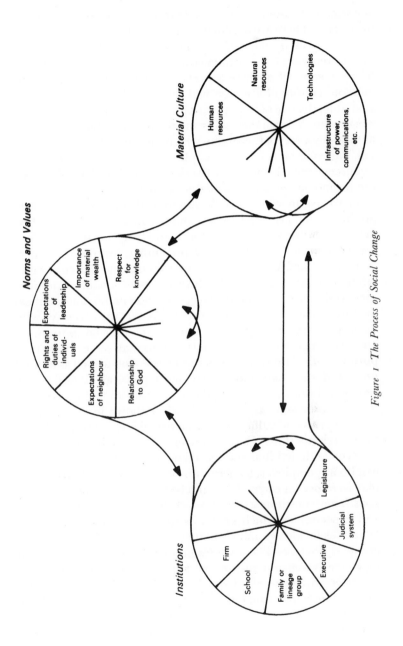

Figure 1  The Process of Social Change

of norms and values, each of which is represented in the diagram by a circle. There are of course many aspects of material culture, many forms of social institution and many different values. These may be represented by segments of the appropriate circle, though by no means all of these aspects are shown. For example the material culture of a nation will relate to the human resources available, the size of its population, the proportion of productive workers, the stock of their skills and so on. It will also relate to the natural resources of the land in which they live, the fertility of the soil, the availability of water supplies and the existence of mineral resources which the people will seek to exploit. And it will include the technology which is available to them in doing so.

The ways in which people organise themselves in order to produce and market their goods and to make use of this and their many other talents to achieve for themselves a particular way of life are shown in the circle representing institutions. These include the family or lineage group; the clan; the church or other religious organisations; the health services; economic institutions such as the firm, the cooperative, the trade union; and political institutions such as the legislature, the party, the executive with its various ministries and field officers; the judicial institutions; and many many more. Some institutions may serve a variety of purposes – the family may be a production unit as well as a social unit, and the trade union may be a political as well as an economic institution. Among the many institutions in a society is the education system. Some of these are shown in the diagram.

The norms and values of the society will include those relating to the relationships which exist, or it is thought should exist, between an individual and his fellow men – whether as relative, neighbour, employer, leader or any other of the many roles they play in respect of each other – and between a man and his god or gods. They constitute a complex web of obligations, rights, duties and expectations which set limits to the freedom of a man to behave as he pleases and regulate conduct in the interests of the group as a whole. These values may find expression in art and language as well as in institutions and social customs. Sometimes we refer to the world view of a society – the religious and philosophic stance which the society assumes in dealing with the material world of which it is part. As we have noted, a modernising society is likely to consist of a number of cultures;

consequently there is unlikely to be a single set of norms and values which apply with equal effect in all respects to all members of a national society, and there may well be certain norms and values not as yet widely accepted which national leaderships will seek to promote.

These three dimensions of a society and the many aspects of each dimension are integral and interdependent parts of the whole way of life of the society. Consequently any change which takes place for whatever reason in any one aspect is likely to lead to further change in other aspects. For example, the introduction of new farming methods, improved communications or new sources of power may lead to an increase in agricultural production through better exploitation of natural resources. Increasing production in turn may enable a larger population to be supported and a growing population may spread more widely over the land area. As this happens new forms of social organisation may be developed to link more widely scattered communities. At the same time new patterns of organisation may be introduced to make the production, distribution and exchange of produce more efficient and specialisation of function may develop. Individual producers may band themselves together to form a cooperative, or a firm may come into existence which will collect, process and market the production of others. The consequence may be that new kinds of relationship between individuals emerge. Producers may become more dependent upon (and possibly employed by) those who take up their products and these new dependency relationships may be reflected in differential distribution of wealth and power. Changes may be induced in the pattern of norms and values of the society, with perhaps the acceptance of inegalitarian values, of a belief that it is right and proper that individuals should have different amounts of rights and duties. In turn this shift in values may be reflected in institutions. Decision-making power may move away from the traditional institutions of government and come to reside more in powerful economic institutions, the authority of the chief and the elders may be reduced by the fact that many fundamental decisions may now be taken by those who manage firms often some distance away. A continuing process of change affecting many aspects of the society in all its dimensions may have thus been initiated.

This hypothetical example is not of course an accurate description of what may happen nor a description of the whole range of possible changes which may occur in such a situation. Certainly there is no inevitability about the process. Change is not a simple linear process of cause leading to effect and effect becoming the cause of a further change, such as may be implied in this crude example. A single instance of change is likely to be rooted in a number of different causes and modifying factors – population growth may result from improved health practices as well as from an increase in the capacity of men to support their children. The extent of population growth may well be moderated by other factors acting in a contrary direction. For example, changing value systems consequent upon industrial and urban development may favour the small nuclear family rather than the larger extended family. The consequences of that single change may be many and affect several different dimensions and sectors of a society, interacting with other factors in a highly complex way. The outcomes are then highly unpredictable. To throw a single stone into a pool of water will set up a fairly simple ripple effect, but where many stones are thrown at once a far more complicated ripple pattern will be set up and this pattern will be affected by the physical configuration of the pool, its shape, the presence of vegetation, small outcrops of rock, the varying depth of the pool as well as by the varying size of the stones and their scatter.

This very crude model which we have been considering cannot satisfactorily describe the actual process of change in a particular situation but it may assist the reader to begin to grasp the nature of the process. It can of course be interpreted in various ways. Some would use it to stress the adjustive, equilibrium-seeking qualities of a society, seeing change as a process in which a society as an organic whole seeks to absorb and incorporate change whilst preserving its essential wholeness. Others would wish to argue that change is not a simple adaptive or reactive process in a society which is essentially cohesive but a process resulting from conflict between elements within a society. In this view conflict, not equilibrium, is the normal condition of a society and the occasions for conflict increase as a society becomes more complex. Others would argue that such a model over-stresses the importance of systems and structures and under-values the importance of the individual who should be seen as not merely acted upon by change but as an active initiator of change through his own self-interest and perception of what is happening around him. We are not here concerned with seeking to reconcile and harmonise these differing interpretations nor with arguing for one or other particular interpretation, but merely with noting that there is no agreed viewpoint.

However, as we turn to consider the place of education in the process of social change and development, one important conclusion may be drawn which is sometimes overlooked. Many of us have grown accustomed to thinking in terms of education as an instrument of social change. We have seen education as one of the main levers for bringing about change and perhaps it is so. As the World Bank was advised in 1978,

> At bottom, what is meant by 'development' is a process of enabling people to accomplish things that they could not do before – that is, to learn and apply information, attitudes, values and skills previously unavailable to them. Learning is not usually enough by itself. Most aspects of development require capital investment and technical processes. But capital and technology are inert without human knowledge and effort. In this sense, human learning is central to development.[8]

But we have sometimes failed to recognise that education is a social institution which is also acted upon by other factors operating in our societies. To a large extent what education is and does is not determined by the educator but by others – individuals and groups with their different perceptions – and the whole social context within which we work will moderate what is achieved by any of us. To use a sporting image, if we conceive of education as a football, we should remember that we educationists are not the only players on the field who are kicking it and that other players, politicians, economists, parents, pupils and others, may be seeking to kick it in different directions. What actually happens to the ball will depend however not simply upon who kicks it or who stops it, but also upon the direction of the wind, the slope of the field and the length of the grass. The wind may represent the general current of change

within a society which some of us will wish to resist and others to
go along with; the slope of the field may represent the resources
which are available to us – where they are limited we may indeed
have an uphill task ahead of us; and long grass may represent the
many factors of inertia existing in our situation (which we shall be
discussing in a later chapter) including clusters of attitudes and
values prevalent in our society contrary to those we are seeking to
implant.

Anderson has used more academic terms to describe this
situation: 'The more useful an education system becomes to its
ambient society, the more manifold become its linkages to other
aspects of social change. Accordingly it becomes progressively
more difficult to make useful judgements about congruence
between particular programmes and desired outcomes.'[9] In
viewing education as an instrument for achieving planned
change we have probably been over-optimistic about our
capacity for ensuring that it achieves what we want and in this
book we shall be very much concerned with this matter. As
educationists we may know or think we know where the goal is.
But can we score and will we win the game?

## References

1. I. Schapera, *Tribal Innovators: Tswana Chiefs and Social Change 1795–1940*
   (London University Press, 1970).
2. L. Mair, *New Nations* (London: Weidenfeld and Nicolson, 1963) p. 15.
3. J. F. A. Ajayi, 'The Impact of Europe on African Cultures and Values',
   paper given to Conference of the African Studies Association of the United
   Kingdom, Liverpool, 1974, p. 15.
4. G. Myrdal, *Asian Drama, an Inquiry into the Poverty of Nations* (Harmondsworth: Penguin Books, 1968) vol. III, appx 2, p. 1871.
5. J. K. Nyerere, Speech to the Dag Hammarskjold Seminar on Education and
   Training and Alternatives in Education in African Countries, Dar es
   Salaam, 20 May 1974.
6. A. Curle, *Education for Liberation* (London: Tavistock, 1973) pp. 118–19.
7. H. C. Brookfield, *Inter-dependent Development* (London: Methuen, 1975) p. 83.
8. D. E. Bell (Chairman), *Report of the External Advisory Panel on Education to the
   World Bank, 31 October 1978*, p. 4.
9. C. A. Anderson, 'Development through Education Seen Dimly', in P.
   Williams (ed.), *Prescription For Progress? A Commentary on the Educational Policy
   of the World Bank* (University of London Institute of Education, 1976) p. 15.

# 2

# Education and Schooling

Having examined at least cursorily the processes of social change and 'modernisation' which are taking place in African societies, we must now give some preliminary consideration to the ways in which the concepts and practices of education have changed both as a consequence of the impact upon them of social change and because of the new roles they have been called upon to play.

What is 'education'? The UNESCO International Standard Classification of Education defines education as comprising organised and sustained communication designed to bring about learning.[1] Communication in the sense implied here requires a relationship between two or more people involving the transfer of information, 'organised' means planned in a sequence with established aims and curricula, and 'sustained' means that the learning experience has duration and continuity. 'Learning' is taken to mean any change in behaviour, knowledge, under-standing, skills or capabilities which the learner retains and which cannot be ascribed simply to physical growth or to the development of inherited behaviour patterns.

How helpful to us is this definition? Clearly what goes on in the institution we call a school is intended to be education in these terms, but equally clearly education may be carried on outside formal schools. We recognise that all societies have at all times sought to develop appropriate behaviour patterns, to spread the possession of knowledge, understanding and skills among their members in ways which possess many of the above characteristics even though the degree of organisation and the extent to which aims were articulated tended to be limited. Anthropologists refer to such practices as socialisation and enculturation, lifelong processes by which an individual is incorporated into the group and made capable of behaving in the ways expected by the society for a person of a particular age, sex or status. Recently educationists have begun to refer to such processes by which an individual learns the culture of his group as 'informal' education, to distinguish between the processes of learning through living in and with the group from processes of learning provided in specially designed learning environments (designated 'formal' education) and processes of more highly specific learning which, though they may not take place in such designed environments, are nevertheless thought of as fundamentally different from normal socialisation patterns ('non-formal' education). In a later chapter we shall be examining formal and non-formal patterns of education more fully but here we are asking in what ways useful distinctions may be made between informal and formal education, in order to begin to understand what 'school' is and why it has come to operate in the way it does.

In so far as we tend to require our schools today to pass on to rising generations the attitudes, values, skills, social understanding and practice of the societies to which they belong, to socialise them and enable them to fit usefully and harmoniously into those societies, is there any difference between what schools do and what has always been done by informal means? Some definitions of formal education deliberately avoid this issue. Malinowski[2] defined schooling as that somewhat restricted part of education which is given by professional educators to those who come under their tutelage in organised institutions of learning, distinguishing formal from informal education in terms of its outward characteristics rather than basic function. Such a distinction is less useful when we consider that many African societies, and particularly those with higher degrees of centralisation of political authority, have long possessed processes of socialisation through age sets, initiation procedures and secret societies. Often these were really quite 'formal', involving from time to time the instruction of the young for an extended period in a withdrawn situation by an experienced elder according to an accepted curriculum and with testing of performance. Some African societies like the Bahaya of East Africa in their Muteko system used these formalistic training periods to identify the more able of their youth and allocate to them positions of status and responsibility. Others established training institutions of a specialised kind such as the wrestling school in Ogoja and the Egbe Akurubegbe-Ekiti school of war, both in Nigeria. Islamic groups have long possessed their hierarchies of Koranic schools and mahadras, up even to university level in some of the older cities of West Africa, for instruction in Arabic, the Koran and some forms of non-religious education. In many of these instances the instructors assumed something of the character of professional staff.

Moreover there are many characteristics of socialisation procedures which closely resemble techniques of education which leading educationists have for many years been advocating as appropriate for formal education. One common feature of the way in which children are brought up in traditional societies is the process of learning by doing, whereby through imitation, identification and co-operation a child learns how to behave as an adult – over the years his play develops imperceptibly into work. Associated with this process is the 'modern' principle that what a child learns should be related to his immediate environment and to his immediate needs at his particular stage of development in that environment. Commonly also there is a body of knowledge and information which the child must learn and remember through an intellectual process – the legends, traditions, folk tales, lullabies, riddles and proverbs which, orally communicated, encapsulate much of the inherited wisdom of the society.

It may appear hardly surprising, therefore, that a number of thinkers including Jomo Kenyatta[3] have wondered why it was necessary to abandon so completely this indigenous educational tradition and to adopt a 'Western' pattern of schooling which, it is suggested, is a far less efficient instrument for enabling a child to fit into his society. Could not the indigenous tradition have been built upon to provide a pattern of education which would serve modern purposes whilst retaining an organic relationship with its cultural matrix? To this question we now turn.

As we do so however we should note that some attempts have in the past been made to do precisely this, notably in Tanzania in the 1920s and 1930s. Bishop Lucas and the Universities Mission to Central Africa in Southern Tanganyika and the Church Missionary Society in central Tanganyika attempted to utilise initiation ceremonies to communicate instruction not simply in Christianity but in modern ways of living including health, hygiene and family life. Such experiments failed essentially because the purposes for which traditional institutions were being used were so different from their original purposes that they became unrecognisable as such. The difference between modern schooling and traditional socialisation is not so much a matter of structures and methodologies as of purpose and the perceptions of their function held by those who use them.

The educational processes of society reflect its nature and its needs and as these change so its educational processes may have to change. In simple, small-scale, isolated and self-sufficient societies, where the security and survival of the group depended upon harmonious co-operation between all members of the group, educational practice tended to stress the transfer to new members of the cultural symbols, values, beliefs, and sanctions upon which personal relationships, patterns of conduct and customs were based. New members also had to learn the technical and vocational skills of the group. In this way they were prepared to play their full part in maintaining the cohesion, stability, survival and well-being of the group. The emphasis in this induction process was naturally upon conformity and obedience and there was relatively little concern for developing the unique talents of the individual, for encouraging qualities which would differentiate the individual from his peers, since individualism would put at risk the stability of the group. In the same way concern for the intellectual development of the person was subordinated to other aspects of his training. The individual was to be prepared to fit comfortably into the existing pattern of his society, to fulfil roles as a member of that society which were largely ascribed to him by custom and which were clearly understood by those around him who were responsible for his training. Members of such societies normally did not actively seek change, since change might again threaten the security and stability of the society, and their educational processes were not therefore concerned with preparing individuals to initiate or adapt to change but rather with reinforcing the existing social framework.

This is not to argue that such societies were static and unchanging. The model of the simple society we have been considering may never have existed in Africa in a pure form. As we have argued earlier, some changes must always have been necessitated by external forces, whether natural or human, and there must always have been strains within societies which have required adjustments. The processes of change outlined earlier must have been true in some degree of all societies. However, as Lloyd suggests for West Africa, the extent and pace of change in many of the relatively simply-structured and small-scale societies which predominated in Africa was in the past fairly limited. Local groups have survived the rise and fall of empires and dynasties with but little change in their social and political organisation.[4] More recently these pressures for change, both external and internal, have been violently accelerated, notably through the impact of colonialism.

The enforced formation of larger political units embracing often large numbers of different cultures and social groups had an impact upon local cultures more far-reaching than those of earlier empires for two reasons in particular. The first was the systematic character of the new centralised administrations which reached out into local communities more regularly and efficiently than had previously been the case. But the second was even more significant. The new administrations were actively concerned with bringing about change. Colonial governments on the whole brought with them a belief in 'progress', in the ability of man to solve his problems, and particularly in the capacity of new technologies and managerial structures to provide man with increasing mastery of his environment. The consequences were complex and far reaching, taking the form of patterns of change such as we have earlier discussed. In the post-independence years national political leaders endorsed these beliefs in change and progress and adopted more recent concepts of planned and directed modernisation in recognition of the desirability of mobilising the whole power of the nation in order to achieve the desired progress. At the same time wider consciousness of the need to control undesirable aspects of change, to preserve things of value in traditional cultures which were being undermined, to create a nation from the heterogeneous groups within the national boundaries, introduced new dimensions to the process by which societies were being transformed.

Education in consequence assumed a new significance and new roles. Formerly an instrument for promoting social stability and continuity, it increasingly had to serve as an instrument for promoting and controlling change, for creating discontinuities.

Previously an instrument for communicating the values and skills possessed by the adult members of a culture, it now had to transmit new national values and new economic and other skills which most adults might well not possess. Previously a means for incorporating an individual into a society possessing to a considerable extent a common consensus of beliefs and preparing him for roles which society would assign to him, it had now to be a means of incorporating him into a rapidly changing national society with pluralistic patterns of belief and preparing him for a highly fluid situation in which he would have to make his own way, achieve his own selected roles and adapt to ongoing change.

For such purposes the old informal procedures of socialisation and enculturation would no longer suffice. Formal processes such as had been developed in large-scale and complex Western societies and to a lesser extent in many of the larger and more centralised societies of Africa were perhaps inevitably called into service. Equally inevitably the particular form which these processes took was derived from the schooling tradition of the colonising powers. Because of the speed with which change was taking place and because adult society appeared resistant to change, largely in consequence of the way in which it had been socialised, education in the form of schooling became essentially focused on the young, ceased to be co-terminous with life and became future-oriented, a preparation for life and to a large extent a process of accumulating knowledge for later application. Because of the range of demands which would be placed upon the individual in his future life in a rapidly changing and complex society, the experience which he was to gain in school was highly concentrated and more theoretical in nature than the process of learning by living and doing. Because much of the knowledge and skills which he would need were not to be found and experienced at first hand in his environment, education became largely a matter of vicarious experience through such media as teacher talk and the book, and partly because alternative resources were limited education became teacher-centred. Because of the range of knowledge and experience which was available through such means was enormous, education became a highly selected process with a prescribed curriculum and detailed syllabuses. Because such patterns of education were expensive and because the needs of the occupational structure did not demand that all workers should receive the same amounts of education, education became discriminatory, very largely a process by means of which the more talented pupils were identified and selected out for further education or for employment through a process of examination and certification.

Since the school in Western society had been traditionally called upon to perform socialising functions, it was not surprising that this role was also commonly given to it in Africa (even though customary socialisation remained strong and healthy) but for two main reasons it has been unable to carry it out in practice. First, the school, despite what has been said about its similarity in some respects to more formal elements in traditional practice, essentially embodied a new and different culture and was therefore ill-adapted to conveying a local culture. Second, because a new national framework had been imposed upon local societies which were largely based upon very different values and practices, the main socialisation role of the school lay in terms of the modern national society. But because no very clear consensus existed as to what these values were or should be (in spite of more recent talk of 'national' cultures), and because the schools were allocated other roles in addition to that of socialisation, in practice the schools tended to give greater importance to vocational and skill training. That the schools continued to socialise their pupils into certain patterns of belief and attitude is not questioned but they did so in an unplanned, incidental way rather than in conscious performance of the allocated role.

The suggestion that schools in practice developed a skill-training orientation may require clarification. Since the product of the school might enter into any one of an increasingly wide range of occupations and social roles, the skills with which the schools were principally concerned were not necessarily narrowly vocational but those which were more generalisable, of which the most important were literacy and numeracy. However since these particular skills were also those which might be provided most cheaply and since they were associated with the more prestigious occupations, other more practical skills tended to be neglected and schooling took on the literary character for which it has been frequently, and often unfairly, criticised. Since these more prestigious occupations were principally to be found in the growing modern sector of society, schools tended to become modern-sector oriented, no longer serving to prepare children for life in their own local communities so much as to fit some children for new roles in the national sphere.

In yet another way education took on a new form. The trends of social change which we have noted had placed new emphasis on the role of individuals, in that those who received an education were expected to take up positions in society in which they would not merely have to be adaptable to change but would also serve as initiators of change. Since they would lack a clear body of custom to guide them, it was necessary that education should place greater stress on their intellectual preparation to enable them to think and act logically on the basis of evidence and to be prepared to find out what they did not know. Although it cannot be pretended that the school has always been successful in this (or indeed in other respects) education could no longer be conceived of as a process whereby knowledge could be transmitted, but had to become a means whereby new knowledge might be generated. In so far as they undertook this task, schools deliberately set a distance between the pupil and his local community and culture in order that he might understand it better. Thereby the values and practices of the community were presented as open to question. At this point it is necessary to note that the functions discussed above have not necessarily been completely or overtly understood and accepted by those who are responsible for operating school systems. The school is surrounded by a confusion of ideas both old and new as to what it should be doing, and it is this confusion which largely accounts for inefficiencies in schooling and for discrepancies between theory and practice.

Broadly speaking there are three basic philosophies of schooling. The first is essentially conservative, in that it regards the main function of the school as being to reflect the society it serves and to convey to rising generations the accumulated values and wisdom of that society – a socialising function not dissimilar to that of traditional patterns of informal education. The second is innovative, in that it sees the school as an instrument for purposively initiating, controlling and directing change in society. And the third may be regarded as liberative, concerned with freeing individuals from their cultural and intellectual blinkers, enabling them to think logically and independently, to identify and solve problems, to take responsibility for initiating change, but not seeking to limit their freedom or constrain their own decisions by imposing upon them a plan which will predetermine what they must decide to do. If we examine statements of educational goals in our countries we are likely to find all three philosophies standing side by side with little recognition of the basic conflict which exists between them, no clear indication of which theme is to be dominant, or guidance as to how far each function is to be served. We shall return to this question later.

There is also some danger that in focussing our attention on the potentiality and functions of the school we shall assume that formal schooling has in fact replaced traditional socialisation, assumed its function and in some mysterious way killed it off.

We must remember that formal schooling is essentially a supplement to patterns of informal education in the home and the community. It does not replace it even though some of its functions are similar. Although many children, if by no means all, will no longer experience, for example, initiation rites, and though other aspects of informal education will be of declining significance (at least for those children who spend much of their time in school), it is probably true that for virtually all children the education they receive from their parents and from living in a community is going to have a highly significant, possibly even dominant, effect upon their behaviour in later life. There is universal recognition of the importance of influences to which a child is subject during his early years which is reflected in African sayings: 'mtoto umleavyo ndivyo akuavyo' – as the child is raised, so will he be (or as the twig is bent, so grows the tree). Many of the fundamental beliefs, attitudes and ways of thinking which a child will carry with him into adult life will be inculcated in him long before he goes to school. Furthermore much of this early learning is so highly internalised that it may remain impervious to and be little affected by later schooling. This becomes particularly serious where the attitudes and values prevalent in the community and communicated to its children run counter to those which the school has been charged with developing. Two examples will illustrate the problem.

It is, as suggested above, frequently the responsibility of the school to equip individuals with a capacity for making independent judgements, for tackling and solving problems.

Schools, we often believe, should normally seek to encourage children to find out answers to problems for themselves and to test their conclusions in discussion with the teacher. However in many cultures it is unacceptable for young people to challenge and question what their elders say since this constitutes disrespect. In consequence schools may find it no easy task to encourage these qualities in their pupils.

A second example is the effort of schools to inculcate scientific views of causality among the children of a society holding incompatible patterns of belief. A number of researchers have suggested that traditional views of causality which children bring to school are particularly resistant to education. Yet we also know that children have a great capacity for learning what is taught and for passing their examinations without ever actually internalising this teaching and basing their conduct upon it. Musgrove has warned teachers to beware of the intellectualist fallacy of assuming that children have internalised what they have learned.[5] Where knowledge and belief conflict, knowledge is likely to yield to belief.

The two situations just described are examples of cognitive dissonance, where children are required to hold two sets of conflicting views simultaneously. It leads to the schools being criticised on two grounds. In so far as children do not behave in the manner intended when they leave school and enter employment, the school is accused of having failed; in so far as the school succeeds, parents may accuse the school of having spoiled their children and it will be suggested that the schools are divorcing children from their culture.

It is apparent that in spite of confusion over function, the school has been called upon to serve some functions which are very different from those of traditional informal education, and in some respects the opposite. Consequently not only were traditional procedures of the more informal kind unsuited to the new functions but those more formal procedures such as the koranic school which were geared to traditional socialisation purposes and which had a specifically culture-conserving function, were highly resistant to being adapted to serve new functions in the cause of modernisation. The justification of the formal schooling tradition in Africa must largely lie in the claim that such functions as have been described can only or at least can best be provided in a formal institution. As Nyerere has argued: 'It is quite clear that in Africa at any rate, the problem of integrating education with the society cannot be solved by abandoning a formal education structure. We cannot go back to an exclusive dependence upon the traditional system of . . ."learning by living and doing".'[6]

In the later chapters of this book we shall be asking how efficient the school as an institution is in performing the various roles allocated to it. At this point we must take up the point made by Nyerere regarding the problem of integrating education with its society and consider through the further use of a historical perspective how far the school as we know it is alien to Africa and whether it might itself have developed a more truly African form.

## The Adaptation of Schooling

The school systems of Africa have been much criticised in recent years for their failure to achieve many of the goals which have been set for them and for the harmful nature of much of their impact upon their societies. Their curricula are said to be bookish, oriented towards higher levels of education which are beyond the reach of the majority of their pupils, divorced from the life and culture of the local people and consequently unsuited for preparing the child for life in his own community. The methods of teaching in use are said to be examination centred, authoritarian, restrictive of the growing child, failing to produce original thinking or problem-solving ability on the one hand and genuine commitment to the service of the community on the other. The selection and allocation functions performed by the schools, it is argued, have encouraged a selfish elitism and individualism alien to the traditions of African society and at variance with the egalitarian principles which are being espoused by the new national societies. Education in the current mould encourages a 'white collar mentality' and a contempt for manual labour, is responsible for a profound cleavage between educated elites and the masses, has encouraged a drift of young people to the towns, the loosening of moral standards and the decay of much that is valued in traditional society. The most complete critique of many school systems is probably to be found in Nyerere's own *Education for Self-Reliance*.[7]

Underlying such criticisms of the school systems is commonly the assumption that the basic reason for their failings is the fact that they were alien instruments, torn from their European context and set down by colonial powers in societies to which they were unrelated. The problem, it appears, is how to reform them, to make them more 'relevant', to root them more completely in the culture of the society and to produce an 'African' school capable of preparing young people for their modernising role without divorcing them from their culture. It is the contention of the writer that whilst there is considerable room for reform in education systems, there is also considerable danger in assuming too readily that their faults derive essentially from their imported character whereas in reality schools have become very much an integral and living part of the African societies they serve, and their distinctive problems derive largely from this fact. If the problem were simply one of alien characteristics unsuited to local needs or irreconcilable with local cultural patterns, then it might be readily solved. The alien characteristics would tend to wither like seeds planted in unsuitable soil. But in fact these characteristics we complain of have not withered and the seeds have rooted and show every appearance of flourishing. If we fail to analyse the local roots of our problems and instead endorse over-simplistic interpretations of their origin, we are unlikely to arrive at solutions which will meet our need.

The problems we face are not new, indeed many current criticisms (such as those contained in *Education for Self-Reliance*) are to be found, frequently expressed in not dissimilar terms, by past educationists in the literature of the last half century or more. And the fact that our predecessors have failed to deal effectively with the problems should warn us of the complexity and difficulty of the situation we now face, for their failure was not due simply to blindness or stupidity or ill-intention but to the intractable nature of the problem. If we examine their experience carefully we may arrive at a fuller understanding of the problem. In this chapter we shall examine briefly one body of experience and shall be suggesting that properly conducted historical studies of other such bodies of experience have a valuable part to play in the design of future educational policies.

Concern that the content of education was largely irrelevant to the real needs of the colonial peoples receiving it was expressed as early as 1847 when Kaye-Shuttleworth and the Education Committee of the Privy Council in London urged the inclusion of practical studies related to agriculture and rural industries. This thinking was eventually embodied in the Education Ordinances for Sierra Leone in 1881 and the Gold Coast in 1882. A similar emphasis on manual training was urged for Nigeria and led to the short-lived experiment by Hans Vischer who sought to introduce agriculture and craft into the koranic schools of the north.

Following the First World War, at a time when there was growing consciousness of the value and significance of traditional cultures and increasing respect for their individuality, this somewhat narrow strand in educational thought was incorporated into a more comprehensive philosophy of education adapted to the nature of African societies. At this time it was widely believed that even the very limited amount of schooling which then existed in African dependencies was undermining the traditional fabric of local societies. Whether intended for the production of manpower for the administration and the economy or for evangelistic purposes, the embryonic school systems were thought to be producing large numbers of 'detribalised' young people who were tending to reject the authority of their elders and the traditional constraints of their societies, and who had developed selfish aspirations ill-matched with either their level of education or the intentions of those who had taught them. In the search for white collar occupations they were deserting their own people and drifting into the towns where they presented a potential source of social and political problems in so far as they were unable to fulfil their aspirations. It was feared that African societies were fragile, threatened with destruction, and in danger of being replaced by a fragmented society characterised by disorientation, rootlessness, self-seeking individualism and blind copying of Western ways. It was argued that the healthy modernisation of these societies required opportunities for them to evolve without losing their own identity, and that a reformed school and education system might serve to cement and strengthen those aspects of traditional societies which would enable them to adapt to change and come to terms with the modern world through stable, integrated community progress. From this belief arose the philosophy of educational adaptation best represented in the British dependencies by the reports of the

Phelps-Stokes Commissions which visited West and South Africa in 1921–2 and East and Central Africa in 1924[8] and in the policy document, *Education Policy in British Tropical Africa*, subsequently produced by the Colonial Office in 1925. This philosophy was also reflected, though differently interpreted, in the Antonetti Circular relating to French Equatorial Africa and a Belgian report on educational policy in the Congo, both, significantly, also appearing in 1925.

The key statement of the British policy statement was the following:

> Education should be adapted to the mentality, aptitudes, occupations and traditions of the various peoples, conserving as far as possible all sound and healthy elements in the fabric of their social life, adapting them where necessary to changed circumstances and progressive ideas, as an agent of natural growth and evolution.[9]

Three aims were defined for education, 'to render the individual more efficient in his or her condition of life', 'to promote the advancement of the community as a whole through the improvement of agriculture, the development of native industries, the improvement of health, the training of the people in the management of their own affairs and the inculcation of true ideals of citizenship and service', and 'the raising up of capable, trustworthy, public-spirited leaders of the people belonging to their own race'.

The central idea was thus to promote the evolution of the community as an integrated whole. Education so conceived would 'narrow the hiatus between the educated class and the rest of the community whether chiefs or peasantry' and whilst the education of leadership was important and the door of advancement through higher education was to be kept open, the main thrust was to enable the bulk of the people to benefit and to ensure that those in leadership positions remained in spirit and culture part of their evolving society.

The Phelps-Stokes Commissions, representing government and missionary bodies and including notably James Aggrey, the most distinguished African educationist of his day, suggested ways in which these principles might be implemented. The teaching of school subjects should be linked to the study of the local community and the curriculum should include health, the use of the environment in agriculture and industry, and preparation for an improved home life and for better use of leisure time. The school itself should be so organised as to bridge the gap between the new world to which his studies would inevitably introduce the child and the older world from which he came and to which he would return better equipped to play his part in its evolution. This might be achieved by rethinking the construction, administrative pattern and daily life of the school in accordance with local custom and tradition, by the use of vernacular languages of instruction, and by methodologies which related theory more closely to practice.

Equally fundamental to this thinking was the concept of the simultaneous education of the adult community through a variety of activities in order to ensure that the older generation would not be out of tune with and left behind by the younger generations who would be benefitting from schooling. This principle was more emphatically spelled out by a later (1935) policy memorandum on the education of African communities which stated:

> the progress of a backward community will be greater and more rapid if the education of the adults is taken in hand simultaneously with that of the young . . . efforts to educate the young are often largely wasted unless a simultaneous effort is made to improve the life of the community as a whole.[10]

In these and a series of other documents emanating from government offices and international conferences between 1920 and 1960 a steady flow of ideas was spelled out about the ways in which education might be more effectively rooted in local societies and develop distinctively African forms whilst serving the modernisation function. In many parts of Africa experimental developments in the design of schools and school systems, of curricula and methodologies, of community education facilities and of management systems involving local people were undertaken. And yet, in spite of the constant reiteration of ideas which in many respects still have the ring of modernity about them and in spite of considerable genuine effort to put the ideas into practice, by the mid-1950s the education systems of Africa presented a very conventional appearance, seemingly far more closely modelled on European lines than those of the 1920s and 1930s. The kinds of criticism to which they were subject in those early days continued to be expressed alongside other common criticisms of inadequacy of scale and racially segregated provision. What had gone wrong? British experience may provide some of the answers.

Since the Colonial Office memoranda possessed only advisory status, the application of their principles depended upon the imagination and enthusiasm of educationists in the various British dependencies, and consequently varied widely. In Tanganyika a considerable range of experiments was initiated with the support of the then Director of Education, S. Rivers-Smith. Schools built and organised on 'tribal' lines were opened – for instance, the CMS girls' school at Buigiri and the government schools developed by Mumford at Bukoba and later Malangali. Under the Directorship of A. A. M. Isherwood and with the strong backing of administrative officers a serious attempt was made in the 1930s to encourage the Native Authorities to develop their own tribal schools. An excellent response was met with, particularly in Unyamwezi and Usukuma where the schools at Ibadakuli and Kizigo were held up as models of this new kind of schooling. The Agricultural Department also sought to utilise the traditional Kwaya schools of the Sukuma. In no other African dependency was such a wholehearted effort made to adapt education, although notable experimental developments were initiated elsewhere.

In the Gold Coast the development of Achimota as an all-age school combining theoretical with practical work on the farm and in the workshop was matched by Guggisberg's trade schools and other experiments. In Nigeria J. D. Clarke established a school at Omu which, like Mumford's Malangali, sought to relate buildings and organisation as well as curriculum to local community tradition. In Kenya, Nyasaland and Northern Rhodesia, and in a not dissimilar form in Nigeria, Jeanes Schools were established to train supervisory teachers to disseminate the new community-oriented curriculum ideas. In several countries special schools for the sons of traditional chiefs were established in the belief that more enlightened leadership would promote modernisation whilst preserving the integrity of local society and culture. At Bakht er Ruda in the Sudan V. L. Griffiths initiated a notable experiment in the ruralisation of teacher education.

In French, Belgian and Portuguese dependencies the application of adaptationist concepts took different forms. The French remained wedded to their assimilationist policy whereby the elites were to be introduced through their education to French culture. Consequently, whilst village schools like those in British dependencies stressed vocational training, higher schools were not adapted but were modelled very closely on French schools. Belgian and Portuguese policy was to promote the wide extension of rural primary and technical schools but to defer the development of post-primary schooling until this base had been sufficiently established as to avoid the dangers of elite creation.

Whilst the theory made much of the concept of integrated advancement of local communities, there was already developing in colonial dependencies a nation-wide modern sector concerned with administration and trade for which local manpower was needed. In effect a dual society was already coming into existence within which the school was being given a dual role – both to prepare the minority for service in the modern sector and to prepare the majority for lives in the more traditional sector. As modern sector demands grew, particularly after the effects of the depression of the early 1930s had been shaken off, the schools found themselves required to place growing emphasis on the literary, general education needed for modern sector employment. The steadily growing demand for people with a secondary, or even (though to a more limited extent) a tertiary, education led to the creation of more advanced institutions offering certification of an internationally acceptable kind. These institutions had the effect of biassing the curriculum of lower schools towards preparation for entry to the next higher level. These lower schools thus found themselves primarily concerned with selecting out the more talented, serving as instruments of differentiation rather than of homogenisation.

Moreover the planners had failed sufficiently to take into account the nature of the aspirations of African peoples and very considerably underestimated the power of these aspirations. The adaptation of education to local cultures and needs as perceived by the expatriate educationists was not necessarily acceptable to the people. Africans were often shrewdly aware of what it was they expected of education in schools. As Ndabaningi Sithole put it, 'to us education meant reading books, writing and talking English, and doing arithmetic . . . At our homes we had done a lot of ploughing, planting, weeding and harvesting . . . We knew how to do these things. What we knew was not education, education was what we did not know.'[11]

Since modern sector jobs offered many attractions not found in rural communities, it was not unnatural that as awareness of the opportunities grew people should wish to take advantage of them, and since it was literary education which led to the kinds of clerical occupations which were more generally available and desired at the time, not unnaturally it was this kind of education which was demanded. This is reflected in the terms used for schooling in some vernacular languages. The Ibo term 'emo-ekwokwo' may be translated as 'book learning', and also in Nigeria the Ibibio term 'udiönö-nwed' as 'knowing book'. 'We wanted', said Sithole 'as we said in Ndebele, "to learn the book until it remained in our heads, to speak English until we could speak it through our noses".'

Under pressure from their clienteles, many schools which set out to develop a genuinely practical and local orientation found themselves serving a different set of felt needs and gradually having to modify their approaches in order to meet these pressures. The experimental 'tribal' schools such as those established by Mumford at Bukoba and Malangali in Tanganyika were very quickly conventionalised by subtle social pressures and the agricultural secondary school set up at Nyakato in that country was very speedily compelled to return to 'literary' studies by parents withholding their children from school and campaigning vigorously against the school. Vernacular language policies also tended to be thrust aside as pressure grew for the establishment of more advanced levels of schooling, and the lower levels became preparatory for the higher, losing their community orientation.

Adapted forms of schooling were necessarily different from those which the expatriates had themselves experienced and were therefore seen as being inferior, likely to deny Africans access to the kinds of knowledge and skill from which the colonial authorities derived their power and to confine Africans to those sectors of the national life which were most remote from the exercise of that power. Politically conscious Africans tended to demand the same opportunities as Europeans in order that they might demonstrate their equal capacity on the colonialists' own ground. European officers consistently failed to take account of the extent to which they themselves served as normative figures. The adoption of European ways by educated Africans which was so frequently interpreted as a deplorable rejection of their own culture was really, at least in part, an assertion that Africans could be the equals of their masters. Efforts by Europeans to discourage this tendency were bound to be seen as an attempt by them to withhold things of value.

Moreover colonial officials who were primarily concerned with the mass of the people still living according to custom under their traditional rulers in the countryside and were seeking the kind of integrated community progress we have described, tended to see the educated and more articulate urban African minority as a threat to this policy, in so far as that minority was often impatient with and critical of the constraints of custom and traditional authority. It was easy to see this minority as self-seeking and disruptive, and consequently the colonial authorities failed fully to recognise the extent to which many Africans were determined to win understanding of, and a capacity to use, the new national instruments of government in order to protect themselves and secure for themselves a position in which they could influence the decisions which would affect their lives. Perhaps the most remarkable instance of this was the establishment by the Kikuyu people of Kenya of their own school system independent of the government. Kikuyu leaders such as Harry Thuku and Jomo Kenyatta emphasised the importance of Africans learning English and becoming well enough educated to be able to fight for their land both in the courts and by making representations directly to the British Government.[12]

It should further be noted that the main thrust of the experimental adaptations mentioned was towards reforming the school. In practice the school remained by far the most important educational agency, drawing to itself the lion's share of effort and resources. The parallel development of adult education which had been envisaged and which had been intended to keep the adult community in step with its young people was almost universally neglected by comparison, attracting little in the way of either resources or original thinking. This was partly the result of the insistent demands of the economy and the administration for schooled manpower, and partly the consequence of the general absence of popular support. Whilst African communities were increasingly willing to make sacrifices to support schools for their children, they were often hostile to, or at best apathetic towards, other developments which might divert effort from the expansion of schooling. The staff of Educational Departments were themselves usually unfamiliar with adult education and unsure of ways in which the education of the community might be undertaken. In consequence real responsibility for adult education was left in the hands of the natural resources and medical departments which operated centralised extension services. These services suffered from under-financing (which was particularly serious in view of the labour-intensive nature of the process) and often from the use of authoritarian practices which tended to alienate the people they were intended to benefit. Moreover they remained for the most part uncoordinated and unevenly distributed. Generally it became accepted that the most appropriate way of diffusing modern ideas of farming, hygiene and health, community and family living, was through the education of rising generations in school. In this way the school became further entrenched as the principal agency of education, a tendency which was further strengthened by its success in meeting, not the intentions of the adaptationists, but the aspirations of those who were fortunate enough to pass through it.

It is conceivable that given time and different circumstances the adaptationist approach might have succeeded. But it was essentially predicated on the assumption of slow and steady social change, it envisaged gradual evolution in which the pace would be dictated by the capacity of societies to absorb change whilst maintaining their cultural integrity. In the event the pace of economic, social and political change was to be very much faster than was anticipated and the capacity of the authorities to control its direction proved very much weaker than had been believed. The educational outcome was in the post-war years a very rapid expansion of formal education in the attempt to keep up with the growing demands of modern sector employment and of the people themselves. Whilst the belief in the need for adaptation remained strong, and whilst policy statements continued to endorse the fundamental principles enunciated earlier, in practice experimental developments were largely swept away by the need to devote all efforts to simply extending the school systems. The increasingly conventional form which schooling took for these reasons was reinforced in the post-war years by advocacy of the provision of primary education as a human right, by the somewhat later recognition of the need for investment in secondary and tertiary education to promote economic growth and by the establishment of independent national governments which were committed to responding to the demands of their people for more education. Up to this time the main, though by no means the only, source of criticism of the way in which schooling was functioning in relation to society as a whole was the international community of educationists: it was when schooling failed to achieve the goals set for it by the new national leaderships that African criticism arose and the contemporary call for relevance and authenticity, for distinctively African forms of education, really began to develop.

The conclusion to be drawn from this experience is that attempts to bridge the gap between education and African culture have in the past proved abortive not simply because these attempts were undertaken by expatriates operating in ignorance of that culture but because in fact the school had, unlike alternative institutions and approaches, been readily absorbed by African society and utilised by the individuals making up that society for their own purposes. The school must now be considered an African institution; its characteristic features and functions are now firmly rooted in the local African context, deriving their strength not simply from a foreign tradition but predominantly from the perception of local people as to their needs and the capacity of the school to meet those needs. If we are now to pursue the effort to adapt schooling in particular, and education in general, to various African societies, success will largely depend upon the ability of African educationists and decision-makers to analyse their own situations, and to recognise that one of the main obstacles to contemporary adaptation is that in the eyes of their clienteles, far from being failures, the schools (at least until recently) have been notably successful.

In the following chapters we shall be examining the extent to which educational systems have been able to achieve the goals set for them and we shall constantly be referring back to these factors and discussing them further.

## References

1. UNESCO, *International Standard Classification of Education*, (abridged edition) (UNESCO, July 1975) p. 2.
2. B. Malinowski, in the *American Journal of Sociology*, vol. 48 (1943), p. 649, quoted in J. A. Akinpelu, 'The Educative Processes in Non-literate Societies: An Essay in the Anthropological Foundations of Education', *West African Journal of Education*, vol. XVIII no. 3 (October 1974) p. 415.
3. J. Kenyatta, *Facing Mount Kenya* (London: Mercury Books, 1961) pp. 98–129.
4. P. C. Lloyd, *Africa in Social Change*, (Harmondsworth: Penguin, 1967) pp. 29–30.
5. F. Musgrove, 'Education and the Culture Concept', *Africa*, vol. XXIII (1953) p. 110.
6. J. K. Nyerere, Speech to the Dag Hammarskjold Seminar on Education and Training and Alternatives in Education in African Countries, Dar es Salaam, 20 May 1974.
7. J. K. Nyerere, *Education for Self-Reliance*, (Dar es Salaam: Government Printer 1967).
8. *Education in Africa: A Study of West, South and Equatorial Africa by the African Education Commission*; and *Education in East Africa: A study of East, Central and South Africa by the Second African Education Commission*; under the auspices of the Phelps-Stokes Fund in cooperation with the International Education Board. These reports have been republished in an abridged form in L. J. Lewis, *The Phelps-Stokes Reports on Education in Africa* (London: Oxford University Press, 1962).
9. Advisory Committee on Native Education in British Tropical African Dependencies, *Education Policy in British Tropical Africa*, Cmd 2374 (HMSO, 1925), reproduced in L. G. Cowan, J. O'Connell, and D. G. Scanlon (eds) *Education and Nation Building in Africa* (New York: Praeger, 1965); the Antonetti Circular No. 8 concerning the organisation of public education in French Equatorial Africa is also reproduced (pp. 53–9) and the Belgian *Projet d'organisation de l'enseignement libre au Congo Belge* (pp. 59–77).
10. Advisory Committee on Education in the Colonies, *Memorandum on the Education of African Communities*, Col. No. 103 (HMSO, 1935).
11. N. Sithole, *African Nationalism* (Cape Town, 1959) quoted in T. Ranger, 'African Attempts to Control Education in East and Central Africa 1900–1939', *Past and Present*, no. 32 (December 1965) p. 68. See this article for further discussion of the strength and direction of African aspirations.
12. J. Anderson, *The Struggle for the School* (London: Longman, 1970) p. 117.

# Part II

# Some Basic Issues

# 3

# Politics and Education

## Education as a Political Agent

Educationists who have been brought up in a Western tradition, as have most African educationists, are often resentful of any manifestations of political control or 'interference', as it is often termed. This is largely because in multi-party democracies we do not wish to see our schools used as pawns in the pursuit of electoral advantage or educational policies subjected to frequent change according to the party in power. We tend to argue that education is a basic human right and that its function is to develop the talents of the individual to the fullest extent possible to enable him to participate freely within a free society. Whilst all school systems seek to inculcate certain basic values and attitudes, such as honesty, respect for truth and for other individuals, self-discipline, and the capacity to identify right from wrong according to criteria of principle and not of expediency, we resist the idea that the individual should be indoctrinated with party-political creeds or moulded in highly specific casts, recognising the danger that such a function may be abused.

However in recent years we have increasingly come to recognise, though with some misgivings, that education cannot be divorced from political concerns and that we as educationists must recognise the legitimate interest of political bodies in what we do. We must recognise that the growing scale and complexity of educational provision necessitates some form of centralised co-ordination and planning, that the rising costs of education must be met largely from the public purse and must therefore be subject to political accountability, and that, if education is a human right, governments have a responsibility to ensure that their citizens are not deprived of that right. In developing countries it has long been recognised that education is a

47

fundamental lever for social change, that investment in education is an essential feature of national development, and that where resources are scarce the nature of that investment must be carefully planned together with other aspects of national development planning. Consequently the amounts and kinds of education which are to be provided must be largely determined by those who have the overall responsibility for deciding what form national development is to take. Finally, as Michael Manley, formerly Prime Minister of Jamaica, said: 'even in a multi-party situation, the central truth remains that education is a political agent because it must, in its very nature, either tend to preserve the status quo or promote change, depending on how it is organised, who organises it and the purpose to which it is put.'[1] This is an important statement which merits further examination. In recent years there has been increasing recognition of the fact that education systems, being integral parts of the total social structure, tend naturally to reinforce that structure and to buttress what exists, even though we may recognise that the structure is inefficient, unfair and needs to be changed. Schools do this because in most societies they are the principal instrument through which those individuals who are to take up positions of leadership, power, privilege and status within the society are selected. This being so, whatever other functions the school may be called upon to serve, the school tends to socialise its products towards maintaining the system. Those who are successful in school and obtain positions of privilege and influence are inclined to feel that it is only right that they should have been rewarded in this manner. They have worked hard, have competed successfully against others, have proved themselves to possess some qualities which others do not possess in the same measure – are they not entitled to rewards? They may not be inclined to question whether the rewards should take the form of privilege. If privileged positions exist in their society, then who is better entitled to such positions than they are. They may not be inclined to ask whether the qualities which they have demonstrated during their education are relevant to the positions which they now hold. If employers place great store by possession of certificates, then so must they, and in their turn as employers they will be inclined to require similar certificates of those they select to join them, since to select by other criteria might undermine their own position by causing others to question the nature of their own qualifications. Parents and young people in school see that certification through schooling is the high road to success in life. They are inclined not to question whether this should be so since they do not see any alternative ways whereby social rewards may be allocated which would be fairer than competitive schooling. The school opens doors to them and they are happy to use them. In these ways schooling and certification tend to legitimate the social system. Adam Curle argues that for these reasons 'education enslaves', binding men to the service of the system, and the best schools serve the system most efficiently.[2]

Schools tend to reinforce existing social systems because of their very existence, because they function as instruments for the allocation of rewards, and not necessarily because what they actually teach is designed to maintain the system (although that may be so as well). Nyerere has argued that a child may be taught in school that the supreme virtue is co-operation with others and service to those less fortunate than himself. But the

> facts of life will teach all the pupils that while co-operation may be a religious virtue the pursuit of self interest is what determines a man's status, his income, and his power. Two things will have taught this lesson. First the very existence of privilege in the society and second the basis on which selection is made for that privilege.[3]

Manley is probably right therefore when he argues that education has a political function whether or not this function is deliberately and consciously planned. The conclusion he reaches is that it is therefore necessary to plan consciously the political function of education since there are few societies in which we are content with the status quo. If we wish to change our societies we must recognise that decisions about the ways in which they should be changed are political decisions, the most fundamental of which are to be taken by legitimately constituted political authorities. Manley argues that 'education is always an extension of political purpose and must be seen as a primary, perhaps the primary agent that is available to that purpose'.[4] Whilst we may accept the first part of this statement, later we shall be considering how far the second part is true. At this point, however, we must consider further the possible implications of the first part of the statement, and note some questions and reservations.

If education is to be used to promote certain kinds of change, it may be argued that the first task is to define precisely what kind of society it is that we wish to create and that then, and only then, shall we be in a position to decide how we can use education to bring about that society. This could be interpreted as adopting a Napoleonic conception of education as 'public instruction' designed to 'throw an entire generation into an identical mould'.

In this age of national development planning, for which precise aims and objectives are assumed and in which debate tends to focus simply upon alternative strategies of achieving the objectives, it is still legitimate to ask how far this is the way in which societies have developed in the past or can be expected to develop in the future. When we were considering the nature of development and of social change we were concerned to stress the enormous complexity of the process, the limited extent of our understanding of the ways in which change occurs and the inadequacies of our current techniques for directing and controlling it. Can we legitimately seek to define the society which we wish to create other than in terms of a limited number of broad principles – such as liberty, equality and fraternity, for instance? How far can we hope to be able to determine the form of the social institutions which will enshrine these principles? Can we and should we try to define precisely the attitudes and skills which individuals should possess in order to bring about the desired society? How far does development stem from the efforts of individuals and from the challenge of ideas which may run counter to prevailing custom and received opinion amongst political leadership?

Even if we believe we can direct and control change and define the skills, attitudes and values which all members of the society should possess, how far are the decision-makers entitled to impose their conception of the future and of the appropriate strategy for achieving it upon the rest of their fellow citizens. This is an age-old and familiar question, one which we have all considered in an abstract and philosophic manner in the course of our professional training. But whilst it is not possible to give lengthy consideration to it here, the writer would argue that it is essential that all those

who are concerned with the role of education in development
should seek to come to terms with it, since many fundamental
decisions as to how we go about our everyday work will depend
upon the view we take, and the views taken by our political
leaders. How far are we concerned with liberating the minds of
our students by making them aware of the ways in which their
society works and assisting them to reach their own conclusions
by training them to think logically and independently on the
basis of valid evidence, as Curle might argue? How far are we
concerned not simply with 'awareness' but with 'conscien-
tisation' which will encourage young people to take
action against what they see as oppressive elements in their
society, as Freire would urge? How far are we concerned with
simple inculcation of attitudes and values thought to be 'relevant'
and 'appropriate' by political decision makers? This latter
question may appear to be largely academic, for although in
declarations of educational policy we frequently come across
statements of the need for the 'inculcation of the right type of
values and attitudes' and for the acquisition of 'appropriate skills,
abilities and competencies',[5] usually these lack precise definition
or are matched with more reassuring statements of 'faith in man's
ability to make rational decisions'.[6]

Sometimes, however, they are remarkably specific, as for
example: 'To promote the attitude that a nation of educated
farmers living in villages of an optimum size will become a model
of a stable and happy society'.[7] And occasionally we find very
strong statements which may be interpreted as rejecting concepts
of liberation of the individual through education, such as
President Sekou Touré's declaration that 'We shall not hesitate
to sacrifice, if it is necessary, the individual for the benefit of the
community',[8] or even the assertion of the Second National
Development Plan for Nigeria that 'a country like Nigeria
cannot allow education to be left to the whims and caprices of
individual choice'.[9] However, even in countries strongly dedicated to communalism and seeking to form their emerging
societies in more precisely defined moulds, education still tends to
be seen as a means of harnessing men and women to the
communal goals through an appeal to their reason. Nyerere, for
example, draws a very clear distinction between 'a system of
education which makes liberated men and women into skilful

users of tools, and a system of education which turns men and women into tools'.[10]

It is probably true to say that educationists in most African countries do not feel unduly constrained or threatened by such statements of policy which, perhaps sadly, have made little impact upon practice. It is probably true to say that in the African countries to which this book is directed the vision of the future society which is held by political leadership is not one which is usually very precisely defined. The main objectives of Nigeria as stated in the Second National Development Plan may be taken as an example. They comprise the building of a free and democratic, just and egalitarian society, a united, strong and self-reliant nation, a great and dynamic economy and a land of bright and full opportunities for all citizens. Such statements may readily be endorsed by all, and since they are susceptible of a variety of interpretations, educators are in practice broadly free to educate in accordance with the dictates of their personal consciences or philosophies. We should, however, periodically re-examine our consciences and re-define our philosophies. In the view of the writer we have a professional responsibility to go further than this and to make political leadership clearly aware of our views on these as on other educational issues. If we do not and if policy trends are not to our liking, we may ourselves be largely to blame.

The questions we are raising are more likely to assume significance when, having completed their education with us, our students express opinions or take actions which political authorities do not welcome. The outcome – which may take the form of a temporary closure of a university or the abolition of student organisations or overt criticism of education for failing to prevent the development of dysfunctional thinking – may be viewed as a clear instruction to educators that there are limits to their freedom and as a direction concerning the goals they should in future pursue. Whilst the writer would argue that the general trend in thinking is away from narrow patterns of schooling which, intentionally or not, force students into pre-determined moulds and towards other patterns which seek to liberate them, leaving them aware but with personal responsibility undiminished, there are not infrequently crisis situations which temporarily reverse the trend or slow its movement.

## Political Goals of Education

To this point we have been examining in what ways it is legitimate to regard the school as an instrument for achieving political purposes. We must now turn to some of the more important specific political objectives of national development in Africa and examine how far and in what ways the school may help to achieve them. It is probably true to say that in the first decade or so after independence the predominant concern of our policy-makers was with economic growth. Experience of the difficulties encountered in stimulating economic growth and growing understanding of some of the problems which it may create have brought us to a situation in which the parallel and possibly overriding political concerns of our nations are being reasserted. Material progress is largely dependent upon political stability. Yet political stability may itself be undermined by some of the manifestations of economic development, notably the failure of economic development to meet the rapidly expanding aspirations of our peoples, the increasingly evident inequalities in our societies, and the gulf which has emerged (and may be widening) between the elites of the modern sector and the mass of the people. Our countries have therefore asserted that economic growth must go hand in hand with the creation of a more egalitarian society (which is very different from what has happened in most countries in the past, where economic development has only very belatedly been followed by attempts to redistribute the benefits more equitably) and have come to a fuller understanding of the necessity of creating a stable and healthy national political system which will unify the country and mobilise all the potential of the nation in a co-operative effort for progress.

NATIONAL UNITY

The new nations of Africa embrace within artificially created frontiers a large number of subcultures upon which in more recent years have been overlaid broader distinctions: between Christian, Muslim and the more traditional faiths; between those who speak English as a second language and those who do not; between those who have entered into modern-sector employment and those who have not; and between those who operate on the national or international plane and those whose life is still essentially lived on a local plane. The ethnic and cultural differences which exist between groups and individuals are in themselves passive sources of disunity but may become serious threats to coherent and co-operative national development and, as we have seen in Nigeria and Ethiopia in recent years, even to national stability when crisis situations arise from other causes. Such situations which impel groups and individuals to fall back upon fundamental belonging identities have tended to arise where one group believes it is subject to unfair treatment, unequal opportunities or some other form of under-privilege. The strength of these fundamental loyalties has been demonstrated in much longer established states and indeed in states which have a long tradition of both political stability and economic progress. They may be observed in Britain, Belgium and Canada as well as in Africa. This fact testifies to the difficulty of eradicating such sources of disunity and of creating strong feelings of national belonging. The problems of Africa are particularly acute however. As Ajayi has put it, 'In contrast to nineteenth century Europe where the basic aim of nationalism was to fit people who shared the same culture and language into a nation state, the fundamental yearning of African nationalism has been to weld peoples speaking different languages and having different traditional cultures into one nation state.'[11] Indeed the differences between groups within a single nation are so great and so fundamental that recent policies of seeking national integration on the basis of communal integration, and the attempt to create a common national culture and a shared belonging identity, have been questioned and the alternative approach of seeking functional integration in which groups are held together by common interest and agreement has been seen as more likely to prove valid.[12]

Whichever strategy is dominant in nation-building policy, education has been seen as a major instrument for achieving the goals of unity, political stability and equality of opportunity and for circumventing situations which may give rise to conflict. This is partly because the problem is seen as being in large part, though not entirely, in the minds of men and the hope has been that young people may be effectively socialised into the national culture or made aware of the desirability of maintaining the national political framework through the formal education they may receive. It is partly of course because of the lack of alternative machinery to deal with the problem that so much faith has been pinned on the schools. We must however consider carefully whether the school is an appropriate instrument for this purpose, capable of reinforcing and stabilising the national framework.

We might begin by examining how the school has functioned in this respect in the past, and it is possible to argue that the schools have been a very positive influence for unity in at least two main ways. First, during the pre-independence years the school played a highly important role in recruiting and socialising the leadership for national political organisations. It fostered the rise of a new politically oriented elite which was to demand the transfer of power from colonial regimes by equipping it with the means to challenge that regime on its own terms, notably by providing the intellectual basis for its position and the organisational concepts upon which effective political action could be taken. Through bringing together men of high ability from many different cultural backgrounds in such schools as Kings College in Lagos, Katsina High School in northern Nigeria, Achimota college in Ghana, Tabora School in Tanzania and Munali College in Zambia, common educational experience helped to confirm in them a belief in themselves as a leadership elite and laid the foundations for working together in later life. Secondly, through schooling the development of a common language was encouraged which facilitated effective political communication and underpinned national administrative and economic activity.

It might therefore be argued that the school may continue to play this kind of role and that deliberate mixing of pupils from various cultural and regional backgrounds within a national school system may generate mutual understanding and respect and promote a common national outlook. Such a policy might be feasible at secondary level and we may see an attempt to apply it in Nigeria where every secondary school is expected to function as a unity school by enrolling pupils from other areas and states, and where each state has two federal government colleges for which the intake consists of an equal quota from each state. However at primary level the need for schools to be close to the homes of young pupils, to be cheap (and therefore to be day schools), to provide the early years of schooling with a strong practical and environmentally oriented basis, and perhaps also for the language of instruction to be the mother tongue (at least in the early years), would render such a policy largely impracticable across the whole nation. Yet primary schooling is all the formal education that the majority of children can expect to receive; to confine the policy to secondary schools would to a considerable extent mean socialising those who in any case are likely to join the nationally oriented elites and ignoring the major problem of the masses.

There are, however, even at secondary level deeper considerations. How far in the past was the socialising role of common schooling made possible by the circumstances within which the school was operating? How far did common opposition to colonial government and common aspirations for political independence dominate all other sectional concerns and conceal differences which under other circumstances might have become prominent? Will the contemporary common enemies of ignorance, poverty and disease provide as effective a rallying point as did colonialism? In any case it is surely true that common political attitudes of anti-colonialism were not created by the school even though the school may have enabled these attitudes to be rationalised and expressed. In effect was not the school simply canalising tendencies which were already in existence outside, in society at large? A number of research studies in Africa and other parts of the world suggest that whilst the school may well be good at confirming, reinforcing and extending attitudes which are already prominent in society, it is questionable how successful the school can be in inculcating attitudes which are not prominent outside its walls, or indeed which may run counter to those current in society.[13] The conclusion may be that the school is a potent influence for national unity where the general trend is in favour of unity, but where it is not and where factors for disunity are strong and active, common schooling may not be strong enough to counter them. Indeed under certain circumstances it is easy to see how it may exacerbate differences between groups.

Numerous instances may be cited where feelings of difference between groups have been strengthened by separate schooling.

remain remarkable disparities in the distribution of formal educational opportunities which have had profound political consequences and which are extremely difficult to remedy. An early advantage in terms of educational opportunity tends to reinforce itself since not only does the possession of education enable a community to benefit more readily from further educational opportunities but it puts that community in a stronger position to demand those further opportunities . Consequently the opportunity gap between an advantaged and a disadvantaged group tends to widen. Arising in large measure from the uneven distribution of educational facilities is the further factor that in some areas demand for educational facilities was both an expression of group and culture consciousness and a process which heightened feelings of difference, rivalry and competition between groups, bringing ethnic and religious differences which existed in the society closer to the surface. Whereas in the past villages competed for primary schools, more recently regions within countries have competed for universities.

However possibly the most significant way in which the schools have played a divisive role has been through serving as a means for selecting and labelling those who are to become members of one or other of the national elites. Traditional patterns of socialisation were primarily concerned with maintaining the integrity of society and children were taught the behaviour and skills which would enable them to fit productively into the society, subordinating their individuality to preserve the security and stability of the group. Schooling, on the other hand, has consciously sought to make distinctions between individuals, to develop their individual talents, and has been the instrument whereby men are set apart from and placed in new relationships to their fellows. In fulfilling this differentiating and allocative function, schooling has taken on an internally competitive nature and, despite the efforts of educators to promote attitudes of service to others and respect for the less fortunate, has helped economic forces to undermine the communalism and relative egalitarianism of most traditional societies.

We should perhaps remind ourselves that the schools, whilst serving as the instruments through which new elites came into existence, did not initiate the process. Elites are no new phenomenon in Africa but in general distinctions in traditional societies were not wide and stratification was often minimal. The new elites which we see today, and the trend towards a stratified society which has been so pronounced in West Africa in particular, have been a consequence of the general modernisation process which colonialism served to catalyse. Economic development has not merely increased the total wealth of societies but increased disparities of wealth between individuals and groups. The greater scale of the political unit has increased the disparity of power between leaderships and the man in the street. Modernisation has brought into being new categories of leadership in the governmental, commercial, intellectual and military fields. Whereas traditional elites were on the whole well integrated with their societies, modern elites have tended to become increasingly remote and socially separate, operating essentially in the modern sector of employment and in the national sphere.

It has been a matter of concern to many observers that there has been a tendency for the gaps between modern sector elites and the masses to widen and for access to the elites to become significantly more restricted by comparison with the numbers now claiming qualifications for entry. Not unnaturally there has been a tendency on the part of new elites to self-perpetuation, in some cases by resisting the efforts of rising elite aspirants, often with higher educational qualifications than existing elite members, to gain the share of power and status to which they believe themselves entitled. The friction between university and secondary school students and the authorities in some countries may largely be attributed to resentment on the part of the former that their access to positions of power, status and privilege is restricted by the fact that many of those who assumed positions in the immediate post-independence years were relatively youthful; it may be some time before a more normal pattern of entry, promotion and retirement is established in the occupational structure.

Elite members will also seek for their own children the best education available and are in an excellent position to ensure their eventual access to elite positions. It has been suggested, for example by Schiman in respect of Ghana,[17] that children from higher socio-economic groups are over-represented in secondary and tertiary education. A number of reasons can be advanced to account for this. The practice of charging fees, coupled with the cost to parents in the rural areas of doing without the services of their children on the farm, works to the advantage of the more wealthy and the urban worker. The existence of fee-paying private schools often geared to the passing of selection examinations is a further mechanism for increasing the degree of social selection. Additionally, of course, there is the advantage children of elite parents have in coping with the demands which schooling makes as compared to children of uneducated parents – a literate home environment, parental assistance and encouragement, and the existence of patterns of achievement-motivation in the home which are likely to lead to greater success in schooling.

It may be argued that in many African countries the development of new elites and the tendency towards stratification which has been noted are as yet only incipient, potential but not yet actual sources of political disunity and instability. This is due to the fact that the predominantly rural nature of society has inhibited the development of class consciousness among the underprivileged because kinship ties provide a strong bond between the rich and the poor within the extended family, preventing the development of clear social class demarcations, and because, until recently, there has been considerable opportunity for upwards social mobility. Because of the small size of elite groups, most students in secondary and tertiary educational institutions are still likely to come from relatively under-privileged backgrounds. Insofar as disadvantaged groups have been conscious of their disadvantage, it has been suggested, their dissatisfaction has been expressed in demands for more and longer schooling in order that their children may have improved opportunities of obtaining good modern sector employment rather than in the demand for the reduction of privilege and for more equal distribution of the direct benefits of economic development.[18] However this situation is already changing. The possibilities of conflict are likely to grow where increases in job opportunities do not keep pace with the numbers of qualified job seekers and if efforts are made to adopt development strategies which may involve possibly temporary restrictions on the expansion of formal education facilities or replacement of these by other patterns of educational provision which do not appear to the clientele to offer equal opportunities to those offered by the school in the past. It must be added that concern to maintain political stability which may be threatened by such developments is coupled with very genuine belief in the need for social justice and for creating egalitarian societies.

## POLITICAL PARTICIPATION

It is widely accepted in Africa that healthy political development, and in particular the achievement of stable egalitarian societies, is adversely affected by the mal-distribution of education. Democratic political processes have been threatened and undermined in many countries by the fact that political leadership has not been constrained by its electorate owing to the lack of general awareness of national development issues and the limited capacity of the mass of the people to participate in decision making, even in ways open to them, because of their widespread ignorance of the law, of their rights under the law and of the procedures which they might use to influence those who act on their behalf and in their name. Democratic government is currently being restored in Nigeria, Ghana and the Ivory Coast, and the need to strengthen democracy in other countries where civilian rule has survived, though sometimes precariously, is commonly recognised. Yet, as Brigadier Shehu pointed out in Nigeria during the lengthy period of debate on the form of the new constitution, which involved the widely publicised debates of a Constituent Assembly and the creation of a new electoral roll, 'A significant number of our people are still on the periphery of the constitutional debate and activity'.[19]

This is a situation which exists in many countries with the consequence that the health of the governmental structure has been dependent upon the honesty, acumen and devotion of individual politicians operating without the constraints of an informed and politically conscious electorate in a context which offers considerable personal rewards for the pursuit of personal or sectional interests. It is hardly surprising that many political leaders have failed the test, that leadership in some cases has become authoritarian, often tinged with corruption, and has frequently given the impression of having lost touch with the needs and wishes of the mass of the people. Political organisation has generally been weak. Whilst Tanzania offers an example of a country which has established a party organisation which reaches down to the level of individual households, for the most part political activity has been confined to elite groups and characterised by crude appeals to sectional interest behind a smokescreen of lip service to high national ideals. In many countries where the activities of politicians have become suspect, there has been a widespread loss of confidence in the capacity of democratic processes to remedy the situation and recourse to action by the military has become almost acceptable and popular.

Attempts to strengthen democratic processes in many countries have become characterised recently by a consciousness of the need to devolve decision-making power to levels closer to and more susceptible of control by the people. Underlying the Sierra Leone Development Plan 1974/5–1978/9, is what the President has termed 'the concept of the people's participation in development in partnership with the Government'.[20] Similar thinking lay behind the reorganisation of local government machinery by Nigeria's former military rulers, who asserted the need to establish sound political activity at local level in order that the reintroduction of civilian rule at national level might be more soundly based, and also behind the adoption in Tanzania and other countries of the principle of decentralising decision making.

For such measures to be effective requires that education systems, in addition to removing as far as possible the sources of political instability for which they are partly responsible, seek more effectively than has been the case in the past to create a politically aware electorate with a genuine capacity to participate in political processes. It may be that one way in which this may be achieved is through the decentralisation of responsibility in respect of education itself. The Gambian government has recognised the extent to which the success of its policy of making education more meaningful to what is almost entirely an agricultural and rural community 'calls for the active participation of a larger number of people in the determination and administration of the educational facilities in each region'.[21] In a number of ways in a number of countries we are seeing the foundations of a national policy for the development of a self-reliant nation being expressed in terms of educational administration.

## Implications for Education

It has been argued in the foregoing pages that there is good reason for concern about the ways in which current education systems operate and more than sufficient reason for examining further in what ways education systems may be modified in order better to assist in achieving the political aspirations of African states. We must now examine some of the solutions which have been mooted and ask ourselves how far these are likely to be successful.

### THE DEMOCRATISATION OF EDUCATION

One particular thrust of educational reform which has been seen as offering more effective means of harnessing the total human resources of the nation, of removing some of the major internal sources of dissension and of improving the capacity of the people as a whole to participate in the management of their own affairs, is that of widening access to education and of making it available to all citizens, both old and young. Concern to maintain political stability is thus allied with the concern of many to promote social justice and to create more egalitarian societies, through the provision of more equal opportunities. It should perhaps be noted that such aims may be interpreted in very different ways by states possessing different political ideologies. It is probably true that over much of Africa it has been generally accepted, even if not explicitly stated, that inequalities of wealth, status and power are inevitable since the occupational structure makes some degree of stratification inevitable. It is also accepted that the fairest way of allocating these privileges is on the basis of merit, and education has been seen as the most appropriate means of assessing merit. A meritocracy will therefore seek political stability and social justice by extending educational opportunities in order that all members of the society have equal opportunity to compete for the limited number of positions of privilege. It is believed that through economic development a growing number of such positions will become available and that the leadership of the few will lead the majority forward to a position in which their basic needs and aspirations will be satisfied and the differentials between the elites and the mass of the people will be reduced. It may further be argued that the existence of continuing inequalities is not merely inevitable but to some degree desirable as a means of motivating the people to make the fullest use of whatever talents they possess. The 1974–8 Development Plan of Kenya, for example, clearly embodies this principle:

> the present plan provides opportunities for everyone to participate actively in the economy and in so doing improve his standard of living. Such improvements are bound to be achieved more quickly by some than by others, however. Equal income for everyone is therefore not the object of this plan. Differences in skill, effort and initiative need to be recognised and rewarded.[22]

The success of such a strategy clearly depends upon the availability of equal educational opportunity and upon the extent to which economic development appears to offer the people real hope of stisfying their aspirations eventually, if not immediately.

Such a strategy is not universally accepted, however. Tanzania has adopted a policy of widening access to education from a very different standpoint. Inequality is not accepted as inevitable nor as a desirable means of mobilising the effort and talents of the people. Instead a direct attack is being made on the existence of privilege to ensure that the benefits of development are more equitably distributed immediately. Such a policy will take time to achieve its desired effects and the practical measures which may more readily be taken relate to control of material rewards. Since privilege may equally be associated with power and status as with wealth, and since any country, whatever its ideology, is likely to require bureaucrats and technocrats operating on the national plane, it will be no easy matter to achieve genuine social equality or to persuade people that privilege no longer exists. Consequently Tanzania's extension of educational opportunity is characterised by two features which are not commonly found elsewhere. The first of these is the use of education for overt political socialisation to promote understanding of the national ideology, to promote respect for political and social equality and reduce the tendency for the possession of high-order skill to be regarded as an entitlement to privilege. To this matter we will turn in a later section. The second is to limit the education provided to the great majority to that required by them for life in their village communities and to provide further education only to the small number needed to meet the high-level manpower needs of the nation, selecting this small number not simply on the basis of academic merit but also on the basis of demonstrated qualities of commitment to their fellow men in the context of the national ideology of 'ujamaa' or 'familyhood'.

It is not our concern here to debate the merits of these strategies but simply to note the danger of assuming that the democratisation of education will have the same purposes, take the same form, and normally involve the provision of universal primary education in the first stage and later the provision of universal post-primary education according to conventional international models. Indeed of late there has been much discussion of alternative models for the provision of mass education, stemming in part from the concern of advocates of fundamental education that education should be viewed as a lifelong process and not neglect the needs of the adult, and in part also from the desire of the de-schoolers that formal structures of education should no longer reinforce existing inequalities and injustices in society. In recent years the focus of discussion has been largely upon the potentiality of non-formal education to complement and supplement formal education. It is probable that the prevailing commitment to formal education will continue for a number of reasons. First, the school has won widespread and passionate acceptance so that it is likely to be politically impossible for African governments to abandon school systems. Secondly, it is not clear what alternatives may be feasible in the African context, although some clarification may emerge from Guinea-Bissau where Paulo Freire is currently advising on educational development. Thirdly, where commitment to meritocracy is strong the schools with their examinations and certificates offer a simple and widely acceptable means of determining merit. And fourthly, the school system appears more susceptible to control and manipulation than non-formal provision might be. Whilst Senegal has decided deliberately to restrict primary education to 50 per cent of the appropriate age group, at least until the end of this century, the great majority of

African states still accept the commitment to universal primary education into which they entered following the Addis Ababa Conference of 1960. Nigeria, in its relative affluence, has already committed itself to extending junior secondary education from 1981. It appears likely that the pattern which will emerge in most African countries is one in which the attempt will be made to provide all children with a minimum period of basic formal education to be followed by a diversity of provision in which formal and non-formal elements will be combined to provide a system of mass education closely geared to prevailing conceptions of national need. It is probable that for the majority of African children formal education will cease at the end of the minimum period.

We now turn to consider how far such systems of basic education as exist or are likely to emerge can provide equality of opportunity. Since the formal component of such systems is likely to be the fundamental determinant of success in the total system, it is upon this component that we shall primarily focus.

Husen has reminded us that there are three aspects to the provision of equality of educational opportunity: to start education on an equal footing; to receive equal treatment during education irrespective of genetic equipment or social origin; and equal opportunity to succeed in and through education.[23] The first concern of educational planners in this respect is likely to be the massive expansion of school facilities, the abolition of fees, and the provision of qualified teachers to all schools, in order that no region of a country may suffer disadvantage. The extent to which finances will permit this is of course crucial, but in view of the immense investment involved we need perhaps to look a little more closely at how far the goal of equality of opportunity will be met by such means. It has been not infrequently pointed out in recent years that merely to admit all children to school will not guarantee that all children will possess the same ability to succeed in and make use of the education they receive. We recognise that children are very different in the range of talents, motivation and experience they bring to school and it may therefore be argued that schools need to provide a great diversity of forms and kinds of experience to cater equally for all children. Advocacy of individualised instruction, of group methods, of enquiry techniques and the like, has largely been based upon the need to enable individual children to learn at their own pace and in the way best suited to them.

However, here we meet with a major problem, over and above that of providing the necessary equipment and skilled teachers. Equality of opportunity is often interpreted as meaning that all children should receive the same treatment, should receive a common education through the same procedures, according to the same syllabuses and subject to the same means of assessment. To treat different children and groups of children differently may not be to treat them equally and may open the door to conferring advantage on some. It is important that the system appears to treat children equally. An unsophisticated clientele will then attribute inequality of performance not to the school but to the child – if he has not shown sufficient merit, then he does not deserve to pass the examination and to obtain a well paid job. Where schools are very different or provide differential education, they are exposed to criticism which may well undermine their credibility. We should also note that there are other arguments favouring the provision of common education, deriving notably from the concern of the planners with generating specific kinds of skill associated with the possession of appropriate attitudes believed to be necessary for overall national economic development.

At this time we are seeing African countries struggling in diverse ways to reconcile these considerations. The comprehensive principle whereby various talents and levels of ability may be provided for within a socially integrating single institution has been enunciated and embodied in a variety of institutions but remains open to the question as to whether, in face of social pressure for academic education of a kind which still leads to the most prestigious posts, adequate status can be given to vocational and practical studies. A senior official in one of Nigeria's states recently explained to the writer that his government had recently decided to revert to a system of specialised secondary academic and technical schools as the only means of ensuring an adequate flow of technically qualified personnel. The solutions which appear to be generally finding favour at secondary level involve the provision of two stages of junior and senior secondary schooling, the first stage providing all students with technical and pre-vocational education and the second stage providing more advanced academic studies for those demonstrating high ability. At primary level it appears that we shall see a continuance of the provision of a common framework for studies but with the schools permitted to provide a limited range of options to enable them to make fuller use of the particular resources to be found in the environment of the school and to meet needs which are of a local nature, particularly in respect of vocational skills.

The outcome will, inevitably, be a compromise, providing only limited equality of opportunity in real terms. However, so long as this remains acceptable to the clientele, and so long as the schools themselves are equitably treated in terms of staffing, plant and equipment, perhaps we cannot hope for more. The ideals of individualised provision to meet the unique needs and talents of individual children and of life long education in accordance with the aspirations of individuals appear likely to demand resources beyond the capacity of even the richest nations. The question, however, is for how long the clientele will remain satisfied with the kind and degree of opportunity offered. It may be asked whether equality of opportunity should be confined merely to opportunities to compete for rewards and how far the concept should not be extended to embrace opportunities to put education into use. Clearly, if employment opportunities are not available to all who qualify we shall face the dual problem of demands for yet more education and of widespread discontent among an articulate and schooled population amongst whom education has generated consumption demands which the economy cannot answer. This issue will be examined in a later chapter. Here we must note the political dangers of such a situation. Although political purposes may lead us to provide mass education, political stability may well be undermined where the extension of education is not matched by a growth in outlets for the products of education. Experience elsewhere in the world suggests that the correlation between the mass provision of education and political stability is by no means as strong as we sometimes believe.

## POLITICAL EDUCATION

This danger has also been long recognised and in response to it a second educational solution has found general favour, that of manipulating the form and content of education to create 'appropriate' attitudes among the rising generations. Repeated official pronouncements about the need to 'decolonise' education, to inculcate a spirit of co-operation, service and self sacrifice, and attitudes of respect for properly constituted authority and for traditional values, can hardly be criticised at face value. These are things which schools everywhere are asked to do. However, these are also things which schools have tended to do very badly for reasons dealt with above. Consequently there has been a tendency to ask the schools to provide overt political socialisation of a more rigorous and purposive kind than most of us in our educational philosophy courses have been led to expect. There are two questions we as responsible educators should ask ourselves: how far should the school be used to inculcate prescribed political attitudes and beliefs, and how far can the school hope to succeed in the task?

It may be helpful in thinking about the first of these questions to recall a statement made at an educational conference by one of Africa's leading political scientists, Professor Ali Mazrui, a few years ago:

> indoctrination in education is desirable in the primary schools; it is defensible in the secondary schools; but it is quite demeaning beyond secondary education. It is desirable at the primary level because children need some guidance as they evolve a capacity for making choices, and the political world can seem mysterious and even frightening without some explanation. Transmission of political values to children at the primary level, *provided the values are broad and rudimentary and basic to the task of living in society*, is in my opinion an education imperative.
>
> At the secondary school level, the transmission of values should become more sophisticated, with a high degree of critical flexibility and individual choice permitted within the system. The higher levels of secondary education may begin to dispense with political education as a process of socialisation, and embark on political analysis as a more detached and independent approach to the understanding of politics.
>
> By the time they complete the sixth form the students have to be treated as intellectual adults from the point of view of

political values. In other words, the emphasis from then on ought to be in perfecting the critical faculties and sharpening individual reasoning, rather than transmitting social values.[24]

It is important to note the qualifications with which this statement is hedged and which I have italicised. What are the basic values to which Mazrui refers? He himself defines them as 'Tolerance, Toil and Teamwork', values which are clearly far removed from party creed and which most educationists would accept. But are these the values which will be stressed by political leadership, particularly where they are faced by crisis situations which threaten the success and continuance of the policies they are pursuing? For example the syllabuses on political education produced by the United National Independence Party in Zambia clearly seek to build up support for the party and for its current leadership: 'The Party, being the only mass movement in the country, has demonstrated beyond doubt the support it enjoys from the people of Zambia. This, however, should not be taken for granted as such support, if not backed by political education on a wide scale, can very easily fade away overnight.'[25] There is no shortage in the world around us of examples of political education which, no doubt for the best of motives, seek to shape the minds of young people in far more explicit moulds than Mazrui envisages, which seek not mere understanding but commitment, and which do not differentiate between policies and personalities.

It is interesting also that whilst Mazrui would emphasise the transmission of his broad and rudimentary values at primary level and would seek to increasingly develop critical and individual judgement at secondary level, in practice where states have sought to implement political education they have tended to concentrate upon the transmission of values at secondary level. Clearly this implies a desire to form the minds and outlook of those who are most likely to assume positions of leadership in the society. To many of us this must be a good deal more worrying if we believe that the future of our societies must depend upon the character of the contribution of a wide range of individuals. It is also worrying that many of the political problems which our countries face concern the primary school leavers who have not been able to move into secondary education, the numbers of whom are likely to rise very considerably as universal primary education policies are implemented. We may well feel that it would be unwise not to provide some form of political education to primary pupils even though we may not wish the overt socialisation element to go beyond the Mazrui prescription.

We educationists are often curiously ambivalent when we come to defining how far we ourselves would wish to go in seeking to inculcate prescribed attitudes and values. Many of us would argue that the school plays its role in modernising society by equipping individuals with the skills they will need if they are to understand, adapt to and exert influence upon the changing circumstances in which they will live. Whilst the nature of change is so ill-understood and the factors which will bring about future change are not easily to be anticipated, we find it difficult to view education as a process which will simply produce the social components for the economic and political systems which await them or which are being designed for them. We believe that educated people will be better able than their uneducated fellows to channel and direct the processes of change and by their efforts promote those changes which they believe to be desirable and inhibit those which are not. What Africa needs, says Hanson, are 'unconventional minds capable of finding unconventional answers to problems certain to stagger any but the most imaginative.'[26]

If education is to equip people in this way it seems clear that schools cannot seek to crib, cabin and confine the growing minds entrusted to them in an attempt to determine precisely their pattern of behaviour. They cannot seek to limit the range of enquiry in which young people may wish to engage, to keep them selectively ignorant and to inculcate in them passive and conforming attitudes. Such a policy would not produce the kind of people the modernisation of Africa demands. As Nyerere has said, 'Africa needs change; and change needs to start somewhere'.[27] (We have previously referred to his distinction between a system of education which makes liberated men and women into skilful users of tools, and a system of education which turns men and women into tools.)

However, if education is to seek to raise the capacity of men to adapt to change and to respond purposively and positively to new pressures and to old constraints, it must seek to develop in young people the capacity to enquire, to challenge, to question and to weigh evidence before arriving at independent conclusions. This is of course the kind of statement which has been the stock-in-trade of educationists and national leaders for a very long time but all too often we have not thought out its implications sufficiently clearly. If young people are to think in these ways then we cannot expect, and far less guarantee, that they will think as we do or as our political leadership would have them think. Even the kind of basic values advocated by Mazrui will be acceptable to them only in so far as their own reason convinces them they are a sound basis upon which to base their lives. And it is clear also that young people who do think independently and insist on subjecting the values and behaviour of their elders to critical scrutiny are not necessarily going to fit comfortably back into the society from which they have come. Yet teachers and civic leaders all over the world are confused and worried by the fact that the younger generations whom they have trained to think for themselves are inclined to reject, or at least to question, many of the principles and values which they themselves hold most dear. The incorporation of educated young people into a society can never be easy and free from strains. Indeed it may well be argued that in societies which genuinely seek change it is a fundamental task of the school to set up strains, to ensure that current institutions, processes and principles are constantly re-evaluated in order that healthy adjustment may take place.

Clearly there must be limits to the freedom with which individuals may act in accordance with their judgement. Where societies make adequate provision for the expression of individual opinion many of us would accept that opinion should be expressed through the legitimate channels thereby made available, a point of view which in recent years has become unfashionable amongst those who seek the rapid achievement of their political aspirations and who see in violence and revolution more effective means for their purposes. Whilst no legally constituted government can be expected to condone illegal action, those in authority in Africa and elsewhere have a responsibility to ensure that the legal channels available are sufficient and effective, and in particular to accept as a normal feature of political life political protest which is the legitimate expression of concern. Sadly this has not always been the case, and in particular the expression of non-conforming student opinion has too often been regarded as unworthy and ungrateful troublemaking.

How successful is political socialisation in the schools likely to be in terms of removing dysfunctional attitudes and aspirations and implanting more generally desirable patterns? Most educationists would probably argue that the school can certainly make an impact in the cognitive domain and would not question that there is a body of political information and understanding which can and should be included in the school curriculum. But they would be far less sure that, even if they were fully committed to making an impact in the affective domain, their efforts could bring about permanent change in the patterns of behaviour of their pupils, so long as the social climate and employment structures remain as they are.

It appears likely that schooling will be no more efficient in this respect than in the past when schools have been expected to persuade young people of the dignity of labour and the desirability of returning to their homes and placing themselves at the service of their communities. Coleman has suggested that pre-second world war Japan and the Soviet Union are two examples of countries which sought to use education for deliberate and systematic political socialisation and which succeeded in creating a technically competent but loyal and submissive population. This success, however, he would argue, was attributable not so much to the use of education for this purpose as to the existence of ample and alternative channels of upwards social mobility created by relatively advanced and rapidly expanding economies.[28] Could even the Soviet Union and Japan have succeeded in an economic situation involving the widespread frustration of the natural aspirations of people for such social mobility or where the political ideas taught in the school were substantially less in tune with the prevailing currents of aspiration and belief in the adult community?

Clearly much would depend upon the capacity of teachers both to organise and teach political content and to communicate appropriate political attitudes by personal example. We should not underestimate the difficulty of the former task if we intend more than a mere civics course and if political consciousness is to pervade the whole curriculum. There is also the question of how teachers themselves should be appropriately socialised through their own personal and professional education, both pre-service and in-service. In Tanzania political commitment is taken into account in the selection of teachers but we are all aware of how difficult such commitment is to assess, particularly in face of the pressures presented by acute teacher shortage. Is political indoctrination appropriate to teacher education which otherwise aims to prepare teachers to play a genuinely professional role? Mazrui with his views on secondary and tertiary education would certainly reject overt socialisation. Furthermore teachers commonly regard themselves as a disadvantaged elite group and cannot be assumed to possess the political attitudes which leadership may seek to promote. Finally, where large numbers of expatriates are employed in teaching, particularly in secondary and teacher education, a further set of problems may arise.

Certainly little attitudinal change is likely to be achieved through exhortation alone, whether from political leadership or teachers. Pupils and their parents possess a very shrewd understanding of where their own interests lie and have learned what value to place upon the statements of those who, having won their places in the sun, attempt to persuade others of the virtues of living in the shade. Yet whilst political education has been developed as a reasonably efficient tool in those contexts where the struggle against colonialism has continued into recent years, in few countries has it been effectively developed to cope with the post-colonial explosion of demands and expectations. Tanzania is perhaps the major exception and it is worthwhile examining briefly how this country has set about inculcating socialist attitudes among its people.

The key to the Tanzanian approach, despite statements to the contrary and the much publicised inclusion of political education in the curriculum of university and schools, lies in the attempt to revolutionise the social context through the ujamaa villagisation policy. Essentially the people of Tanzania are to learn about socialism and are to appreciate its virtue not through expositions of the theory but through living socialism in their day to day lives. The ujamaa villages in which the great majority of the people will continue to live are not yet socialist communities but they are expected to evolve towards socialism as the people, through practising elements of it, come to recognise that it works and as their understanding of their experience is sharpened by extensive programmes of adult education. As society itself moves towards more completely socialist forms, the formal educational institutions will find themselves playing the role to which they are best suited, reinforcing and confirming the dominant political trends in their societal context, no longer being called upon to preach principles not being practised outside their walls. The schools themselves are being called upon not merely to explain but to practise socialism by becoming working communities in miniature and by integrating themselves more completely with the evolving communities they serve. In this way the school and the ujamaa community will, it is hoped, become mutually reinforcing agencies. Since, in theory at least, the number of pupils moving on to secondary education will be small (the demands of Tanzania's modern sector also being small) and since those who receive secondary and further education will be selected according not merely to academic criteria but also on the basis of their commitment to their communities as assessed by their fellow members of those communities, the school will no longer present itself as a means of escape from the village and will no longer encourage the dysfunctional selfish and competitive attitudes so commonly complained of elsewhere.

This at least is the theory but Tanzanians would readily admit that it will take considerable time before the reality is achieved. As Nyerere, who has himself been bluntly critical of the limited progress made so far, has said 'if we state that some new Jerusalem is where we are going, and then we begin the journey, our friends should not be disappointed when they find that we are still in the desert.'[29]

The Tanzanian strategy may well not be appropriate in other African countries. Tanzania is a poor country in which inequalities of wealth and opportunities for personal advancement have for some time been far less than those existing in neighbouring countries. Its political leadership has been relatively unchallenged and possesses a clear vision of the future, but its few resources limit the range of alternatives open to its people. Nevertheless other countries can learn from the clarity of its theoretical analysis of its situation and from its experience in translating theory into practice.

But if, as seems clear, there are serious difficulties of turning policy into successful practice in Tanzania, where major efforts have been made to reform society and the school simultaneously, how much more serious are the difficulties likely to be in countries where social divisions and inequalities are more extreme and deeply rooted? The writer is inclined to believe that deliberate political socialisation of a narrow and doctrinal kind has a highly variable and unpredictable impact upon pupils, and that this impact is likely to depend not so much upon programmes of study conducted within the school as upon the climate prevailing in the social context, the strength of reinforcing or negating influences outside the school. Education, it may be argued, may make a man capable of political participation but cannot guarantee the direction of that participation.

CULTURAL IDENTITY

A final set of political considerations should now be noted. Among the concerns of political leadership has been the desire to establish national cultural identity and individuality in the face of tremendous pressures from the outside world which appear to be undermining many valued aspects of traditional culture and promoting the growth of discordant materialism and individualism. In particular the rejection by young people of traditional sanctions and constraints and the growth among them of aggressive and intolerant patterns of behaviour have been widely condemned. The spread of what is termed indiscipline in schools has been a recent preoccupation of educationists and others in Nigeria in particular.

There has in consequence been a widespread effort on the part of leadership to reconcile and synthesise the drive towards modernisation with the conservation of the cultural matrix, as a means both of maintaining social discipline and of channelling the energies of the people in constructive directions through the appeal to their pride in their unique cultural identity. Even major social changes such as villagisation in Tanzania have been justified as a return to enduring traditional values. New philosophies of national development have been proclaimed which seek modernisation in the name of traditional symbols and values. President Kaunda in Zambia has explained that the Humanist philosophy of that country 'must be understood against the background of what we know to have been the way of life enjoyed by our forefathers'.[30] (Yet in Ghana the former head of State General Acheampong, speaking of the Charter of the National Redemption Council, said 'it is our aim to attack the foundations of our society, to remove the factors militating against our rapid and orderly development and to create conditions for the emergence of a new man . . . We have embarked upon a revolution in our culture and values.'[31])

Statements of national goals often echo the thinking of the 1925 memorandum in appearing to propose the selection of worthy elements in traditional life for preservation and the discarding of those elements which appear likely to impede development but, as we have seen, human society has so far defied the efforts of leadership to manipulate particular elements within its dynamic whole. The very fact that national leaders seek to do so through national machinery which is itself remote from traditional reality and in the light of value systems not derived from that reality may be sufficient to render their efforts in this direction abortive.

It must be questioned how far political philosophies which appeal to tradition, such as Zambian Humanism and Tanzanian Socialism, can be genuinely rooted in the shifting cultures of their society and how far they reflect the present will of the people. It may well be argued that appeals to tradition viewed as a means of mobilising the people behind coherent and planned modernisation have as yet proved relatively undynamic and ineffective. Yet efforts to avoid the complete destruction of traditional culture and to ensure that the new national societies of Africa may possess the stability, strength and confidence which may be derived from feelings of continuity with the past and from strong belonging identity, are both noble and expedient.

The central question, however, remains that asked by Kaunda 'How do we preserve what is good in our traditions and at the same time allow ourselves to benefit from the science and technology of our friends?'[32] To this question there are as yet no very clear answers. Inevitably, perhaps, leadership has looked to the educational system to provide at least part of the answer. From some educationists we have heard the call for the teaching of aspects of traditional cultures in the schools, for the inclusion of dance and song, stories, legends and riddles, things previously taught in the homes which it is now feared may no longer be so, and which in the schools may serve as effective vehicles for more modern educational purposes. Few would doubt that we should not deny to African children what after all is part of the birthright of all children in all societies; nevertheless it may be questioned how far such measures will make the kind of strong socialising impact which is envisaged upon the minds of young people already firmly caught up in the excitement of the modernising process and attracted by the new and non-traditional possibilities to which their education and the changing world around them will already have introduced them. We have also heard calls for the reconstruction of syllabuses in the humanities and social studies areas to stress local, environmental and national studies, and to reduce the attention paid to 'irrelevant' studies of the history and geography of other parts of the world. Again few would doubt that in the past schooling has purveyed an unbalanced diet and left children not merely ignorant of many things in their own society which they need to know but also with a distorted view of the relative significance of their own culture and those of distant peoples. However in redressing the balance there is some danger in going to the other extreme and there are strong objections to an education which confines the child too narrowly within his own culture. It has been said that it was probably not the fish which discovered the existence of water. Whilst African children will certainly need a deep and accurate understanding of the society within which they live, it is unlikely that they will arrive at the necessary knowledge and understanding and appreciate the nature of the changes taking place around them unless their education seeks at least in part to take them outside their own society, to provide them with a broader frame of reference for their thinking. A properly balanced education for the citizen of tomorrow must immerse the child in his society but at the same time set a distance between the child and his society in order that he may arrive at a truer understanding of its needs and potentiality.

In respect of cultural identity, as with the other political goals we have considered, the educational implications are by no means simple and clearcut. Compromise there must be in other respects also. In this chapter we have been considering some of the political goals which education systems are called upon to promote. In the following chapter we shall be studying some of the economic goals set for education. There it will become apparent that in crucial respects the achievement of economic goals appears to require measures which may well operate against the achievement of political goals and vice versa.

## References

1. M. Manley, 'Politics, Society and the Total School', keynote address, *Report of the Sixth Commonwealth Education Conference*, Jamaica, 1974 (Commonwealth Secretariat, 1974).
2. A. Curle, *Education for Liberation* (London: Tavistock Publications, 1973) pp. 12–13.
3. J. K. Nyerere, Speech to the Dag Hammarskjold Seminar on Education and Training and Alternatives in Education in African Countries, Dar es Salaam, 20 May 1974.
4. Manley, 'Politics, Society and the Total School'.
5. Federal Republic of Nigeria, *National Policy on Education* (Lagos: Federal Ministry of Information, 1977) p. 4.
6. *Ibid.*
7. The Gambia, *Education Policy 1974/5–1984/5*, Third Draft, Education Philosophy, Aims and Objectives, para 1.1.3.6 (n.d.).
8. Quoted in L. Adamalekun, *Sekou Touré's Guinea* (London: Methuen, 1977).
9. Federal Republic of Nigeria, *Second National Development Plan, 1970–74*, (Lagos: Ministry of Information, 1970) p. 235.
10. Nyerere, Speech to the Dag Hammarskjold Seminar.
11. F. A. Ajayi, 'The place of African History and Culture in the Process of Nation Building in Africa South of the Sahara', in I. Wallerstein (ed.), *Education and Social Change in the Colonial Situation* (Wiley and Sons, 1966) p. 606.
12. See D. Ronen, 'Alternative Patterns of Integration in African States', *Journal of Modern African Studies*, vol. 14 no. 4 (1976) pp. 577–96.
13. See O. Klineberg and M. Zavalloni, *Nationalism and Tribalism among African Students* (Brussels: Mouton et Cie, 1969) for Ghana, Ethiopia, Senegal, Uganda, Zaire; also N. K. Onuoha, 'The role of Education in Nation Building: A Case Study of Nigeria', *West African Journal of Education*, vol. XIX no. 3 (October 1975).
14. 'The Politics of UPE', *West Africa*, no. 3140 (12 September 1977) p. 1854.
15. Reported in Correspondence, *West Africa*, no. 3014 (31 March 1977) p. 371.
16. P. J. Foster, 'Ethnicity and the Schools in Ghana', *Comparative Education Review*, October 1962, p. 127.
17. D. A. Schiman, 'Selection for Secondary School in Ghana', *West African Journal of Education*, vol. XV no. 3 (October 1971).
18. See G. E. Hurd, 'Education in Social Development', in J. Lowe, N. Grant, and T. D. Williams, *Education and Nation Building in the Third World* (Edinburgh: Scottish Academic Press, 1971) p. 129: also S. P. Heyneman,

'Why Impoverished Children do Well in Ugandan Schools', *Comparative Education*, vol. 15 no. 2 (June 1979).

19. Shehu Musa Yar 'Adua, reported in *West Africa*, no. 3149 (14 November 1977) p. 2325.

20. S. Stevens, 'Message', *National Development Plan 1974/5–1978/9* (Freetown: Ministry of Development and Economic Planning, 1974) p. iii.

21. The Gambia, *Education Policy*, Introduction, p. ii.

22. Republic of Kenya, *Development Plan 1974–1978*, Part 1, (Nairobi: Government Printer, 1974) p. 3. See also discussion in D. Court, *Development Policy and Educational Opportunity: the experience of Kenya and Tanzania* (Paris: IIEP UNESCO, 1978).

23. T. Husen, *Social Background and Educational Career* (OECD, 1972) pp. 14–15.

24. A. Mazrui, 'National Goals and Political Philosophies in Africa: the Implications for Teacher Education', in S. Kajubi, *Reform of the Professional Education of Teachers in Africa*, Report of the Conference of the Association for Teacher Education in Africa (Makerere, 1973) p. 105.

25. United National Independence Party, *Syllabuses on Political Education in Zambia* (Lusaka: Office of the Secretary-General of the Party, 1975) p. iv.

26. J. W. Hanson, *Imagination and Hallucination in African Education* (Michigan State University, Institute for International Studies in Education, 1965) p. 3.

27. Nyerere, Speech to the Dag Hammarskjold Seminar.

28. J. S. Coleman, *Education and Political Development* (Princeton University Press, 1965) p. 232.

29. J. K. Nyerere, interview with David Martin, *New Internationalist*, May 1973, p. 7.

30. K. Kaunda, *Humanism in Zambia*, vol. 1, (Lusaka: Zambia Information Services, n.d.) p. 5.

31. I. K. Acheampong, 'Guide to the Study of the Charter of the National Redemption Council' (February 1972).

32. Kaunda, *Humanism in Zambia*, p. 9.

# 4

# Economics and Education

## Investment in Education

The publication in 1960 of the report of a commission on higher education in Nigeria headed by Sir Eric Ashby may be said to have marked the beginning of a new era in thinking about the role of education in development in West Africa. The report bore the title 'Investment in Education' and embodied clear recognition of the intimate relationship which exists between education and economic development. It was largely based upon a survey of manpower needs conducted by Frederick Harbison and sought to establish by what kinds of educational development these needs might be met. It clearly perceived educational planning as no longer the exclusive concern of ministries of education but as an integral part of general development planning.[1] Today, when the concepts of integrated development planning and of education as a form of economic investment are commonplace and the technique of planning according to manpower needs has become almost unquestioned orthodoxy, the reader may be surprised that the 'new era' referred to is of such recent origin. Since in the following chapters the reader is to be invited to question the relevance and validity of these concepts, he should perhaps begin with some understanding of the way in which they came to assume their current importance.

It is necessary first of all to realise that the responsibility of governments to involve themselves directly in economic activities and to plan the economic development of their societies was not as widely and fully recognised in the past as it is today. Of course from a very early date colonial governments were engaged in providing social 'services' such as schools, medical facilities and guidance to farmers and other producers through extension activities of various government departments, but until the mid-

1930s the dominant conception of government held by the colonial powers was a considerably more limited one than would be acceptable today. Governments, it was held, should seek to provide sound administration, maintain law and order, and build up the infrastructure of communications, power supplies and other services – to provide the framework necessary for economic development to take place – but responsibility for that development was to be largely left to private enterprise. The idea that government should actively participate in economic development through planning and directing the process and through direct investment in it was one which, whilst perhaps never completely absent in the African dependencies, developed only relatively slowly. In addition it would not be unfair to suggest that concern for economic development itself was muted by the deep concern felt in the years following the First World War about the need to protect subject people from exploitation and to enable their traditional societies to adapt to the impact of the modern world whilst maintaining the essential integrity of their cultures. The nature of this concern among the international community which established the League of Nations is possibly best revealed in the terms of the various mandates awarded to colonial powers to administer former German colonies. These mandates emphasised the protection of subject peoples from abuses and had relatively little to say about their economic development or preparation for sharing in political power. In the 1920s paternalism and gradualism held sway, and this was reflected in the budgetary arrangements for British dependencies. As a later statement on Colonial Development and Welfare was to put it, the provision of the services needed to underpin development was limited by 'the old principle that a Colony should have only those services which it can afford to maintain out of its own resources'.[2] Whilst the metropolitan government might well provide grants-in-aid to assist colonial governments to balance their budgets, not until the 1929 Colonial Development Act were substantial funds made available by the British government to finance purposive development activities.

In consequence education and other services were financed from recurrent revenue which, since this revenue was acutely subject to fluctuation year by year, effectively inhibited forward planning. In any case education was regarded as essentially a spending service and only to a limited extent as an investment in the human resources of the dependency. It is of course true that governments customarily supported or provided schooling in order, in large part, to ensure itself of a supply of local staff to man the government machine. It is also true that colonial administrators not infrequently discussed the desirability of relating educational provision to the manpower demands of the economy. But the absence of effective statistical services and the virtual impossibility of forecasting needs sufficiently far in advance in conditions of considerable economic uncertainty effectively ruled this out. Even the 1929 Colonial Development Act did not see education in a broad sense as a means for stimulating economic development, and made funds available only for certain specifically vocational or technical forms of education. The 1935 Colonial Office Memorandum on the Education of African Communities, a highly important restatement of colonial education policy for British possessions, included the statement: 'There is obviously an intimate connection between educational policy and the economic development of a territory'. But it went on to define this connection in very limited terms: 'The improvement of economic conditions may have to precede the extension of educational facilities as a means of providing the indispensable foundation for the latter.'[3] This pattern of thinking, which became very unfashionable in the post-Ashby era, was paralleled by considerable concern about the experience of India and Ceylon where large numbers of school leavers were unable to obtain paid employment and causing considerable social unrest in consequence.

By 1940 the inadequacy of earlier thinking was being more fully recognised. Social and political changes were taking place which far outstripped the conceptions of the old gradualist policies. The Colonial Development and Welfare Act of 1940 embraced the principle of promoting rapid and comprehensive development through the injection of substantial financial aid, and though the Second World War delayed the application of the principle, it was substantially extended by the later Act of 1945. Colonial governments were called upon to prepare ten-year comprehensive development plans to take effect from 1945. However, if planned investment in development by governments was now fully respectable, it was not to be expected that planning techniques of any great sophistication were available for use. The outcome was what may broadly be termed sectoral planning, with individual ministries submitting lists of projects which they wished to undertake and competing for slices of the financial cake, with final allocations being made by co-ordinating committees arbitrating between claims. These committees did so in accordance with some broad notions of development priorities but in the absence of either an adequate statistical base or fully worked out conceptions of strategy. Consequently the education plans were drawn up with only the roughest appreciation of manpower needs and priorities, and the prevailing assumption remained that direct investment in economic development should take prior place. Education continued to be regarded as essentially an item of social consumption, largely distinct from considerations of economic investment.

In these early post-war years educationists in Africa, and indeed all over the developing world, were still feeling their way hesitantly through the new development climate which had resulted from the acceptance of state direction and coordination of planning and the increasing availability of external aid. UNESCO was urging the importance of free and compulsory primary education in accordance with the 1948 Universal Declaration of Human Rights, and the general concern was with providing more educational facilities as quickly as possible. Earlier insistence on developing appropriate models of educational provision were to a considerable extent swept aside and internationally conventional models assumed a greater apparent validity.

General development theory was also passing through a somewhat confused stage. There remained for many years an assumption (which, though questioned, survived largely intact) that the colonial dependencies, now committed to speedy economic development, would follow the same industrial road as had more developed nations before them. It was believed that the dependencies possessed a real advantage in that their late modernisation would permit them to avoid the mistakes made by countries which had developed much earlier and to take technological short cuts by borrowing from these countries. In pursuit of industrialisation it was thought that what the dependencies lacked was sufficient capital and that if this could be provided, with the support of existing 'know how' in more advanced countries, development would take place. Rostow later hypothesised that developing countries would need substantial assistance in order to reach the point of economic take-off, the stage at which their economies would be capable of self-sustaining growth. This point would be reached when the infrastructure of power and communications had been established, when the country had achieved a sufficient degree of technical readiness to enable it to service as well as use machinery, and when the country was able to invest from its own resources a sum equivalent to 10 per cent of its annual national income.[4]

Experience during the early 1950s tended to suggest that the point of take-off would not be so readily achieved as had earlier been thought, and that making available material resources would not alone be sufficient for the purpose. The focus of attention then largely switched to human resources. It may surprise the reader that the pioneering work, of T. W. Schulz in particular, in this field only became influential in the late 1950s. Many educationists had for some time, though in an insufficiently rigorously worked out way, been asserting the importance of education in the development process but the significance of education as investment had continued to be obscured by its traditional function of transmitting the cultural heritage and social mores of the group and by the social welfare context in which it was normally considered. Economic theory had continued to stress the importance of other factors of production, notably of course capital, regarding labour as a more or less homogeneous input which could be assessed simply in quantitative terms. In the late 1950s and early 1960s a reassesment took place which stressed the qualitative aspects of the labour force and stemmed from several different kinds of study.

Historical evidence deriving from studies of more advanced countries during their periods of rapid economic growth, and notably of the United States, the Soviet Union, Denmark and Japan, suggested that there had been a very significant relationship between their economic growth and the amounts and kinds of education provided to their workforces. A number of other studies had indicated a certain correlation between the increase in national expenditure on education and the increase in the gross national product (GNP). Harbison and Myers in a very influential study found significant statistical relationships between levels of human resource development on the one hand and levels of GNP on the other for 75 countries grouped according to the former criterion.[5] It was easy, in retrospect perhaps too easy, to assume a causal relationship here which attributed economic growth largely to investment in education, but in the climate of the time and in the light of other new evidence such an assumption appeared justified. Other studies of instances of economic growth were demonstrating that measurable inputs of the traditional factors such as physical capital and man-hours of labour left much of that growth unexplained. Indeed it was confidently asserted that in the manufacturing sector less than a quarter of the growth in production achieved could be explained in this way. There must therefore be a 'residual' factor which would explain the balance of the growth, and it was widely accepted that this residual factor must include organisational improvement and human factors including the health, morale and level of education of the workforce. In spite of continuing difficulty in identifying specific components of the residual factor and of measuring their respective contributions to increased productivity, often quite specific assertions have been made, notably by Soviet researchers, as to the contribution of education.

As we shall see many of the conclusions drawn from such research as the above were questionable and have in fact been seriously challenged in the light of later research and experience. However the speed with which educational and development planners siezed upon the concept of education as a national economic investment is fully understandable. The development of this thinking between 1957 and 1965 coincided with the achievement of independence by the majority of the former African dependencies. The new nationalist governments were committed to speeding up development and also to extending educational opportunities to their peoples. The assurance that large investments in education would pay off in economic terms reinforced their long-standing faith in education as a means of remedying a whole range of social, economic and political problems and justified their responding to the clamour of their electorate for greater educational opportunities. The need to replace expatriate staff demanded the rapid expansion of secondary and tertiary education: immediate and acute manpower shortages in almost all fields tended to dominate longer term considerations.

The new wave of thinking about investment in education was largely generated by UNESCO through a series of international conferences on educational planning held for various regions of the world at Karachi, Tokyo, Santiago, and for Africa at Addis Ababa in 1961. Whilst the latter conference proclaimed that 'The right of young people to acquire education and understanding must never be completely sacrificed to economic needs',[6] it nevertheless firmly grasped the concept that education was an investment in productivity – 'there is no disputing that expenditure on some forms of education is an investment which more than pays for itself even in the narrowest economic terms'[7] – and urged that educational provision should be henceforth planned continuously in relation to manpower needs at all levels. As Harbison pointed out 'the country which rapidly increases its national income through productive investment in development of skilled manpower may reach its goal of universal primary education more rapidly than if it were to neglect the early investment in secondary and higher education.'[8] In consequence, whilst participating countries agreed to aim at achieving universal primary education by the apparently remote date of 1980 and rejected the view that in the shorter run primary school production should not be allowed to outrun the rate at which the agricultural sector of the economy, which would have to absorb the majority of primary school leavers, was adopting appropriate techniques to accomodate them, it was to secondary education that first priority was assigned for the immediate future.

Secondary education, it was noted, occupied a pivotal position in the school system: it utilised the primary school output, fed the tertiary institutions, provided directly and indirectly through other institutions the high and intermediate level manpower needed by the economy, and incidentally supplied the school system with teachers, permitting it to develop further. By 1980, it was agreed, some 30 per cent of the primary school output should receive secondary education in which there should be a shift away from philosophic and literary studies towards the natural and applied sciences. It was argued by Arthur Lewis that one of the major failures of underdeveloped countries was to make adequate provision for secondary and post-secondary education other than in universities. Economic development requires only a very small number of graduates and it can proceed quite rapidly, despite a surprisingly high level of illiteracy. What is fatal is a shortage of intermediate level personnel, that is of technician or executive grade staff.[9]

The Addis Ababa conference set a target of 20 per cent of the secondary level output to go on to a higher education by 1980. Although the conference noted that adult education was the form of education most closely geared to economic development and recommended that 'adequate priority' should be accorded it, perhaps inevitably the focus of its discussions was on the formal system. Overall a substantial stepping up of the expenditure on education was required to around 6 per cent of national income by 1980. In addition it was assumed that overseas aid exceeding $1000 million per annum would be required by 1970.

The implementation of the policies agreed at Addis Ababa varied considerably from country to country according to the capacity of each to invest from its own resources or to attract foreign aid, and according to the interpretation placed on the policies by each country in the light of its own circumstances. However between 1960 and 1972 the average percentage of GNP allocated to education in 44 African countries rose from 2.8 per cent to 4.7 per cent, half as fast again as growth in GNP itself. Budgetary allocations to education rose generally to between 20 and 25 per cent, and in some instances to over 30 per cent.

Yet in 1976 Amadou-Mahtar M'Bow, the Director-General of UNESCO, had to inform a conference of African Ministers of Education that despite all these efforts the long term target set at Addis Ababa that primary education should be universal, compulsory and free by 1980 would not be achieved. Enrolment rates in 1975 had risen to 59.1 per cent and at the current rate of progress would by 1980 only have reached 59.5 per cent after which they would begin to fall. There was, he noted, a race between population increase, which was rapidly rising towards 3 per cent per annum in Africa as a whole, and efforts to increase enrolments. At the same time the absolute number of illiterates was rising even though the percentage of illiteracy had fallen between 1961 and 1970 from 81 per cent to 73.7 per cent. Only at the level of higher education had the Addis Ababa targets been exceeded.[10] A number of countries, reviewing their rates of progress, determined in the mid-1970s to make a major effort to speed up educational expansion, hoping to learn from the experience of earlier pioneering schemes of universal primary education which had not been completely successful, as in the Western Region of Nigeria in the 1950s and in Ghana from 1961. Nigeria, with its massive oil revenues, embarked upon its long heralded universal primary education programme for no fewer than fifteen million children, many of whom would for the first time be given access to schooling. Tanzania, which had from the early 1960s pursued a policy of containing the expansion of primary education in order to develop its post-primary provision in line with the Addis Ababa strategy determined also to move rapidly towards the universal primary education which it regarded as an essential concomitant of its 'ujamaa' policy, in spite of the poverty of its resources. Other countries commenced rather more cautious reviews of education policy but with the same end in view. There were not lacking, however, voices which asked for how long education budgets could continue to expand, or even be sustained at the same level, and whether the money might not be more advantageously spent in other ways.

However, if the educational picture was worrying, the overall economic situation appeared even more so. By 1970 the alarm bells were already sounding loudly. The first United Nations Development Decade which ended in that year had set what had been described as a fundamentally realistic target of a real growth in national economies of 5 per cent per annum during the decade. At the end of the decade it was found that the great majority of African countries were still far from achieving this rate of growth. Although substantial economic progress had in fact been achieved and economies had grown on average by more than 5 per cent per annum, high rates of population growth had reduced the real rate of growth per capita to half this figure. From the mid-1970s recession in the economies of the more developed nations coupled with world wide inflation, and in particular the rising price of oil, presented developing countries with soaring costs of imports and unfavourable markets for exports and threatened the continuance of even this limited rate of growth.

At the same time concern was being expressed about a number of problems which had largely resulted from the development strategies being pursued. The first of these problems was that economic growth was not reaching the poorest sectors of national societies and, perhaps equally significant, that the poorest sections of the population were not significantly contributing to national growth. The problem was not confined to Africa. Robert McNamara, President of the World Bank Group, pointed out in 1973 that among 40 developing countries surveyed the richest 20 per cent of the population received 55 per cent of the national income whilst the poorest 20 per cent received only 5 per cent.[11] Figures commonly quoted to show the overall economic development of the country such as growth in GNP or GNP per capita tended to hide discrepancies of distribution of wealth which the development strategies being pursued appeared likely to exacerbate rather than ameliorate.

The major source of concern, however, and one to which leaderships reacted with some degree of shock, was the extent and rate of growth of unemployment among young school leavers. After all attention had been focussed for some time upon the acute shortages of skilled manpower and in the drive to 'Africanise' jobs there was a tendency to disregard early warning signals about the growing competition for employment among the less well qualified school leavers and about the rate with which they were migrating to the urban areas in search of work. A study conducted in Kenya in 1966 showed that only about 90 000 of the 150 000 children leaving school each year at the end of the seven-year primary course could hope to obtain further education or employment of any kind, and to this number of school completers there had to be added the very considerable number who dropped out of school before completing the course.[12] A case study in Western Nigeria conducted by the International Labour Office at government request in 1967 revealed that each year almost 97 000 pupils were completing either primary or secondary education and a further 124 000 were leaving without completing their courses. This total figure of almost 221 000 school leavers each year in Western Nigeria alone was contrasted with the overall figure for the whole of Nigeria of half a million wage and salary earners in government, the professions, and the larger industrial and commercial firms. There were in addition calculated to be something over two million young Nigerians in some form of apprenticeship. It was concluded that at best only about half of the school leavers could be absorbed in the non-agricultural sector. Yet in a local case study it appeared that about 60 per cent of village children between the ages of 15 and 19 had already left the villages for the towns and large cities. Scarce resources had been expended on their education in order to promote economic development. Now it appeared that not only were many of them unable to repay the cost of their schooling by engaging in productive activity but they represented a major drain on the resources of society through the funds and energies diverted to their upkeep and through the social problems presented by their presence in large numbers in the towns.[13]

As consciousness of the problem grew, growing concern was expressed about the danger to law and order, and indeed to political stability, which might result from the steady build-up of unemployed youth in the urban areas, and about the possible reduction in the capacity of rural areas to progress when the most able and vigorous young people deserted them in this way. A rate of population growth rising towards 3 per cent per annum meant that 60 – 65 per cent of the population was likely to be under the age of 25 whilst 40 – 50 per cent were likely to be in school and about to join the employment-seeking category. Since a very high proportion of those migrating to the towns were believed to be school leavers, attention largely focused upon what might be done through education to persuade young people to remain in the rural areas and to take up farming. The schools became subjected to a barrage of criticism that the content of their syllabuses was urban-oriented, that children were being taught to despise rural occupations and encouraged to aspire to white-collar occupations, and that by increasing the probability of obtaining paid employment education was encouraging migration to the towns. It may be noted in passing that these somewhat blinkered responses to the problem stemmed largely from uncertainty about its real nature and extent. Time would be required to obtain the necessary information. In the meantime could not the tide of migration be stemmed by more 'relevant' education?

Mounting disillusion with these aspects of the development strategy being pursued and with the contribution being made by the school system was accompanied by other worries. These were summed up by Siaka Stevens, the President of Sierra Leone, when in 1974 he told delegates to a conference of his ruling party:

> The most serious danger which confronts us today as a people is the danger of losing our hold on our traditional past and heritage while we have not yet fully grasped the cultures and traditions presented to us. . . . Most of us are 'displaced persons' from the educational and cultural point of view.[14]

Many voices had been raised for some time in criticism of patterns of development which were mere emulation of the more developed nations. These had not only failed to bring the anticipated returns but had introduced Western values in the train of Western technology, had exposed traditional societies to the influence of commercialism and materialism and had posed a threat to the distinctive cultural identities of Africa. There was a reassertion of the older view that whatever development strategy was pursued, it should be a distinctively African one, using African techniques to deal with African problems and to achieve African objectives. If Western technologies were to be success-fully absorbed and assimilated by Africa, the foundations of African society had to be secure and confident. Once again criticism of forms of education which were based upon alien value systems and encouraged dysfunctional tendencies was being heard and was accompanied by calls for major reforms of the structure and content of education systems.

The education systems upon which so much had been spent and upon which such high hopes had been placed by the planners and by the clienteles of the schools appeared to have failed. What had gone wrong? To begin to answer the question we must re-examine some of the basic assumptions upon which the strategy of investment in education had been based.

## The Theory of Investment in Human Resources Re-examined

It must be remembered that most of the research upon which the strategy was based had been, as it still is, conducted in the more advanced countries. These had followed an industrial pattern of development and the lessons of their experience inevitably implied that such a pattern should be followed. We are however becoming increasingly aware that the evidence derived from these historical examples regarding the significance of education is unclear. We are reminded that the United Kingdom amd most European nations carried through their agricultural and industrial revolutions without the aid of universal or even widely distributed education. The Soviet Union, which has been particularly vocal in urging the importance of education in its own massive industrial revolution, nevertheless as late as 1959 had a workforce with an average of only four years of formal education. Anderson and Bowman in examining the relationship between provision of education and economic development in the USA and around the world have concluded that the evidence suggests that the expansion of educational provision may have resulted from the generation of wealth through economic development just as clearly as the reverse conclusion.[15] We are also reminded of the dangers of assuming that the developing countries today are in a similar state of economic readiness to that of major industrial nations prior to their industrial take-off. The Soviet Union was a major industrial power long before political revolution made education widely available. It has been suggested that the success of modernisation during the Meiji era in Japan may largely be attributed to the unusually advantageous conditions confronting Japanese agriculture in the later part of the nineteenth century and that the level of development from which most developing countries have had to start was lower by as much as one-third than that of pre-industrial Europe.

Hoselitz noted that the countries in which returns to investment in human resources had been found to be high possessed five sets of common characteristics. First, they had highly developed economies with negligible or tiny subsistence sectors and highly important exchange sectors. Secondly, they had highly diversified occupational structures with a considerable degree of specialisation and hence with substantial need for elaborate training programmes. Thirdly, they had relatively full employment and efficient labour markets. Fourthly, they had highly developed communication systems dependent upon assumed universal literacy. Fifthly, they displayed a high degree of social and occupational mobility yet with sufficient stability as to ensure a strong correlation between the training an individual might receive and the career which he might actually pursue. These conditions, he argued, applied only to a limited extent in many developing countries and in some hardly at all.[16]

It has also been argued that we have failed to take into account the very significant difference between the world economic situation at the time when the major industrial powers were developing and the situation which confronts developing countries in the second half of the twentieth century, which may require developing countries to possess very different amounts, levels and *kinds* of education if they are to be able to play an effective part in the international trading system. In order to compete, industrially, developing countries have sought to introduce advanced technologies directly into largely pre-technical societies rather than pursue the slow development of technical readiness in their populations: consequently these populations are being called upon to understand and use far more complex technologies than did people in the more developed countries at a similar stage in their development. Because few of the developing countries possess a viable domestic market and because they are not able to produce for themselves all the manufactured goods and tools for production they need, they are compelled to enter into a cruelly competitive international trading situation in which not merely do they have to compete with more advanced countries but also with each other because of the limited range of primary produce which many of them have to offer. Consequently they require greater entrepreneurial and marketing skills and general economic understanding than was necessary, for example, in the late nineteenth century.

It has also been clear for some time that the simple importation of technology cannot meet the needs of developing countries. At this particular stage in their development, it has been suggested, they do not necessarily need the advanced technology appropriate to more developed nations but technology appropriate to their own social and economic circumstances, which in large measure they must be able to create for themselves. Until they can create their own technical capacity, developing countries are likely to be unable to catch up on the more developed nations and furthermore may be condemned to falling further behind because of the speed with which technology begets more advanced technology elsewhere in the world. The educational implications of the situation in which African countries find themselves are clearly immensely different from those of nations which developed earlier. Yet as we shall see the educational patterns which have grown up in Africa are not merely those of nations very differently situated but correspond largely to the patterns which existed in those countries in the past.

However we should not yield to the temptation of assuming that the failure of our educational systems to achieve all that we expected of them is due simply to the adoption of obsolete 'western' models. It has been argued in an earlier chapter that such models were not simply blind adoptions but to a considerable extent evolved in Africa in response to local factors which were and remain very strong. It must also be suggested that the failure of school systems can easily be exaggerated and that insofar as there has been failure it may be attributed to our expecting schools to perform functions for which they are ill-suited. To these points we will return but at this point we must examine some of the particular problems which have arisen in connection with the investment conception of education.

It had perhaps been too readily assumed that expenditure on education would more than pay for itself by the economic activity it would generate. As Arthur Lewis[17] and others have pointed out, in the circumstances of a poor country the amount of education which will pay for itself in economic terms is bound to be limited (at least in the short run) because of the limited absorptive capacity of the economy. Education systems can very easily produce more educated people than the economy can profitably employ for a number of reasons. The first reason may be that the education system is producing people with the wrong kind of skills, with the consequence that it is not uncommonly found that large numbers of educated people are unemployed whilst employers complain that they are unable to recruit people with the skills they need. It is not sufficient to argue that this is a consequence of the 'classical', 'literary' or 'academic' tradition which has prevailed in the schools.

One reason why such traditions have survived, despite the constant efforts to introduce into schools a more practical and vocationally oriented form of curriculum, is that in the past it was the more literary and general forms of education which led directly into the kinds of employment which were available (these being mainly of a clerical or administrative nature). Indeed, today it is this type of education which leads to those positions which possess the greatest social status and economic rewards. In most African countries the lawyer, the doctor and the administrator rank highest in public esteem above the engineer and the agriculturist, the industrialist and the trader. Even at the intermediate levels of employment, clerical occupations rank higher than technical and commercial occupations. Acheampong, whatever his other failings as a national leader, put his finger on this when he declared in 1976 that, 'A society gets the education it deserves. It is no use blaming the educational system for failing to respond to particular manpower needs if society does not accord such needs due recognition'.[18]

Consequently, well-intentioned efforts to diversify the school curriculum and to produce skilled people for technical and craft occupations have tended to wither away, partly because they were often more costly in terms of plant and equipment and demanded teachers possessed of skills which were in short supply, but mainly because pupils and their parents saw vocationally biassed courses as leading to dead-ends by comparison with the academic courses which offered entry to higher education and thence to more rewarding occupations. Chances of success were limited but one could always try, and the possession of even a modest academic education often gave preferential opportunities for entry into employment or training in competition with those whose education was more narrowly practical and craft oriented.

As a result the status of technical subjects, and indeed of the teachers responsible for teaching them, tended to remain low and to attract the lower-ability pupils and the failures from the academic streams, and even within the practical courses the tendency was for increasing emphasis to be placed upon the theoretical aspects and the literary studies which accompanied them in order that pupils might win a 'second chance' to rejoin the academic mainstream or to secure clerical employment. However there were also other reasons for this situation, to which we shall pay more attention in later chapters. The immense difficulty of forecasting what kinds and quantities of different

skills and abilities would be required by the economy in the years
ahead, when children currently in school would be ready to seek
employment, was compounded by the fact that even had it been
possible accurately to forecast manpower needs, school systems
proved not to be capable of the fine tuning and rapid reorien-
tations which would have been required for them to meet the
needs as precisely as planners tended to demand. In consequence
schools sought to provide a general education which, in theory at
least, would equip the child to take advantage of whatever
employment or training opportunities would confront him on
leaving school. The poor match achieved between employment
opportunities and the products of the school was thus at least as
much a matter of inappropriate aspirations as of qualifications,
and over the former the school had little influence.

A second reason for the inability of developing countries to
absorb easily all their school leavers is that education in itself does
not create jobs, except of course for school teachers. If the
products of the schools are to be able to use their education and to
assist in the process of creating wealth, it is not sufficient to equip
them with relevant skills. The jobs themselves must be available.
Unfortunately the creation of a modern economy is by no means
a speedy process and even where a satisfactory rate of economic
growth is achieved the rate of job creation may be considerably
slower than the rate of growth in national income (probably
about half). For example, between 1963 and 1967 when Nigeria
had the advantage of a relatively fast growing economy, GDP
grew at an average rate of 5.1 per cent per annum but wage
employment by only 3 per cent per annum. In its current five-
year plan, backed by massive oil revenues, Nigeria envisages the
creation of four million jobs mainly in the building, manufacturing and service industries. This would be a remarkable
achievement, but when this figure is compared with the number
of young Nigerians who will be emerging each year from the
universal primary education system and expanding secondary
school system the outlook is by no means encouraging. In its first
and second national development plans Zambia assumed that
20 000 new jobs would be created each year but the actual rate
proved to be about half this, and it declined at a time when the
annual output of the school system was rising to well over
100 000. In some other African countries manufacturing employ-

ment appears in fact to have been falling. Harbison has stated bluntly that,

> unemployment is associated with unbalanced economic progress. It appears to be a by-product of growth, a disease of industrialisation, and a consequence of the introduction of modern ideas and institutions. Its roots lie not in failure to achieve high levels of investment and economic growth but rather in progress towards achievement of these very goals. In short, modernization is a generator of unemployment.[19]

Why should this be so and how may a country achieve more balanced economic progress? The root causes of the situation are rapid population growth, the expansion of formal education (which has generated expectations among the growing population that their aspirations can be satisfied), and urban–industrial emphasis in economic development, which by its nature has been unable to absorb the potential labour force. The main reason for this latter point is connected with the kind of technology employed in the industrial sector. In order that African industries may be competitive and produce the quality of output which will project a modern national image, capital-intensive technology has been employed. This technology has been imported from more developed countries, countries which have been concerned with reducing production costs in the high wage situation they face by employing fewer workers and replacing them with automated production processes.

There is an absurdity about the application of capital-intensive technologies in countries which have a shortage of capital but an abundance of labour which has been emphatically pointed out by Schumacher and others. Whereas in the early stages of its industrial revolution Britain used industrial processes which required a capital investment per employee equivalent to the wages of that employee for about four months, the corresponding investment in some industrial developments in the developing countries is equivalent to about thirty years income. Schumacher has called for a deliberate policy of creating work places cheap enough to offer employment to many more people through the development of simple production methods which would minimise the demand for high-level skills. The need was for new 'intermediate' or 'alternative' technologies to be developed largely by the developing countries themselves which would enable individuals and communities to create their own work places. Capital-intensive technologies by their very nature could not be spread widely or have any demonstration effect which would mobilise the people through the use of their own resources. It was argued that opportunities to use such intermediate technologies existed particularly in industries producing consumer goods (including building and building materials) and also in agriculture and rural industries servicing agricultural communities. Goods and services produced in this way would, it is further argued, be sufficiently cheap for local people to buy, and the development of a healthy domestic market would promote the extension of the intermediate technologies.

It should be noted, however, that partly as a reaction to the sometimes unrealistic claims which have been advanced on behalf of intermediate technology, some commentators are beginning to stress the need for a more balanced assessment of the place of conventional urban-based industrial processes in the total strategy. Intermediate technology may well have a vitally important part to play in creating balanced development but it must complement rather than seek to replace the use of more advanced technologies. Indeed Caldwell has suggested that manufacturing industry in West Africa is likely to suffer from the high cost of production for many years to come and that costs can only be held down by a concentration of industrialisation on the largest towns.[20] Louis Emmerij, Director of the World Employment Programme, has advocated the continuing employment of capital-intensive technology to increase production, but suggested that this should be accompanied by a restructuring of employment so that more individual workers can be employed, each working for a shorter time.[21] In any case the development of new intermediate technologies, even with the assistance of such organisations as the London-based Intermediate Technology Development group founded by Dr. Schumacher, will be no speedy process and its success may be dependent upon attitudinal change and the spread of relevant skills among the rural peoples who are the intended beneficiaries.

It is not our purpose here to examine these complex arguments in depth, merely to note some of the reasons why massive investment in education, involving of course less investment in other aspects of the economy which might take up the products of the school, has not generated the anticipated economic development. We must now note other factors. One of the most important reasons why developing economies have been unable to absorb all the products of the schools has been the high cost of using educated manpower. In poor countries the salaries paid to educated personnel are substantially higher by comparison with average per capita income than is the case in richer countries, particularly where colonial or international salary scales have been applied to local workers and the substantial inducement element included in the former has been retained. Poor countries may be in desperate need of the services of highly trained personnel but cannot afford to pay them in large numbers. We may note this most clearly in our own field of education where the possibility of employing more highly qualified teachers in primary education is ruled out so long as it is necessary to pay such teachers the salaries to which their qualifications under existing arrangements would entitle them. As several economists have argued, manpower planning needs to be complemented by an appropriate control and setting of wages and incomes, but it would probably be politically impossible in most countries to adjust disparities of income by reducing that of the highest salary earners since these are the people who exercise the most power.

At the Addis Ababa Conference Arthur Lewis had argued that a surplus of educated persons tends to be self-adjusting through the reactions it sets up. Some of the surplus may emigrate, some may use their education in new ways, so increasing productive capacity, some may lower their sights and accept less remunerative employment than they had previously aspired to, in some cases the educational requirements for entry into occupations may be raised, and finally some of the educated may bring about political change which will accelerate development.[22] Experience has made us less sanguine about the operation of these factors. The 'brain drain' has tended to affect categories of skilled personnel such as medical staff who are in highest demand at home. The ability of educated people to generate their own employment has proved largely dependent upon the existence of a buoyant and expanding economy, upon the availability of loans and grants to assist them initially and upon trading situations favourable to the small entrepreneur – conditions which have not been sufficiently satisfied in many African countries. Whilst in the long term it is likely that educated young people will accommodate themselves realistically to whatever job opportunities are actually available, this now appears unlikely to be a speedy or painless process. Consequently the political effects of the process of adjustment are likely to promote instability rather than constructive change. Finally it has been found that the process whereby employers raise the educational qualifications required, may lead to higher qualifications being demanded than are actually needed. Job-seekers are in consequence inclined to seek higher and yet higher levels of education in order to compete effectively for the jobs which are available, and countries may be forced into providing more of the more costly higher levels of education than they can really afford and than is needed for the efficient performance of the jobs taken up. As Dore has pointed out, this process is associated with 'qualificationism' or 'the diploma disease' whereby efficient education and training may be corrupted into mere certificate winning because of the importance ascribed by employers in both appointing and thereafter promoting employees to the qualifications they hold.[23]

This thought brings us a further consideration, that the cost of providing education in developing countries generally is higher relative to national income than in more developed countries, and therefore it is correspondingly more difficult to make it pay in economic terms. One reason for the high relative costs which prevail, despite low costs in absolute terms, is the low internal efficiency of the school systems. High drop-out rates mean that the unit cost of producing one completer of an educational stage is much higher than it should be. High repetition and failure rates, which result largely from poor quality of instruction but also from the application in a mass education situation of syllabuses and curricula derived from the earlier highly selective system, mean even higher unit costs. A further major reason for the relatively high cost of education provision relates to teachers' salaries. Education is a labour-intensive industry and between 70 per cent and 90 per cent of education budgets is normally expended on paying these salaries. These salaries, which we so often complain are unfairly low by comparison with similarly qualified personnel in other occupations, are in fact much higher by comparison with average per capita income than teachers in far wealthier countries receive. Consequently the cost to the nation of providing a basic course of education to all children is considerably higher in Africa than in more developed parts of the world. At present many African governments are investing in education substantially higher proportions of available revenue than are governments in richer countries and yet they find themselves unable to provide as much education as they think necessary.

Of course our governments are not simply concerned with economic investment. Insofar as we are concerned with creating equality of opportunity and with preparing our peoples to participate in democratic political processes we may well find it necessary to spend a great deal of money on the extension of primary education. This may in itself not be the most economically productive form of education particularly where the high and intermediate level manpower needs are pressing and where extension work and community development work among the adult population is starved of funds. Insofar as we are concerned with political stability, our governments may have to respond to public demand for education which may well not coincide with economic need. They may have to choose to invest resources in regions of the country or sections of the community which may not yield very high economic returns at the expense of depriving other regions or sections where the economic benefits might be more immediate. Consequently, insofar as educational development is pursued for such non-economic reasons, the efficiency with which education meets economic needs may be substantially reduced in two main ways. First, scarce resources may be consumed which might otherwise be invested in transport, power, communications and other forms of economic infrastructure or more directly in production activities. Secondly, investment of this kind may result in the production of large numbers of people who cannot be employed in the modern sector of the economy and who may, if they do not find alternative outlets for their skills, rather than constituting a pool of talent which might be construed as an economic strength in fact constitute a further drain on the resources of the nation through the consumption demands they make.

The experience of the years since Ashby and Addis Ababa has taught us to question our many assumptions more rigorously regarding the relationship of education and economic development: unfortunately it has produced little in the way of answers. In September 1971 the World Bank, examining the situation at the end of the first development decade, noted: 'Not only is [education] not directly revenue producing; in the present state of our knowledge its economic return is not accurately measurable'.[24]

It is recognised that the contribution education may make to economic development will vary according to the particular circumstances of a particular country, the stage of development which it has reached, the development strategy being pursued and the forms of education being utilised. As Vaizey pointed out some years ago, education may well be a potent weapon in economic modernisation, but only if the conditions are right: 'by itself it probably consumes more resources than it produces'.[25] Certainly we have learned that education is but one facet of overall development and that its importance to the overall strategy requires some qualifications, though even in advancing such qualifications we must be clear that in the present state of our knowledge these remain but hypotheses.

## Education and Rural Development

With these considerations in mind we now return to the question of achieving more balanced development and in particular of promoting the development of the rural areas in which the majority of the populations of African countries currently live. Guy Hunter has recently argued that we have been unduly alarmed about the process of migration to the towns:

> The movement from country to town is absolutely natural and absolutely essential; it is not a disease, it is a very right and proper economic activity. In East Africa urban proportions of population are about 9 %; in Nigeria it is something like 21 %, Ghana, 28 % urban at the last census now ought to be over 30 %. So there is a long way to go.[26]

He argues that the vision of future development which we should adopt is one in which approximately equal numbers of people live and work in urban and rural areas. However this is not a view which is as yet widely current and in general it is probably true to say that national policies follow the lines expressed as early as 1966 at the important Kericho Conference: 'Despite the considerable investment in the industrial sector of the economy, it is increasingly apparent that a productive life for the mass of young people must depend on opportunities in the rural sector, in agriculture and associated employment.'[27]

Concern for the rural areas and recognition of the importance of meeting the needs of predominantly rural peoples was of course nothing new. As we have seen official policy for half a century and more had consistently stressed the need for developing agriculture as the economic backbone of African countries, for encouraging the steady evolution of rural communities towards more satisfying ways of life, and for enabling them to maintain their social and cultural integrity whilst mobilising their innate capacity to contribute to their own development. But there can be little doubt that in recent years, despite repeated expressions of concern for rural peoples, development had been largely conceived of in narrow economic terms with a new emphasis on rapid modernisation. In the new era of economic planning with targets being defined in terms of growth in national income, social aspects of development tended to be lost sight of and salvation was sought through those sectors of the national economy which promised the greatest returns in the shortest period of time. Development policies consequently focussed primarily on the modern industrial sector and were largely dominated by the requirements of the articulate and progressive urban populations. Investment in the rural areas tended to be concentrated upon large scale cash crop developments which could feed the modern sector of the economy most efficiently.

The policy adopted has been described as essentially a bridgehead strategy, whereby, in pursuit of rapid industrial development and the creation of a modern national image, advanced manufacturing and other technologies together with the most up-to-date social institutions had been imported to constitute bridgeheads of modernity within broadly unmodernised societies. Computerised accounting procedures might be brought into use within a few yards of traditional market places where business was conducted by illiterate market women, high technology production might take place in factories outside the walls of which the roadside production of household necessities continued to employ the simplest of tools and materials, new hospitals equipped with graduate doctors and modern medical facilities looked out on streets where sanitation remained appalling and the traditional herbalist remained in great demand, and shining new universities taught advanced science and technology in close proximity to roadside koranic schools and children preparing for initiation ceremonies. In the towns concrete buildings shone their electric light out across the darkened countryside. The benefits of these islands of modernity would, it was assumed, in the course of time trickle down to all sectors of society. The wealth created by the new industrial and commercial enterprises would eventually enable the government to provide fuller services to the countryside and to invest in the remoter and less privileged areas. The greater concentration of limited resources upon the more productive sectors represented not a neglect of the needs of the mass of the people but a short cut towards meeting them more effectively.

Such a strategy appeared to have much to recommend it but experience rapidly revealed some of its more important problems and limitations. Essentially it conceived of a dual economy and a dual society in which the modern industrial sector would be fed by the rural sector, would receive its produce and process and market it, enabling government either through ownership of major commercial enterprises or through taxation to obtain the resources for a further stage of development. Its success would be measured by the extent to which these resources would spread the benefits of development more widely over the course of time. This depended upon, first, the allocation of a sufficient proportion of the new wealth to rural development and, second, the selection of appropriate strategies for investment in the rural areas. It may be argued that for reasons which are not necessarily disreputable the first of these conditions was rarely achieved. Taxation creamed off only a part of the new wealth. Much of it went elsewhere, into private pockets, thereby enlarging the gulf between the way of life of people associated with the modern sector and that of the great majority of the people. Much of the wealth, instead of being reinvested in local development, tended to be used for the purchase of goods and services often of a luxury nature, not unnaturally demanded by the modern sector elites. This has been the subject of much comment and has led to the mounting concern for social justice which we have mentioned. Possibly more significant, however, is the fact that much of the reinvestment that has taken place has been in the further development of the modern sector, which has a voracious appetite for capital. Such reinvestment could easily be justified as being the means whereby, at the cost of immediate sacrifice by the majority of the people, further increments of wealth might be achieved, enabling far greater benefits to be afforded them at some later date.

It is perhaps not difficult to understand why this strategy should have been so widely adopted. Experience tended to suggest that the existing conditions under which agriculture was carried on offered little hope of rapid or of substantial improvement. The majority of the farming population were subsistence farmers, often barely able to meet their own food needs from small, fragmented and scattered land holdings with the use of rudimentary tools and techniques. Poor levels of production were often accompanied by deterioration of the soil. Where animals were kept, they were not normally integrated into the overall farming system. Facilities for the storage, transportation and marketing of food crops were often so poor and expensive as to discourage farmers from producing more than they needed for their own subsistence. Cash crop production was viewed as essentially subsidiary to the production of food and undertaken in a similar way. The agricultural pattern as a whole appeared to be uneconomic and capable of maintaining only a low standard of living for rural populations whilst being unlikely to meet the expanding demands of the towns for foodstuffs and cash crops.

Moreover change in this picture through the evolutionary strategy appeared improbable. The argument has been summed up as follows;

> Illiteracy makes it difficult to teach new techniques, poverty prevents investment in new facilities, and a land tenure system which does not establish legal land boundaries and security of

tenure deprives the farmer of an asset against which to raise loans and gives him no incentive to invest in long term improvements. Add to this a variety of social and economic prejudices and there emerges a picture of farming as an occupation associated with illiteracy, low income, heavy manual labour, and lack of social amenities.[28]

This vicious circle, it was argued, could be broken only by starting anew. Improved skills and habits could be learned, new organisation developed and the necessary supervision provided only by adopting transformational approaches involving the creation of major land-settlement schemes utilising advanced production technology. In addition such settlement schemes would be of a particular value where the rural population was too widely dispersed in homesteads for support to be readily afforded and where growing population pressure demanded that new and marginal land be broken in.

The spectacular success of the Gezira settlement scheme in the Sudan appeared to testify to what might be achieved in this way. Beginning in the 1920s and based upon the irrigated cultivation of cotton, the scheme had by the 1970s extended to nearly two million acres and 75 000 families, diversifying successfully into a range of other crops. Other examples of apparently successful land settlement schemes were to be found in Niger, Tanzania and Zaire. Consequently there was a rapid growth in the number of such schemes in many parts of Africa but equally quickly their deficiencies were revealed. They were found to suffer from sociological problems associated with the formation of new communities and from dependence upon expert management, which was in short supply. Their main disadvantage however was that they proved inordinately expensive. Whilst it was demonstrated that they had a significant place in rural development, notably in terms of the rapid expansion of the production of cash crops, the general conclusion reached was that it would be prohibitively expensive to resettle more than a tiny proportion of the farming populations and that land settlement could not therefore solve the underlying basic problem of the rural areas.

By the end of the first United Nations Development Decade there was widespread disappointment with the results of concentration upon industrial development and large scale mechanised agriculture. Awareness was growing that the modern sectors of national economies were proving largely unable to support the process of balanced and comprehensive national development. Added to this was world wide concern over the rate at which natural resources and particularly non-renewable natural resources such as oil and other minerals were being depleted, a concern which found echoes in those countries such as Zambia and Zaire, and rather more recently Nigeria, which relied heavily upon the exploitation of such resources. Unless means could urgently be found whereby the income from such resources could be effectively invested in agriculture, the long-term viability of their economies was seriously threatened. At the same time there was growing awareness that a new relationship between the agricultural and industrial sectors of an economy must be arrived at. As Harbison has put it, 'In most developing countries . . . a rural transformation is necessary to foster growth in other sectors . . . rural transformation is a necessary prerequisite for rapid economic growth as well as the principal means of creating more productive employment.'[29]

A further dimension of the problem was the fact that at a time when there was need to diversify forms of employment in the rural areas both to absorb growing populations and to contribute to improving the quality of life in those areas, traditional small-scale rural industries were already in danger of being killed off by competition from modern industry. Clearly the emphasis upon the rural areas as markets for urban products was but one facet of the need: the prosperity of rural areas depended upon the maintenance of a balance between farming and other occupations within those areas. Much interest was being shown in Chinese experience with the devolution of industrial development to the rural areas and the promotion of low-technology service industries.

Recognition of the extent to which manufacturing and agricultural production are interdependent parts of a single economic system demanding appropriately balanced investment did not mask the fact that further balances had to be struck between investment in large-scale mechanised agriculture and in small-scale peasant farming, and between cash crop and foodstuffs production. Unfortunately experimentation with large scale mechanised techniques and a parallel concentration upon the production of cash crops had often resulted in a continuing neglect of the subsistence sector and of food production. Resources were thinly spread and efforts to arrest the long-term decline in the fertility of the soil, to stem the ravages of soil erosion and crop disease, and to increase the productivity of the peasant farmer were largely ineffective. Whilst successes were recorded in some areas, as in Kenya with the introduction of new high yield varieties of maize, over much of Africa subsistence farming remained stagnant. Indeed the outcome overall was a decline in agricultural productivity in relation to the growing numbers of people which the rural areas were being called upon to support. In 1977 it was reported that between 1970 and 1975 only 10 out of 40 African countries surveyed had succeeded in raising their per capita rate of agricultural production, and that 90 per cent of Africans were living in countries where the rate had in fact declined.[30] Sierra Leone, for example, had been self-sufficient in rice, its staple food crop, in the 1950s, but in 1974 found it necessary to import rice to the value of £14 million, equivalent to more than nine times the budgetary allocation to agriculture in that year. The growing importation of foodstuffs constituted an increasing drain on the foreign currency reserves of a number of other countries. The Sahelian drought of 1972–4 which required a massive relief operation to bring food to Senegal, Mali, Mauretania, Upper Volta, Niger and Chad, and which brought catastrophe to Ethiopia and Somalia in 1973–5, threw clearly into relief the deficiencies in Africa's existing capacity to feed itself by traditional methods. Campaigns such as Operation Feed Yourself in Ghana and Operation Feed the Nation in Nigeria were hastily mounted but took on much of the character of emergency measures.

At the same time the rural economies of Africa found themselves unable to respond sufficiently rapidly to favourable world market conditions for cash crops such as coffee, tea and cocoa between 1975 and 1977. The Ghana Government found it necessary to set up an enquiry into the Cocoa Marketing Board to establish why, with such favourable circumstances, Ghana's share of world cocoa production should in fact have declined.

Increasingly the argument has been heard that African countries need to look again at the capacity of small-scale peasant farming to provide the strong backbone of national economies. A number of studies have indicated that under the right circumstances small farms can be efficient in terms of production and that they have a greater capacity to absorb large numbers of workers and so to facilitate a fairer distribution of wealth and to promote genuine rural development than have large-scale mechanised state farms and land settlement schemes. So-called traditional society, it was argued, is much more flexible than it is often supposed to be, and we were reminded of the far-reaching revolutions in diet and crop production which have in fact taken place among rural African peoples in recent history. In 1973 Robert McNamara pointed out that

> It has often been suggested that the productivity of small-scale holdings is inherently low. But that is simply not true. Not only do we have the overwhelming evidence of Japan to disprove that proposition, but a number of recent studies on developing countries also demonstrate that, given the proper conditions, small farms can be as productive as large farms.[31]

He cited experience in Guatemala, China, India and Brazil, where output per hectare was substantially greater on small farms than on large ones and concluded that there was ample evidence that modern agricultural technology is divisible and that small-scale operations need be no barrier to raising agricultural yields.

Emphasis on the need for increases in agricultural productivity should not, however, lead us to the conclusion that rural development is simply a matter of raising output, although it would be true to say that until quite recently the two were considered to be virtually synonymous. Currently a broader view is taken which seeks a transformation of both social and economic structures and embraces a range of long term goals including

> the generation of new employment; more equitable access to arable land; more equitable distribution of income; widespread improvements in health, nutrition and housing; greatly broadened opportunities for all individuals to realize their full potential through education; and a strong voice for all rural people in shaping the decisions and actions that affect their lives.[32]

Rural development, like any other form of national development, is extremely complex. All too often we have been unable even to define our aims, save in the most general and rhetorical language, or to draw clear distinctions between the goals we seek to achieve and the instruments, such perhaps as education, which may be necessary for success. Whilst rural development must be a multi-faceted process, we are still uncertain as to which facets of the problem should be dealt with first or merit priority in the allocation of resources. The debate will rage for many years to come but the unsatisfactory results achieved from the methods used in the past suggest some general conclusions. We have discussed briefly the deficiencies in investment in large-scale agriculture which figured prominently in the 1960s, but in view of the new emphasis upon the importance and potential of the small farmer we now need to look briefly at the use of what have been called sectoral programmes to mobilise this potential. To a considerable extent these programmes took the form of the provision of services, of roads and communications, of water supplies, storage and marketing facilities, clinics and dispensaries, schools and community centres, backed by the extension services of the various ministries involved. Such programmes have been criticised for their failure to invest fully even the often limited sums of money made available, for the lack of co-ordination between projects and programmes, and for their failure to focus upon clear cut manageable goals appropriate to particular areas. In particular, attention has frequently been drawn to what were seen as the inadequacies of the field staff employed and the methods adopted by them, particularly their excessive authoritarianism. More significantly, perhaps, there is now growing agreement that whilst such services are essential features of the infrastructure upon which a healthy rural economy must be built and whilst they often reflected the demands made by rural people, the manner in which they were provided tended to undermine the long-term process they were intended to promote – the regeneration of the capacity of rural communities to sustain themselves and to contribute more substantially to their own on-going development. Too often these communities were caught up in a process of pauperisation through which they became increasingly dependent upon remote officialdom, upon government initiatives and government finance to provide for their needs. It may be that attitudes of dependence have developed most markedly in those countries with the most resources. It has been suggested, for example, that 'Zambia has been cursed with ample government resources which have stunted local self-help by making it rational for people, not to help themselves and contribute, but to petition for help'.[33] As Nyerere argued some years ago

> people cannot be developed. They can only develop themselves. For while it is possible for an outsider to build a man's house, an outsider cannot give a man pride and self confidence in himself as a human being. Those things a man has to create in himself by his own actions. He develops himself by what he does; he develops himself by making his own decisions, by increasing his understanding of what he is doing and why; by increasing his own knowledge and ability, and by his own full participation – as an equal – in the life of the community he lives in. Thus for example, a man is developing himself when he grows or earns enough to provide decent conditions for himself and his family; he is not being developed if someone gives him these things.[34]

The farmer needs not only to receive a just share of the national wealth but to earn that share and thereby to contribute to its creation. Only in this way can he effectively participate in the development process and only through his participation can effective development be achieved. This was recognised to a degree in attempts during the 1970s to involve local people in development planning through the creation of provincial and regional development committees as in most East African countries. However, despite claims of popular participation in the process, such committees have rarely achieved substantial success, largely because the overall tendency has been to reserve planning decisions and financial capacity to central bodies and because of the basic difficulty of finding appropriate procedures for involving local people.

A second major conclusion derived from experience with sectoral programmes is that there has been a tendency to envisage the provision of the economic infrastructure as being the first step towards the establishment of a healthy rural economy which would be capable of promoting social development, modernising institutions and transforming the way of living and thinking of rural peoples. It has long been argued, however, that in some respects social development must precede the introduction of new facilities and services in order that these may be effective, or perhaps more correctly that development must take the form of a complex interaction in which both social and economic factors will be present.

It is often pointed out that changes in techniques in the fields of production and marketing, for example, may involve quite fundamental changes in the culture and social institutions of a rural community. Indeed commentators such as Myrdal have suggested that the main obstacles to development are not facilities but social attitudes and that facilities often cannot be effectively used without attitudinal change. Attitudes and values which are reflected in social organisation and institutions often largely reflect the desire of the peasant for security and a natural resistance to change may be associated with arrangements for the apportionment of land, the ways in which it may be held and used, and the procedures by which the produce is distributed. Some writers have spoken of 'accelerators' which in the presence of the kinds of basic facilities which are noted above may bring about more rapid increase in production – for instance credit facilities and co-operative associations – but it is clear from such examples as these that their introduction must involve fundamental changes in the way in which certain peoples view indebtedness and the handing over of responsibility to members of their group. Whilst traditional societies are often more flexible than we sometimes assume, we should not overestimate the extent and the speed with which change may be introduced, at least in its early stages.

It may be that the process by which deep rooted social attitudes may be changed and the ability of people to participate in their own development may be liberated will include two main elements. The first will be the demonstration of the benefits which accrue from the early stages of change. Recognition by rural peoples of the desirability of further change and their consequent willingness to adapt to and accommodate often unforeseen effects of change will very largely depend upon the extent to which they are genuinely receiving benefits and are able to perceive the fact and the causes underlying it. The second will be the application of purposive educational measures which will both assist people in understanding changes which are taking place around them and the potential which exists for further improving the quality of their lives and providing them with the skills they will need to turn this understanding into action. We must now examine some of the principal ways in which attempts have been made to use the education system for this purpose.

For reasons already discussed, the educational response to development needs was dominated by the demands of the modern sector for high-level manpower and consequently by the formal school system. Yet as we have also seen there has been for many years strong consciousness of the need for the schools to serve the rural areas. The basic thinking which survives to the present day is that through primary education in particular, even though it might reach only a part of the population, a cadre of enlightened leadership might be developed both in and for rural communities, a leaven of men and women who possess a more scientific understanding of the cause and effect relationships which lie at the root of improved agriculture and community living, are more aware of the possibilities of change and progress, and have learned sufficient of a variety of simple skills to be able to show the way in farming, nutrition, sanitation and so on to their less progressive neighbours. Such leaders would help to create a climate within which innovation and experiment might flourish, more receptive of whatever assistance might be afforded by specialists from outside the community. At the same time some of those completing primary education would go on to further education and training and join the ranks of these specialists – extension workers, community development officers, medical workers and teachers. A dual strategy was thus being pursued with the school feeding both arms, and each arm dependent upon the other.

From very early days such policies as these proved largely ineffectual and indeed in certain respects counter-productive. Rural peoples varied in their response to the introduction of schooling, some groups even today retaining deep-rooted and justifiable suspicions that education would take their children away from them and spoil the children by inoculating them with ideas and attitudes that would estrange them from their communities and parents. More generally, early reluctance to send children to school turned into vociferous demand for education as the benefits to be gained, particularly in terms of access to paid employment, became apparent. The effect was that the school became less a means of equipping young people for service and life within their communities than an escape hatch whereby they might obtain access to modern sector benefits. The community itself would benefit in terms of the greater security their regular salaries might offer to their parents. Since there appeared little prospect of such benefits being gained by remaining on the land, and since the school constituted virtually the sole means whereby modern-sector employment might be obtained, the process by which the more talented, progressive and able young people regularly moved away to the urban areas tended to deprive the countryside of the leadership the schools had been intended to enhance. The popularity of schooling was largely responsible for the way in which complementary efforts to bring education to adult members of rural communities fell into disfavour and tended to wither away. In consequence the basic strategy lost one of its arms and the effectiveness of the other arm, represented in the extension services, was much reduced.

It had been anticipated that some of these problems would be overcome through the wider provision of schooling so that a higher proportion of educated young people would remain in the rural areas. However rates of migration did not normally diminish and the frustration of young people who, following a period of schooling, failed to satisfy their aspirations and were compelled to return to the land set up strains in their communities which often failed to find profitable outlets. It had long been believed that if the content of schooling could be made more directly relevant to, and in harmony with, life in the rural areas, these problems could be largely overcome. But, as we have seen, early adaptation of both the curriculum and the pattern of school organisation proved unsuccessful, largely because it was unacceptable to rural people, and experimental developments were almost entirely swept away, particularly during the post-war drive to provide needed manpower for the modern sector.

By the mid-1950s it was being argued once again that schooling should be reformed principally through curriculum reform to include more practical and vocational studies. In particular it was believed that practical agriculture should be revived to form a central part of the curriculum. Schools should be equipped with school farms and demonstration plots on which their pupils might practise skills, study the benefits of improved farming methods and develop a useful understanding of the underlying theory. There was little new in these proposals though in one or two instances, notably in the syllabus developed for middle schools in Tanganyika in 1952, the integration of practical with theoretical work was more carefully worked out. It was also felt that other subjects, particularly in the social studies, might be more effectively taught through focussing more closely upon the local community and through drawing upon its resources. It was hoped that combination of practical work and community studies would stand the pupils in good stead as adult members of their communities, whilst the clear recognition implied in these changes that primary education would be terminal for the majority of pupils would help to reduce the selection focus of schooling and minimise feelings of frustration and failure among those not selected for further education. With agricultural skills they would be more inclined to settle on the land and would serve as the means whereby improved farming practices might be more widely diffused.

For many years argument has raged over the value of such developments as these. It was easy to argue that earlier failures in agricultural education were the result of insensitivity on the part of colonial authorities and failure to provide the necessary support and follow-up services. It remains easy today to argue that the main weakness of efforts to revive agriculture in schools lies in a lack of commitment on the part of those responsible. But some very fundamental questions have long been asked and still need to be answered. Can younger children be expected to undertake practical farming activities and to learn purposively from them, or must practical agriculture amount to little more than desultory hoeing and weeding in the hot sun? How far can largely repetitive farming operations serve as a basis upon which to build a sound theoretical understanding? How much science and maths can be learned in this way? How far does the introduction of practical studies not threaten the achievement of high standards in theoretical and academic subjects? Will any of the knowledge gained be retained long enough for it to be put into practice when the pupils become productive farmers? – a particularly worrying question when the motivation of pupils to learn is in question. Will the practice of such improved methods as the school may advocate prove possible for them? Do not many of these methods involve not merely more work, which is discouraging enough, but also equipment and materials which may well be beyond their resources? Will the land be available to them to farm even if they wish to, and will the nature of the land tenure system permit them to apply some of the newer methods? In a society which respects age and customs is it appropriate to hope for the infusion of new techniques through their use by young school leavers, or will not the young farmer be compelled by the weight of custom to follow the practices of his elders? Is the extra cost of training teachers of agriculture, of providing schools with farms and other facilities, and of making available support services of other government departments, a cost which can only be met at the expense of other activities, likely to justify itself so long as the schools retain their traditional dual function and are unable to guarantee that their pupils' aspirations and motivation will provide sufficient interest and effort to result in effective learning?

How effective, then, has formal education been in promoting rural development? It must be admitted that whilst there are many opinions on the subject from often well-informed commentators, very few can claim to be based on rigorously conducted studies. On the question of the contribution of education to agricultural productivity we may quote a few studies from East Africa. Following an investigation conducted between 1964 and 1967 in Sukumaland, northern Tanzania, Heijnen reported that few primary school leavers had any genuine understanding of the simple scientific reasons for the improved farming practices they had been taught in school and consequently they speedily abandoned them. In practice the farming techniques practised by school leavers and even those with eight years of education behind them were on average only a little better than those of illiterate farmers save that extremes of bad practice did not occur among the schooled group. Even eight years of schooling had not provided the peasants with the conceptual inventory and procedural knowledge to make simple cost–benefit calculations to evaluate recommendations for improvement.[35] De Jongh in his parallel study noted that there was no indication of any connection between the extension of cotton growing, the major agricultural innovation in the region, and schooling.[36] The techniques involved were simple, requiring no literacy, and in any case, he commented, the schools did not necessarily teach better techniques. A few years later Hopcraft concluded from a study of small farmer productivity in Kenya that

> There is not much evidence of improved farm productivity attributable directly to the schooling experience, and there is some evidence of the opposite. When it comes to applied knowledge about farming practices and husbandry techniques, there is no evidence that the farmer who has received some formal education is better off than the one who has not.[37]

The studies found it difficult to define and measure the influence of schooling more generally upon social attitudes and customs. Varkevisser in the Sukumaland study regarded the school more as an accelerator than as an initiator of change and he mentioned the slow breakdown of the extended family system and of the Kinamhala, a customary organisation of the older men which had a strongly conservative influence upon community life. He noted strong opposition to the Kisumba, a similar organisation of young men and girls, among school leavers but pointed out that they found it almost impossible to break away from it and within the organisation were forced to conform to the traditional ways of the majority.[38] Both Varkevisser and de Jongh noted the continuing prevalence of belief in witchcraft and the strong influence of societies of medicine men and diviners, which had proved profoundly resistant to either church or school. Schools had remained largely isolated from the central foci of community life but were tending to estrange their products from the community. Hopcraft concluded that the familiar assertation that school tended to alienate people from farming and to orientate them towards the urban job market received some support from his findings but while the gross effect of schooling appeared marginal at best, and might even be negative, there were grounds for some optimism.

> The effect of education, in this view, is above all to broaden horizons and raise expectations. It provides the individual with some familiarity with modern concepts and institutions. When an educated farmer settles down to farming, when he develops some commitment, and abandons the off-farm pre-occupation that also appears to be the result of education, he is likely to be a more aggressively innovative farmer. There is evidence that such a farmer is somewhat more likely to seek out useful knowledge more aggressively from other agencies and institutions where it is available. There is also evidence that he is likely to use modern farming inputs more intensively and, in general, be more commercially oriented.

In Nigeria Ogionwo sought to correlate the innovativeness of a group of farmers with their economic circumstances and certain selected social characteristics including age, level of education, contacts with information, and personal attitudes. He found that those farmers most likely to adopt government-recommended farming practices were those with greater resources (and there-fore perhaps able to take a risk), and those whose personal attitudes included proneness to change and rationality in approaching decision-making. Young farmers were more in-novative than their elders. However, whilst there appeared to be a positive correlation between level of education and innovativeness, it was not very strong. Sixty-two per cent of the sample had been to school but fewer than half of these read newspapers and only about a third received printed materials designed to provide guidance and encouragement to farmers. Most however listened to the radio. Ogionwo concluded that the most effective influences upon the farmers were those of their neighbours and friends, and rather less so the influence of extension officers. Personal contact and the spoken word were the most important things and the literate group with access to printed information did not appear to be notably more inno-vative than the illiterate group.[39]

A study of 20 low income countries conducted for the World

Bank and examining the relationship between levels of education and production efficiency found that, other things being equal, farm productivity increased on average by 6.9 per cent if a farmer had four years of education and that his productivity was likely to be higher in modernising environments than in traditional environments.[40]

Whilst the available evidence is thin, we should not disregard the general conclusions being reached by experienced observers and educationists. Foster has argued that whatever the role that education plays, it is not likely to be a powerful agency of change if all we mean by education is the development of specialised vocational or proto-vocational education in agriculture in lower level schools.[41] Griffiths has stressed that more important than learning elementary skills was the acquisition of certain attitudes of mind and the bases for understanding and co-operating in change. Adding to the quantity of factual knowledge is not the problem but changing the quality of thinking very much is. These attitudes and understandings are not to be taught by adding to the curriculum isolated subjects such as elementary science or agriculture but through permeating all teaching with the desired attitudes, knowledge and qualities of thinking.[42] Anderson has warned of the dangers of developing too strong a practical and distinctively rural orientation in rural schools:

> If primary schools were ruralised, they are more likely to function poorly in preparing farmers for innovative leadership. At the same time, those schools will become inefficient circuitous routes to the main path of general education. Once we abandon the search for a way to make primary pupils practise farming, we can turn to the main task, i.e. the task of identifying the different groups who really need agricultural instruction and of providing it to them in its different kind by more appropriate means.[43]

In effect it appears that again we have been guilty of expecting too much from the school, have failed to identify what its real contribution may be and, whilst condemning it for its inadequacy in other respects, have reduced its efficiency in performing its main task by attempting to adapt it to a task for which it is not well suited. As Brembeck has suggested,

There are certain structural characteristics associated with formal schooling which cannot be ignored in any attempts to improve it. Schools are essentially detached institutions, physically separate from the life and work of the community: they are future oriented institutions preparing pupils for their later lives inevitably devaluing what the pupil can currently put into practice because they are concerned with a step by step build up of understanding and skill towards substantially different future practice; immediate action is largely and properly subordinated to abstract learning and concept building looking towards longer range change. Because they must make the fullest use of experience and understandings which are not to be found in the immediate environment of the school, learning cannot be derived simply from practice but must be achieved through vicarious means necessitating the prior and ongoing learning of abstract languages, literacy and numeracy. Because of the nature of formal instruction schools are ghettos of the young, themselves structured according to age bands, and consequently unsuited to proper representation of normal community life.[44]

This is not to argue that many of these characteristics cannot be modified and learning substantially improved. There are, no doubt, opportunities to link the school more closely with local community life, with the world of work, and for increasing the element and effectiveness of learning by doing. But the strength of the school lies essentially in what is usually termed general education, equipping young people with the tools needed to investigate and enquire, to think, conclude and understand: it is substantially weaker in its capacity to inculcate prescribed attitudes, to train in specific production skills. Probably the school does rely overmuch upon deductive learning derived from study of the disciplines of knowledge and assuming rather too much about the applicability of the disciplinary approach. No doubt a good deal of potential lies in inductive approaches stemming from study of the tasks people undertake and the problems they face in the course of their daily lives, but the basic structural characteristics would remain and would continue to limit the effectiveness of the school as an instrument for serving too wide a diversity of social purposes. If in fact the main role for which the school is suited is to render men more capable of understanding and analysing their situations, then it seems likely that in the initiation and maintaining of progress in rural areas a greater emphasis must be placed on other agencies of change, including other means of meeting the training needs of the community. Only when economic development is proceeding and social changes are already coming about can the schools be expected to play more than a very subsidiary role.

## Urban Development

Although attention has recently focussed very much on the development problems of the rural areas, it must be remembered that there remain acute problems in many urban areas which were largely created by the kinds of development strategy which have been pursued. The most acute problems of the exploding city have not yet affected Africa to anything like the same extent as other parts of the developing world where the situation of cities such as Calcutta, Jakarta, Seoul, São Paulo and Bogota can only be described as terrifying. Yet we should remember that in Lagos Africa possesses the world's second fastest growing city and that the populations of African towns and cities are rising faster than national populations as a whole. The strains which this growth is placing upon urban administrations, which have to provide housing, transportation, sanitation and other social services, are already immense in far smaller cities than Lagos. The problems of feeding and finding work for growing numbers of people are manifest everywhere, and yet we may be only in the early stages of a process which, if the experience of other parts of the world is repeated, seems likely to escalate at a dizzy pace. The shanty towns which surround the small, modern concrete and glass nuclei of so many of our cities are unlikely to disappear and may more probably depict the kinds of lives to which ever-increasing proportions of our national populations will be condemned in years to come if the warning is not heeded.

The reasons for the growth in urban populations are fairly well understood, though only in a general way, and much work remains to be done if effective measures are to be taken to contain the situation. African countries, like their counterparts in Asia and Latin America, are industrialising at a time when their populations are increasing at unprecedented rates, a situation very different from that in which European nations industrialised. Consequently, existing urban populations grow rapidly through natural increase and at rates apparently faster then even rural populations (possibly because of better access to medical services). Moreover, they are joined by large numbers of people moving from the rural areas, attracted by the new life styles and opportunities offered by the cities and to some extent discouraged by real problems of maintaining themselves on the land – the familiar pull-push effect. It is generally recognised that the problems of the towns, the unemployment, the crime and vagrancy – the insecurity and the politically dangerous polaris-ation of rich and poor – cannot be solved in the towns alone but that many of the answers are to be found in rural development.

However there are many problems which can only be solved in the towns themselves and it is being suggested that if we are to cope we shall need to adopt very new ways of looking at them. Up to this time there has been a pronounced tendency to look upon rural–urban migration simply as an evil that must be stopped, to view the inhabitants of the shanty towns, the young men who besiege employers, the hundreds who sleep in the streets, simply as liabilities, and to regard dilapidation of buildings and roads, overcrowded and broken down buses, overflowing drains and piles of refuse, simply as affronts to national and civic dignity which if possible should be hidden from the eyes of visiting dignitaries. The consequent tendency has been to seek to solve the problem by discouraging immigration, by preaching birth control, by bulldozing the shanties (replacing them with concrete block boxes which can at best only house a small minority and which are surely destined to become the next generation of slums). New modern highways are built and traffic controls imposed which permit the elites only the briefest glimpses of the sordid scene around them as they drive to their offices or to the airport. It is not suggested here that such things do not have their place. Alone, however, they may temporarily ameliorate the problem without removing it. The Nigerian spokesman who informed a United Nations population conference in Bucharest that immigration into Lagos 'has not created the massive sociological problems one would have feared' and referred to 'sluggish traffic' as 'the most stupendous manifestation of sprawling urbanism' was merely reflecting the one sided view of the situation which we are describing.[45]

The alternative and more positive way of looking at urban problems must begin, Koenigsberger has suggested, 'with the quest for policies, plans and programmes that accelerate the process of urban settlement rather than oppose it'.[46] Instead of applying standards of town planning more appropriate in affluent societies the aim should be perhaps to accept minimum standards of social services, to provide only the services which people cannot provide for themselves and to release the energy they have already shown themselves to possess in a guided process of self-development. It is clear that not even the apparently appalling conditions under which many of them live will deter them from moving into the cities and from continuing to live there in the majority of cases. They are prepared to accept these conditions so long as the city offers them the things which they most value – the possibility of obtaining paid employment, education for themselves or their children, and a way of life characterised by greater individual freedom than the countryside appears to offer. It is suggested, therefore, that the older social welfare approach which treated people as liabilities and problems should be replaced by one which offers them complete acceptance and values their potential. In practice there may be little alternative since direct government action sufficient to make a real impact on the situation would be far too costly.

The policies of self-reliance and of community self-development which have been widely accepted for rural people may then be equally applicable in urban situations. Clearly, once again there will be an important role for education to play, a catalytic function which will include helping new arrivals to cope with the new values, attitudes and skills of urban living, promoting the integration of diverse cultural groups, improving community and personal relationships, and in essentially practical ways improving the capacity of town dwellers to improve their own situation, to supplement inadequate services, and to satisfy their social and psychological needs.

How these things may be done we shall only learn through trying to do them. Fortunately Africa still has time to learn before the situation gets out of control and the cities place intolerable strain on our precarious national polities and economies. But we may not have as much time as we suppose and it may be that in ten years time we shall all be talking about urban development as desperately as at present we talk about rural development.

## References

1. Federal Ministry of Education, Nigeria, *Investment in Education, the Report of the Commission on Post-School Certificate and Higher Education in Nigeria* (Lagos: Government Printer, 1960).
2. Great Britain, *Statement on Colonial Development and Welfare*, Cmd 6175 (London: HMSO, 1940).
3. Great Britain, *Memorandum on the Education of African Communities*, Col. No. 103 (London: HMSO, 1935).
4. W. W. Rostow, *The Stages of Economic Growth* (Cambridge University Press 1960).
5. F. H. Harbison and C. A. Myers, *Education, Manpower and Economic Growth, Strategies of Human Resource Development* (McGraw Hill, 1964).
6. UN Economic Commission for Africa and UNESCO, Conference of African States on the Development of Education in Africa, Addis Ababa, 15–25 May 1961, *Final Report*, 1961, p. 11.
7. *Ibid.*, p. 9.
8. F. H. Harbison, 'The Process of Educational Planning', in *ibid.*, Annex IV, p. 49.
9. W. A. Lewis, 'Education and Economic Development', in *ibid.*, Annex IV, p. 77.
10. Conference of Ministers of Education of African Member States, Lagos, 27 January – 4 February 1976, *Final Report* (UNESCO, 1976) Appx II, p. 58
11. R. McNamara, 'Address to the Board of Governors, World Bank Group', Nairobi, 24 September 1973, in *World Bank, The Assault on World Poverty*, (Baltimore: Johns Hopkins University Press, 1975) p. 90.
12. Christian Council of Kenya, *After School, What? Further Education, Training and Employment of Primary School Leavers* (Nairobi: CCK and Christian Churches Educational Association, 1966).
13. International Labour Office Mission, *Interim Report on Education in a Rural Area of Western Nigeria*, (Ibadan: Ministry of Economic Planning and Social Development, March 1967).
14. S. Stevens, Address to the Fourth National Delegates Conference of the African Peoples Congress, 1974.
15. C. A. Anderson and M. J. Bowman, 'Concerning the Role of Education in Development', in C. Geertz, (ed.), *The Quest for Modernity in Asia and Africa* (Free Press, 1963).
16. B. F. Hoselitz, 'Investment in Education and its Political Impact', in J. S. Coleman (ed.) *Education and Political Development* (Princeton University Press, 1965).
17. W. A. Lewis, 'Education and Economic Development', *International Social Science Journal*, vol. XIV no. 4 (1962).

18. I. K. Acheampong, reported in *West Africa*, no. 3011 (4 October 1976) p. 1466.
19. F. H. Harbison, 'The Generation of Employment in Newly Developing Countries', in J. R. Sheffield (ed.), *Education, Employment and Rural Development*, (Nairobi: East African Publishing House, 1967) p. 174.
20. J. C. Caldwell (ed.), *Population Growth and Socio-Economic Change in West Africa*, (Columbia University Press, 1976).
21. L. Emmerij, interviewed in *New Internationalist*, no. 43 (September 1976) p. 26.
22. W. A. Lewis, 'Education and Economic Development', p. 72.
23. R. Dore, *The Diploma Disease: Educational Qualifications and Development* (London: Allen & Unwin, 1976).
24. World Bank, 'Education: Sector Working Paper', September 1971, p. 17.
25. J. Vaizey, *The Economics of Education* (Faber, 1962) p. 134.
26. G. Hunter, 'The School Leaver Problem: False Trails and Fresh Thoughts', in P. Williams (ed.), *The School Leavers in Developing Countries* (London University Institute of Education 1976) p. 29.
27. Sheffield, *Education, Employment and Rural Development*, p. ix.
28. M. Kreinen, *Israel and Africa* (New York: Praeger 1964) pp. 58–9.
29. F. H. Harbison, 'The Generation of Employment in Newly Developing Countries'. (see 19) p. 185.
30. UN Economic Commission for Africa, *The Present Situation and Future Prospects* (New York, 1977).
31. McNamara, 'Address to the Board of Governors, World Bank Group', pp. 90–1; see also P. Hill, *Studies in Rural Capitalism in West Africa* (Cambridge University Press, 1970).
32. P. H. Coombs, with M. Ahmed, *Attacking Rural Poverty*, (Baltimore: Johns Hopkins University Press, 1974) p. 13.
33. R. Chambers and D. Belshawe, 'Managing Rural Development, Lessons and Methods from Eastern Africa', Discussion Paper no. 15, University of Sussex Institute of Development Studies (June 1973) p. 4.23.
34. J. K. Nyerere, *Freedom and Development* (Dar es Salaam: Oxford University Press, 1973) p. 60.
35. J. D. Heijnen, 'Socio-Economic Background', in Centre for the Study of Education in Changing Societies (CESO), *Primary Education in Sukumaland, Tanzania* (Wolters-Noordhoff, 1969).
36. J. F. De Jongh, 'Schools and Society in Sukumaland', in *ibid*.
37. P. Hopcraft, 'Does Education increase Farm Productivity', Working Paper no. 279, Institute for Development Studies, Nairobi University (August 1976) p. 2.
38. P. M. Varkevisser, 'Growing up in Sukumaland', in CESO, *Primary Education in Sukumaland*.
39. W. W. Ogionwo, 'The Adoptions of Technical Innovations in Nigeria: A Study of Factors Associated with Adoptions of Farm Practices', Ph.D. thesis, Leeds University, 1969; cited in J. E. Goldthorpe, *Sociology of the Third World*, (Cambridge University Press 1975) p. 222.
40. M. E. Lockheed, D. T. Jamison, and L. J. Lau, *Farmer Education and Farm*

*Efficiency: A Review of the Literature* (World Bank Development Economics Department, 1978).

41. P. J. Foster, Editorial Introduction to *Education and Rural Development, The World Year Book of Education 1974* (Evans 1974) p. 3.

42. V. L. Griffiths, *The Problems of Rural Education*, (UNESCO/IIEP, 1968) pp. 22–3.

43. C. A. Anderson, 'Effective Education for Agriculture', in Foster and Sheffield, *Education and Rural Development*, p. 43.

44. C. S. Brembeck, 'The Strategic Uses of Formal and Non-formal Education', in C. S. Brembeck and T. J. Thompson (eds), *New Strategies for Educational Development* (Lexington and Toronto: Lexington Books, 1973) pp. 58–60.

45. Reported in *West Africa*, 2 September 1974.

46. O. Koenigsberger, 'Urban Pioneers of the New West', in *The Guardian*, 31 May 1976.

# Part III

# Changing School Systems to Meet National Needs

# 5

# Problems in Educational Planning

In the last chapter we noted that the emergence of the concept of investment in education was accompanied by a new understanding of the importance of educational planning. In the 1960s African countries passed through a period when the desirability of planning education in the context of general development planning was generally accepted and when the entire planning process was strongly influenced by economic thinking. As we shall see, in the 1970s political and social considerations began to play a more important role and have given rise to a new and broader conception of what planning should be. In this chapter we shall trace the evolution of thinking about planning and attempt to examine how far the techniques of planning which have been evolved are capable of solving the kinds of problems presented in the previous chapters.

Educational planning according to Coombs is simply 'the application of rational systematic analysis to the process of educational development with the aim of making education more effective and efficient in responding to the needs and goals of its students and of society.'[1] There has always been a degree of planning in this sense associated with educational development, though the term 'planning' tended not to be used and its effectiveness was limited by financial uncertainties and budgetary procedures. Planning as a specialised activity with its own skills and techniques is, however, a much more recent development stemming from the acceptance by governments of fuller responsibility for investing in economic activities, for co-ordinating these activities and for dealing with the problems of consequent social change. The desirability of educational planning was asserted by the economists as they increasingly came to realise that the problems of development were largely problems of human development and by the social scientists as their understanding grew of the ways in which education systems related to social structures and patterns of privilege and disadvantage. Education, as one of the world's fast growing industries, was both too crucial to national development and too costly to be allowed to develop simply through the momentum exerted by social demand. Decisions of a political character, relating to priorities and purposes, had to be tied in with the solution of administrative and practical problems. The process whereby national development plans extending conventionally over five-year periods were prepared – setting out national goals, analysing national resources and constraints and presenting a broad design broken down into programmes and projects within each sector of national development – offered hope that the interrelationships between the various sectors could be taken account of and the most appropriate courses of action chosen in the light of overall goals and means.

Experience, however, did not fulfil this hope and much educational development took place with scant regard to development activity in other sectors. Educational planning has, moreover, been severely criticised for failing to anticipate and give warning about such damaging trends as the escalating costs of educational provision, the inefficient functioning of school systems, the growing numbers of educated unemployed and the failure of schools to reduce inequalities in national societies. We shall examine some of the reasons for this failure. First, however, we should note the significance of the adoption of planning techniques for educationists in our countries. Planning procedures such as have been described meant that educational decisions could no longer be taken by educationists alone. In the circumstances of the 1960s it was perhaps inevitable that this meant that educational decisions were dominated by economic considerations with a corresponding neglect of other considerations close to the hearts of educationists. Educationists have had to come to terms with a situation which was unfamiliar to them and which they did not fully understand. The mystique associated with planning and the degree of specialisation associated with its techniques has been such that many educationists have been inclined to abdicate responsibility and to leave to the specialists, including of course educational planning specialists, the task of gearing the education system to national needs. This has left largely unquestioned the basis on which the plans were made. As Spaulding has observed, 'Educators were hard to find in many educational planning offices. They were often handed a plan and told to implement it.'[2] Planning tended to be viewed at this period as a highly specialist activity demanding no very extensive knowledge of schools and educational processes. Educationists themselves were rarely capable of talking the language of the planners and statisticians and were often bemused by their complicated models. Senior educational administrators have not always found it easy to accept the new importance given to planning experts who were often self-confident young graduates and working relationships often suffered in consequence. We are only now coming to realise that whilst planning has a vital role to play in developing societies, the planning techniques which we have at our disposal are still extremely crude, the basis of understanding of our problems upon which they operate is still highly defective, and that the effectiveness of the planning process will depend very much upon the extent to which the specialised knowledge and understanding of educationists and others whose activities are being planned but who have tended to remain outside the planning process is made available to the decision-makers. Educationists must recognise that their countries have been compelled to engage in planning at a time when all over the world we are still learning what planning means and what we need in order to plan effectively. Planning cannot solve our problems until we have made our contribution to solving the many problems of planning.

Although it must be noted that there have been wide differences between countries as to the agencies used for planning, the degree of integration sought between education and other aspects of development, and the legal and effective status given to plans, three main approaches to planning have been influential. These have been termed the social demand approach, the manpower forecasting approach and the rate of return analysis approach. We will examine these in turn.

## The Social Demand Approach

The social demand approach is essentially a simple planning technique which has been in use in our countries for many years unadorned by this title. It amounts on the one hand to a calculation of what the situation in respect of costs, supply of teachers, plant and resources, and school leaver output will be at the end of a specified planning period if existing school provision remains more or less as it is, and on the other to a calculation of what the situation would be and what would be required if various kinds of social demand were acceded to. Clearly such calculations are of vital importance in establishing the baseline for projecting desirable changes in the system, notably of scale – for example where the aim is to provide universal education at certain levels of the school system or where the principle of doing so has been conceded. Account may be taken of demographic trends in anticipating the resource and administrative implications of such a policy or alternatively, perhaps, of maintaining the provision of schooling for a fixed percentage of the school-age population.

Since political decisions must take into account the need to satisfy the demands of the general public, simple projections of this kind are important in informing the decision-makers of the implications of such demand. However few countries anywhere in the world are in a position to provide as much education as may be demanded and decision-makers must seek to reconcile private demand with public need. Where resources are acutely limited, as in most African countries, and where we are seeking to provide those kinds and quantities of education which will offer the greatest good to the greatest number, such planning techniques, whilst useful, cannot offer all the guidance we need as to how best to meet identified needs.

## The Manpower Forecasting Approach

This approach, focussing upon a major area of need, does appear to offer the kind of guidance lacking in the social demand approach. Simply described, it involves an analysis of the skilled manpower requirements of the economy from which a calculation may be made of the quantities, kinds and levels of education required to meet these requirements. If we know that by a particular target year we shall require a certain number of people in each of a number of crucial employment categories, and if we make certain assumptions about the length and kind of education required for each category, we can in theory set about adjusting the educational system to ensure that the people are available when needed. In practice a more complex procedure must be followed but there is an attractive simplicity about the theory. It is hardly surprising, in view of the strong emphasis given in the 1960s to modern-sector economic development and the great need in the years following independence to replace departing expatriates with local manpower known to be in short supply, that this approach, which appears to promise fairly precise means of calculating the educational provision necessary, should have been the principal form of educational planning adopted in African countries and elsewhere.

The practice of manpower forecasting, though not unknown previously, was in its infancy in the early 1960s and has passed through a number of stages of development. The absence in most African countries of an adequate basis of statistical knowledge about prevailing employment structures initially resulted in the application of international correlations of increasing specificity and the use of various 'rules of thumb' or assumptions about, for example, the relationship which would exist between rates of growth in GDP and in various categories of employment. The second Nigerian development plan of 1970–4 applied Harbison's rule of thumb that employment grows at about half the rate of growth of national income and Tinbergen's calculation that high level manpower has to grow at about the same rate as national income. Such assumptions could only be used effectively in respect of high and intermediate levels of manpower, pro-fessional, sub-professional and technician categories, which in view of the difficulty of precise occupational distinctions could conveniently be defined in terms of the level of education required for each – a university degree, or so many years of schooling. In the event projections based upon such rules of thumb proved highly inaccurate, partly because they were derived from the very different economic and historical context of more highly developed countries and partly because the circum-stances of individual African countries varied so considerably. (However, in respect of certain specific occupations it was possible to arrive at rules of thumb based more soundly upon empirical experience, for example in calculating the need for teachers on the basis of acceptable teacher–pupil ratios, or for doctors on the basis of the size of the population to be served.)

From an early stage, as recommended by the economists, more detailed national manpower surveys were conducted to arrive at a truer understanding of the existing employment structure and stock of skilled manpower as a basis for forecasting future needs. Such surveys incorporated the opinions of employers as to their current and future needs coupled with extrapolations of past trends in the labour market and took into account probable attrition resulting from death and retirement. In some national plans, as in the second national development plan for Nigeria, the more sophisticated approach pioneered in the Mediter-ranean Regional Project was used. A target of economic growth expressed in terms of GDP for the target year is set, this overall target is then broken down into the contributions anticipated from each major sector of the economy – agriculture, manu-facturing, mining, transport, distribution, service industries and so on – and these are then further broken down by individual industries. The labour force requirements of each industry for the target to be reached are then calculated, categorised and converted into educational requirements.

However the apparent simplicity of the theory and the growing sophistication of the procedures were deceptive. 'It would be flattering to call such studies inaccurate', Mark Blaug is reported as saying, 'More nonsense has been talked about this than any other aspect of education.'[3] Experience with manpower planning has proved disillusioning even in more developed countries. In Britain it was stated in 1976 that manpower planning had proved an imprecise tool even in areas such as the supply of teachers and doctors where it was essential, and attempts to apply it to broader areas such as science or engineering had proved impossible.[4] Jolly and Colclough, reviewing over 30 manpower studies conducted in more than 20 African countries between 1960 and 1972 concluded that the planning techniques used were subject to a wide range of technical deficiencies – weakness of data, crude assumptions, and methodological inadequacies.[5] Commonly they projected ex-pansion from baselines incompletely analysed, assumed growth rates in the economy substantially different from those actually to be achieved, tended generally to overestimate the manpower needed and the extent to which the products of schooling would enter into employment. The methods used were in general more suited to projecting requirements in a situation of simple growth whereas in African countries economic development involving substantial change in the industrial and occupational structures was both needed and sought.

Whilst the fundamental problem was that in a situation of world economic uncertainty it was virtually impossible to forecast with any accuracy how far and in what ways the economy would develop, certain of the technical deficiencies merit further brief mention. Employer forecasts are notoriously unreliable as a basis for estimating skill needs. Even allowing for their propensity to change their requirements during the planning period, some employers are likely to demand educational qualifications which they do not in fact need and others to need certain kinds of qualifications without being fully aware of the fact. It is clear that the availability of educated manpower has a considerable influence on the amount and quality of the manpower employers seek to acquire. In a situation of shortage, employers will accept less well qualified manpower than they would wish, but where the education system is producing larger numbers of educated people than the economy can easily absorb they may be tempted to demand higher qualifications than perhaps are required for the job. And of course employers who forecast needs with expansion in view cannot be compelled to undertake this expansion and to take up the manpower prepared for them.

There is an odd circularity about defining manpower categories in terms of levels of education and then seeking to adjust the output of the various levels of education to provide for estimated need which tends to freeze our thinking about the kinds of education required for effective employment. Manpower planning tends to deal in terms of crude levels of education and to say nothing about the wide range of possible combinations of education and training which may equally well meet the need. The possibilities of substituting one level or kind of education for another are known to be very considerable, particularly where work experience is fully recognised as a criterion for promoting workers from one grade or post to another and where workers can qualify themselves for new levels and kinds of work through on-the-job training or through private study outside the formal school system. Moreover efficient production may be attained through a wide range of manpower structures using different combinations of high, intermediate and lower qualifications in their labour forces. The assumptions on which manpower planning is based lend themselves to easy translation into schooling requirements but tend to impose too inflexible a structure upon the use of manpower in industry.

The manpower forecasting approach has been preoccupied with manipulating the supply of initial entrants into employment through directing the flows of people into and out of schooling. It may be that in consequence we have discouraged the development of training and retraining opportunities within employment and so have restricted internal mobility. At the same time entry to occupations at various levels and based upon possession of qualifications has encouraged differentials between grades of employment, has tended to freeze them in a manner not calculated to maintain high morale and encourage greater efficiency, and has promoted a top-down management mentality which does not encourage innovative thinking among employees in the lower echelons. Increasingly, as shortages of educated manpower in many categories disappear the number of people fresh from school who will be absorbed into employment will represent a diminishing proportion of the total number in employment and for this reason it is vital that we pay more attention to ways of managing and deploying the total stock of labour through moving people from areas of over-supply to areas of under-supply and through providing the on-the-job training necessary for this to take place efficiently. As the costs of education mount and as the level of qualification demanded for entry to particular levels of employment rises, we ought perhaps to be asking ourselves how best to combine the minimum level of expensive formal education with the maximum of hopefully less expensive on-the-job training to achieve a sufficient level of competence at minimum cost in wide sectors of our labour forces. Furthermore in economic situations such as those which face many African countries in which diversification of production, the development of labour-intensive modes of production, the encouragement of entrepreneurial activity and the opening up of new markets is urged, implying significant structural change in the economy, it is even more important that the planners be concerned with improving the quality and adaptability of existing manpower stocks.

However, even if it were possible to forecast manpower needs more precisely, there would remain the problem of ensuring an appropriate supply. It is here that the economic planners are at their weakest and that the potential contribution of the educattionist is greatest. The long feed time associated with education – the period of years which it takes to produce the educated man demanded by the employment market – is a major embarrassment to planners. Wastage rates from educational institutions are commonly very high in Africa and the reasons for this are still insufficiently understood. Again it may well be difficult to attract sufficient numbers of students into certain courses geared to perhaps less attractive forms of employment, and thereafter to prevent them from dropping out or from using the qualifications they gain for purposes other than those for which they are intended. The example of teacher education is particularly relevant here. In many African countries it is difficult to fill all the places available for teacher training, we cannot easily forecast how many will successfully complete the course, and we know full well that many of those who qualify will seek to use their qualification to gain another kind of post altogether or to re-enter the formal education system as students. There are many fields of commerce, administration and politics where a teaching qualification and the general education it represents is readily acceptable. In some countries the teaching qualification is given direct equivalence to general education; in Nigeria for instance the Grade II Teachers' Certificate is widely accepted as being equivalent to the School Certificate or Ordinary Level of GCE and is consequently used as such for purposes of gaining entrance to employment, training or even university entrance. Many countries have experience of finding that the products of other kinds of vocational training institutions, designed to meet urgent manpower needs, also melt away into other forms of occupation rather than taking up the opportunities for which they were trained. The precise matching of manpower needs and educational provision is impossible where this can occur, and yet, of course, to a considerable degree it should occur if a flexible and adaptable labour force is to be created.

We should also note the widespread and long-standing concern about the brain drain which occurs when possession of skills and qualifications is given international recognition, and when the shortage of certain categories of manpower in other countries leads them to offer salaries and conditions of service better than those which can be afforded in the country providing the training.

Problems such as these may be inevitable where there are shortages of skilled and educated manpower and may be expected to redress themselves as overall supply rises to meet the level of need, but this is likely to be a slow and sometimes painful process. The tendency of manpower studies to ignore the desirability of providing adequate incentives, perhaps through an incomes policy, to encourage young people both to enter appropriate courses of study and to take up employment where they are needed, has been frequently criticised. In the meantime, if employment needs are to be met the education system may have to overproduce relevantly qualified people and accept both the danger of unemployment among its products and wasteful investment in their training.

We have always known in any case that education systems cannot be other than wasteful in meeting high and intermediate-level manpower needs. If a hundred graduates are needed for certain posts, we cannot simply admit a hundred pupils to primary school and thereafter push them through the programme of education needed. In order to provide a hundred people capable of university level studies we may have to provide secondary education to several hundred people themselves selected from a far larger number of primary school entrants. This wider educational base may itself be substantially ill-matched with the labour market need for people with a secondary or a primary education. A fundamental problem with manpower planning as it has been practised is that it has focussed upon the need of the modern sector of the economy for high and intermediate level manpower. It has had very little to say about the educational needs of lower-level skilled and unskilled manpower engaged for the most part in the traditional and subsistence sector of the economy. An education system designed to produce the manpower which it does specify will therefore produce large quantities of educated products which cannot be absorbed in the sector towards which their education has been focussed, and yet, as we have seen, they cannot easily be absorbed in the agricultural or low-level craft occupations which remain to them, their education having neither provided them with the skills nor the psychological orientation which they may need.

In general manpower forecasting has focussed upon employment needs and has been little concerned with the educational means whereby the manpower might be produced other than in terms of the numbers of graduates needed from the more advanced levels of education systems. Whilst at tertiary level it may have something to say about the desirable balance to be achieved between science/technology and other areas of study, at school level it has said little about the process of education, the kinds of skills needed, the balance between education and training, and the means whereby manpower of an appropriate quality might be produced, other than the frequently reiterated, and to many educationists dubious, recommendation that schooling should be more practical in orientation. This is perhaps not surprising since, as Blaug has put it, 'education to economists is simply a "black box": they do not profess to know what happens to anyone passing through it; all they know is that employers somehow value the experience and are willing to pay for it.'[6] They are not in consequence fully aware of the problems faced by educationists in responding to manpower forecasts.

Educationists for their part are well aware that schools are not assembly lines on which a variety of inputs are combined to produce the desired output and that the schools cannot pre-determine the knowledge, skill and attitudinal makeup of their graduates to any very precise degree. We recognise that the young person who emerges from the school will have been formed by a range of influences of which the school is but one (and not necessarily the most powerful) and over most of which we have little control. We are also aware that the school system, upon which the manpower forecasters have tended to concentrate, is not the only or necessarily the best means of providing the education and training needed for working life and have welcomed the growing interest in non-formal education in recent years. We have argued that education is concerned with far more than inculcating the skills of production and fitting people into employment structures even though we accept the importance of these things, and finally we recognise that institutionalised education involves lengthy and sequential processes which cannot be readily turned on and off like a water tap in response to changing demand. In a later section we shall be examining in more detail why it is that school systems find it difficult to change and adapt in response to planning demands. Here we merely note that manpower forecasting has tended to make assumptions about the capacity of schooling which are not justified.

Finally we must note that manpower forecasting has been primarily concerned with the quantities of manpower needed and not with the cost of producing it. It has not conventionally incorporated cost/benefit analysis, and in consequence in situations where resources are scarce it could well be that the heavy investment in schooling which may be called for may outweigh the economic benefits to be gained. The third planning approach to which we now turn is, however, primarily concerned with calculating the economic returns from investment in education.

## The Rate of Return Approach

Essentially the rate of return approach, sometimes referred to as the cost/benefit analysis approach, is a mode of analysis of current relationships between education and income and not a planning technique, but it is argued that it may provide valuable insights which may be of value in planning the development of education systems. The approach is based upon the assumption that the wages and salaries paid to workers closely reflect differences in their productivity, and that variations in their productivity are primarily the result of differences in the amounts and kinds of education they have received. If we construct age–earnings profiles for various categories of workers, showing their educational background, it can be demonstrated that an individual who invests in his own education rather than choosing to take up employment at an early age can expect to earn more during his working lifetime than he would otherwise have done even though he might have started to earn money sooner had he chosen to work rather than to receive education. By calculating how much his education cost, including both direct costs and the earnings which he otherwise would have received, and by comparing this 'investment' with lifetime earnings we can work out with apparent precision the returns to be gained by individuals from various amounts and kinds of education. Since employers are thought to be rational beings who will only pay higher salaries when they receive equivalent returns in terms of productivity, we may conclude that not only will individuals benefit from investing in additional education but so will society as a whole, since overall productivity will be raised. We may also analyse which kinds and amounts of education yield the greatest returns to the individual and to society, and this may guide us in designing education systems, in determining the shape of the educational pyramid and the balance between general and technical education, for instance. A comparison of the benefits likely to be gained from investing in education with the benefits to be gained from alternative investments, in physical capital for example, may help us to determine to what extent we should devote our resources to education as opposed to other things we need. Clearly this is something that the manpower forecasting or social demand approaches do not pretend to do.

Most of the rate of return studies which have been undertaken have been in the more developed free enterprise societies, particularly the United States, but academic studies have been made in a number of other countries. Jolly and Colclough have surveyed ten such studies undertaken up to 1970 in Africa, in Ghana (1969), Kenya (1968, 1969), Nigeria (1967, 1969), Rhodesia (1960), Uganda (1963, 1967, 1968), and Zambia (1966) but criticised these studies as involving techniques based upon unreasonable assumptions and inadequate data. The studies were also found to be inconsistent, apparently revealing considerable variations in cost/benefit ratios as between countries and even within a single country at different times, as for example in the three Uganda studies.[7] It may be that we are only just reaching the stage when age–earnings profiles for African countries can be defined and it is not surprising that rate of return analysis had had no very great effect upon educational planning in Africa so far. However certain findings from such studies which appear to show that proportionately higher rates of return may be gained from completing primary education than from secondary and higher education have been used to support the current thrust towards mass education and universal basic schooling, although clearly the apparently higher rates of return are likely to owe more to the lower costs of primary education than to higher benefits. Calculations of the considerable financial benefit which individuals personally receive from their education have also been used to support the argument that a higher proportion of the cost of education ought to be shifted back onto the shoulders of those attending school.

The applicability of some of the assumptions of this approach to Africa must be questioned, notably of course the extent to which salaries reflect productivity. In practice in Africa – and elsewhere – salary levels are often artificially determined by reference to what similarly qualified people in other countries receive. Some salary scales have been inflated by the transfer to local staff of salaries previously paid to expatriates without first deducting the substantial element in those salaries which was paid as an inducement to work in Africa and without taking account of the fact that the salaries were determined in relation to what an expatriate would have received in the very different economic context of his own country. Civil service salaries in particular continue to owe much to this and little to productivity considerations. This is significant since very high proportions of educated people are employed directly by their governments and their salaries have a profound influence on salaries paid in the private sector to employees holding comparable educational qualifications. This is recognised by many governments which, though rarely able to impose salary reductions upon their staff, seek to make adjustments as inflation erodes the real value of the salaries paid. Major discrepancies are likely to remain so long as wages and salaries are more closely linked to educational qualifications than to productivity and to the social value of the work performed. Free market forces which might reflect productivity considerations more clearly are unlikely to make speedy inroads into this situation and consequently rate of return analysis is unlikely to be capable of playing a major role in educational planning for some time.

A further set of considerations merits some brief consideration here. Even if the relationship between earnings and productivity in African countries was clear, and even if we were further to accept that formal education is the principal way in which skills and abilities relevant to productive work are and should be produced – which, as we have seen, may be questioned – rate of return analysis can only indicate directions in which education systems should expand to maximise the earning capacity of their products over a limited period. This is because the approach is based upon study of past trends and cannot be assumed to be securely future-oriented. It analyses past and current relationships between the costs of gaining more education and the increase in earnings to which this leads, but it cannot guarantee that salary levels will maintain the same relationship with educational qualification over the period of years required for the acquisition of the qualification. In Africa the financial return from education has been inflated by past scarcity of people with particular levels and kinds of education: if we provide more of that level or kind of education the law of supply and demand is likely eventually to take its course. And if economic change of the radical kind which we are seeking is to occur we can hardly base educational development upon cost/benefit relationship derived from the economic system we are trying to change.

## 'Synthetic' Approaches

Up to this point we have been cursorily examining three basic approaches to the planning of education in relation to economic needs and noting that the techniques available to us as yet are very imperfect. These are not, however, three competing or alternative approaches. Manpower forecasting attempts to tell us how many people with certain kinds of qualifications need to be produced by the education system over a set period: it does not tell us anything about the costs of producing them or whether the investment will pay for itself. The social demand approach seeks to tell us how many people with certain kinds of qualifications will be forthcoming at the end of a planning period but does not tell us whether there will be jobs for them, and whilst saying something about costs does not tell us anything about the probable benefits. Rate of return analysis tells us something about how the demand for and supply of educated people are currently matched but cannot forecast what the situation will be at the end of the planning period. Whilst manpower forecasting has been seen as the most immediately useful technique, we recall the warning given by the British delegation to the Fifth Commonwealth Education Conference that the three approaches should be seen as complementary and that 'planners ignore any one of the three factors only at their peril.'[8] Attention has therefore recently been directed towards so-called 'synthetic' models which seek to combine and draw upon all three approaches to complement each other. We should not underestimate the complexity of the process. Harbison referring to this as human resource assessment has the following to say about it.

The techniques of human resource assessment range far beyond the traditional type of statistical surveys of high level manpower. They involve continuous enumeration of the labor force, tracing of career patterns of school leavers and university graduates, the study of labor absorptive capacity of different industries and activities, the calculation of cost-effectiveness of investments in human resource development, and many other aspects of education and manpower utilization. Indeed, a human resource assessment is really an assessment of the entire national development process from the perspective of human aspirations and the welfare of a nation's people.[9]

## Contextual Problems

So far we have been considering deficiencies in the methodology or process of educational planning. Now we turn to some of the problems which have arisen from the context within which planning is conducted and upon which its effectiveness must largely depend.

The failure of educational planners to anticipate economic trends is understandable. The inability of many African countries to achieve the rates of growth upon which plans were predicted and thereby to create employment for the products of the schools or to create the wealth upon which further educational as well as other investments depended may partly reflect the over-optimism which characterised the 1960s but was also a consequence of international trends such as the decline in the economic situation of major trading partners, the rapid rise in the price of oil and the effects of the Sahelian drought. The last decade has not been conducive to development planning in this respect.

Equally significant difficulties have arisen in the political sphere. The rational procedures of planning have often been undermined by the failure of political leadership to implement plans fully and its tendency to take decisions in capitulation to social demand or sometimes even on the basis of sectional interest. Political instability or uncertainty which has plagued many countries has not encouraged leaders to look beyond short term concerns, yet, as we shall need to stress later, determined and consistent political direction and support is vital for the implementation of longer term development plans.

Planning is clearly dependent upon the formulation of goals and objectives in a manner which clearly tells the planners what is expected of them. The goals should be clearly stated and both understood and as far as possible accepted by all those concerned. Where multiple objectives exist, as is the situation with any education system, the goals should be reasonably consistent with one another and ordered in terms of priorities in order that where choices have to be made this may be done with the minimum of sacrifice. Finally the goals set for the system should be within the capacity of planners to plan and of the system to implement and achieve. Unfortunately these conditions rarely exist. Most of our countries have formulated statements of national and educational goals which are unclear, which contain potential for conflict and in which priorities are inadequately defined.

As we have argued the definition of national and educational goals is primarily a political responsibility. Since the business of politics is largely one of reconciling and satisfying a range of differing views and principles it is hardly surprising that many policy statements emerge which are broad and general, acceptable to most people but susceptible of a variety of interpretations when we seek to implement them. To be realistic we cannot expect statements of national goals to serve as complete and perfect blueprints for action and we must look to the processes through which these goals are interpreted into courses of action and thereafter implemented for means of clarifying issues and resolving conflicts. In this process responsibility is shared between political decision-makers, the planners who have the technical responsibility for designing the strategy for achieving our goals, and the administrative and professional structures which are concerned with implementing the strategies. These three areas of responsibility cannot be completely distinct. Political decision-makers must be guided by advice and information concerning the needs, the resources, the constraints and the alternatives which exist. To a large extent this advice and information must be supplied by the planning and administrative staff. Similarly, planners must be aware of the problems of the administrators in following the courses of action set for them, and will require guidance from the administration and professional specialists both prior to and during the implementation stages in order that adjustments and modifications may be made which will facilitate implementation.

Much therefore depends upon the quality of communication and mutual understanding between the various groups involved. In his analysis of the organisation of educational planning in Nigeria up to 1966 Wheeler noted the difficulties experienced in establishing effective communication and understanding between the National Economic Council consisting of ministers, the Joint Planning Committee consisting of senior officials, and the Economic Planning Unit consisting of specialist planners, resulting from the inability of ministers and officials to understand the language and techniques of the planners, a situation seriously exacerbated by frequent changes of personnel. In consequence the senior bodies, meeting only from time to time and concerned after the initial stages with studying the recommendations of the Economic Planning Unit, tended to content themselves with examining the feasibility of individual programmes and projects which, in the eyes of the planners, constituted a coherent whole. Some of the decisions which were made about individual components of the plan failed to take account of their place in the total plan and vitiated much of the work done by the planners.[10]

Ruscoe, in examining the conditions necessary for success in educational planning, noted the danger that politicians will sometimes involve themselves in technical matters which they will treat as if they were political, reaching decisions which are not based upon full understanding of the technical considerations. It is also possible that when a political body is inactive or inefficient in performing its policy-defining functions, the planners may be forced to enter into policy determination in order that they may get ahead with their technical responsibilities.[11] In such circumstances the difference between policy formulation and policy interpretation is not a clear one, and even in the most favourable circumstances there is bound to be some blurring or confusion of the functions of various bodies which can be overcome only by close and regular contact and by a sufficient degree of mutual understanding. Adequate communication and co-ordination is clearly also vital in the implementation of plans. Here problems arise from the administrative structure, from the degree of autonomy jealously preserved by specialist ministries, and by divisions and departments within ministries. Ministries of Education, for instance, are commonly organised in such a way that primary schools, secondary schools and teacher training institutions are separately administered and often technical education is operated through its own hierarchy of officials. Adult education is normally shared between several ministries whilst universities, operating largely autonomously, may be financed through inter-ministerial grants committees. Whilst co-ordination between ministries and between divisions may be, in theory at least, maintained at the higher levels, it is a good deal more difficult to maintain co-ordination at lower levels and in the field, where officers often find themselves working in relative ignorance of what their colleagues are doing in the same area. It may be argued that understanding of and concern for the overall national and sectoral plan stands in inverse proportion to the degree of direct involvement in project implementation.

Attention has also been drawn to the peculiar function of ministries of finance in the planning process. Whilst exercising tight control over economic decision-making and financial allocation through annual budgeting procedures, such ministries have rarely sought effectively to ensure that development plans once approved have been efficiently implemented and evaluated, confining their function to the simple and occasional allocation of finance. In consequence there has tended to be a lack of overall supervision of the implementation of plans to ensure that separate programmes are kept in phase with one another, that the priorities originally agreed have been kept to, and that competition for resources is kept to the minimum. Dr. Kunle Adamson of the Nigerian Institute of Social and Economic Research has argued for Nigeria that the scale of national economic planning grew five fold between 1962 and 1976, but that its performance declined significantly during the period because economic problems grew in complexity rendering the techniques in use inadequate. His conclusion that there is a limit to the planning capability of Nigeria given limited executive capacity and low levels of efficiency in management is one which should give all our countries cause for thought.[12]

Effective planning is heavily dependent upon the availability of sufficient, appropriate and reliable data and earlier plans in Africa suffered severely from lack of such information. Those of us who have sought to use or who have been involved in supplying or collecting data will be fully aware of the acute problems faced here. The data needed by educational planners will necessarily go far beyond the kinds of conventional educational statistics to which we have been long accustomed in annual reports and will obviously include information regarding demographic trends and the employment structure which has normally been collected together with many other kinds of data by central statistical offices. Since these offices serve a wide range of purposes, the available data may not be well related to the particular purposes of educational planners, not having been collected with their specific needs in view. Manpower studies have usually involved the separate collection of data and have frequently recommended that separate manpower statistical services should be established but there is some danger here of the fragmentation of the information base upon which overall development planning should be conducted. Even basic educational data is by no means easy to obtain where, as is normal, educational and training activities are the responsibility of several ministries, each with its own accounting and statistical procedures. In consequence it may be a difficult matter even to establish the extent and cost of current educational provision in a single country, a problem further complicated by the existence of private schooling, and possible division of responsibilities between federal, state and local authorities.

In the end judgements must be reached on the basis of the data obtained and this is a matter which involves a high degree of skill and expertise, commodities which are commonly in short supply in Africa. It is clear that at each stage in the data-collection process from the design of the questionnaire, through the collation of returns, to the interpretation of results, a high degree of expertise is required and demands that high priority be given to the training of planning personnel.

## Trends in Planning

It seems clear that we are now moving into an era in which the nature and tasks of educational planning are going to change significantly. In part this has resulted from the now generally acknowledged failure of many apparently well-constructed education plans and consequent questioning of the assumptions and techniques on which they were based. In part it has resulted from changing circumstances in which the overall shortages of educated manpower experienced in the early 1960s have given way to substantial surpluses (at least in certain areas) and in which early optimism about the possibilities of rapid economic expansion has been severely shaken. And in part it has resulted from the consequent reassertion of the importance of other than economic considerations in development, with our early preoccupation with the global expansion of education systems being replaced by a growing concern for the equitable distribution of educational opportunity.

Among the changes in the planning process which we can dimly perceive are the following. We are beginning to see a move away from global patterns of planning involving large-scale surveys of needs and the manipulation of flows into and out of the national education system, towards more practical, and possibly more accurate, diffused approaches. Planners are distinguishing between macro-planning, which is concerned with establishing broad goals and determining resource allocation, and micro-planning which seeks means of achieving these goals at a much lower level, in particular sectors of the economy, in particular kinds of occupation, and in particular regions of the country, for example.

We should note in particular the very interesting development in recent years of what has been called 'participatory planning'. This has involved not merely the decentralisation of planning and the involvement of regional and local bodies in the process, although this has been thought of as likely to produce more realistic and locally relevant planning than remote central bodies may be capable of, but the involvement of the people who will be affected by the planning decisions. The participation of teachers, parents and students in the decision-making process, it is argued, will help them to understand what is intended, will assist them in implementing planning decisions, and more than this, will win their acceptance of changes and develop their commitment to making the changes work. People, and notably educated people, are often highly resistant to changes which they do not understand and about which they have not been consulted. Moreover, through being involved in planning it is likely that they will develop their capacity to contribute to effective decision-making and thereby increase the likelihood that decisions will be soundly based. African examples of participatory planning approaches would include the university based Sierra Leone Education Review of 1974, the national debate conducted in Zambia in 1976–7, the national seminar approach used in Nigeria in 1973, the national seminar following the 'educational dialogue' between Ministry and people in Lesotho 1978, the nationwide survey of 10 000 people conducted in Togo and the more diffuse models of discussion and consultation which have been used for ten years in Tanzania.[13] The Zambian example is particularly interesting. A carefully planned schedule of activities was followed involving study visits abroad and special investigations at home by specialist study groups leading to a national report-back seminar and the preparation of a draft statement on Educational Reform which was widely distributed in seven languages. Mass media campaigns paved the way for nationwide seminars and opportunities for individuals and organisations to send written comments. The response was thoroughly evaluated and significantly led to quite substantial and fundamental revisions of the proposals. Participatory approaches are extremely promising in some respects but necessarily must make the process of decision-making more complex, attenuated and possibly more expensive, and will certainly demand far more efficient multi-directional communication between all those involved. It will also mean genuine willingness on the part of politicians to consult and to listen, and on the part of the planners to modify and explain their techniques, otherwise the process could be simply a cosmetic one, increasingly counterproductive as those 'consulted' come to recognise the fact.

The trend we are discussing is, however, of deeper significance than the extension of participation alone. As Foster has put it the place of planning is 'to provide the institutional framework for small scale operative decision-making, not the wholesale making of such decisions.'[14] Thus the former emphasis of planners upon the design of detailed plans intended to direct all development activity in periodic and end-on succession may give way as Weiler suggests[15] to a far more complex concept of planning as a cyclical and on going process of enquiry and illumination intended to inform and facilitate decision-making rather than to take those decisions. This does not necessarily mean that there will be no plans as such but they are likely to take the form of clearer definitions of goals and priorities couched in terms which will, without prescribing all the action which must be taken, given more adequate direction to those who must in their various ways seek to give practical form to the intentions set out. The central planning function will no longer be one largely concerned with detailed design but with co-ordinating and facilitating implementation and with evaluating progress being made. Micro-planning will become increasingly the responsibility of those who are closely involved in implementation.

Clearly there is much that we still need to learn about planning. Some things we will learn from research, others from the analysis of experience. We may be in the early stages of learning how to plan but we have surely no alternative but to continue as best we can, though, as Seth Spaulding suggests, it may be best to approach the future in educational planning 'with a healthy scepticism'. Spaulding fears the 'authoritarianism of the technocrat'.[16] It is the suggestion of this chapter that this fear can only be dispelled and technocratic expertise given its proper place when professional educationists, among others, acquire a fuller understanding of the planning process and are prepared to participate more effectively in the process of making decisions in the areas of their professional competence.

The particular contribution which they need to make is in respect of greater understanding of the way in which the existing educational systems work, of the interrelationships and relative efficiency of their separate parts, of the way in which different combinations of general education and training in formal and non-formal arrangements may meet our needs, of the extent to which economic goals may be combined with political and social goals, of the extent to which client aspiration and background can be purposively modified, and how the impact of changes in structure, institutional patterns, curriculum, examinations, staff development and support services may be maximised. As yet we have very inadequate understanding of these matters, which are crucial to the planning process, and it is clear that we shall need to enlist the specialist assistance of other social scientists in developing the necessary techniques. Without this development, however, no matter how much progress is made in refining the techniques of economic analysis and improving general planning capacity, the planning of education will remain a lopsided and speculative process.

In the following chapters we shall further examine the problems of reforming educational systems in order to clarify some of the crucial issues which demand our attention.

## References

1. P. H. Coombs, *What is Educational Planning?* IIEP Fundamentals of Educational Planning Series no. 1 (UNESCO/IIEP, 1970) p. 14.
2. S. Spaulding, 'Educational Planning: Who Does What to Whom and with What Effect?' *Comparative Education*, vol. 13 no. 1 (March 1977) p. 56.
3. M. Blaug, quoted in P. Hennessy, 'Manpower Plans are Wild Guesses, *Times Higher Education Supplement*, 19 January 1973.
4. G. Fowler, Minister of State for Higher Education, reported in *Times Higher Education Supplement*, 30 January 1976.
5. R. Jolly and C. Coleclough, 'African Manpower Plans: An Evaluation', *International Labour Review*, vol. 106 nos. 2–3 (August–September 1972) pp. 207–64.
6. M. Blaug, *Education and the Employment Problem in Developing Countries* (ILO 1973) pp. 50–1.
7. Jolly and Coleclough, 'African Manpower Plans'.
8. 'Manpower Planning and Education', paper prepared by the manpower planning unit of the Ministry of Overseas Development and presented by the British Government, Fifth Commonwealth Education Conference, p. 1.
9. F. H. Harbison, 'A Human Resource Approach to the Development of African Nations', American Council on Education Overseas Liaison Committee, undated, Washington, p. 23.

10. A. C. R. Wheeler, *The Organisation of Educational Planning in Nigeria*, African Research Monographs no. 13 (Paris: UNESCO/HEP, 1968).

11. G. C. Ruscoe, The conditions for success in educational planning, IIEP Fundamentals of Educational Planning Series no. 12, (UNESCO/IIEP, 1969).

12. K. Adamson, 'Why Nigeria Should Abandon the 1975–80 Development Plan', Paper prepared for National Workshop on Planning in Nigeria, summarised in *West Africa*, 23 January 1978.

13. A very different approach was followed in the Cameroon where the Ministry of Education decided to allow the ruralisation of education programme to proceed without consultation on the grounds that 'There is no point in prematurely alerting and organising majority opinion in connexion with a reform which, when the time comes, will be judged on results'. R. Lallez, *An Experiment in the Ruralisation of Education, IPAR and the Cameroonian Reform* (Paris: UNESCO, 1974) p. 49.

14. P. Foster, 'The Vocational School Fallacy in Development Planning', in M. Blaug, *Economics of Education*, vol. 1 (Harmondsworth: Penguin, 1968) p. 412.

15. H. N. Weiler, 'New Directions in Educational Planning: Implications for Training', Supplement to the *IIEP Bulletin*, December 1976, p. ii.

16. Spaulding, 'Educational Planning', p. 64.

# 6

# Problems of Educational Innovation

In the preceding chapters we have been examining critically some of the purposes which education and particularly the formal school system has been asked to serve in recent years and some of the ways in which educational planning has been conducted. It has been suggested that we need to re-examine the roles to be allocated to various sectors of the education system and that any action we may take in respect of education may have to be regarded as largely complementary to actions which may have to be taken directly upon society if overall national goals are to be achieved and if the school is to be able to play the more limited roles to which it is suited. Later we shall be looking at what these roles might be and what place in the total educational effort should be allocated to schooling and to other kinds of education. First, however, we need to take up an issue raised earlier and ask how easy it is to make changes in schools. It has been argued that planners and policy makers have assumed too readily that the current weaknesses and apparent failings of school systems may readily be corrected by making school systems, institutions, curricula and methodology more 'relevant'. If we assume that certain changes have been agreed upon, and as we have seen even this assumption is questionable, what are the problems of introducing changes and how speedily may this be done? For problems there certainly must be, since much of current discussion regarding reforming the school is not new but has been going on for a very long time, and despite many years of demanding and discussing change the truth is that our schools are fundamentally very little different from what they were twenty-five years ago. This is not because our predecessors were stupid or ill-intentioned but is largely because schools cannot easily be changed.

Consciousness of this fact has grown all over the world in recent years and one of the fastest growing areas of academic concern has been how to manage change in order that desirable innovations may speedily take root. The literature is already considerable, complex analyses have been undertaken and many models formulated. In this chapter we shall attempt to relate some of this international thinking to the African situation.

It is generally agreed that there are three main sets of factors which we need to take into account in considering innovation. These are the characteristics of the target system which it is intended to change, in this case the education system, the characteristics of the social context within which the target system operates, and the characteristics of the innovation and the innovation process. We shall examine these in turn.

## Characteristics of the School System

Havelock and Huberman, analysing barriers to educational innovation, concluded that inadequate planning, failing to take into account the nature of the system into which the innovation is being introduced, was the most important 'dimension' of these.[1]

It has been suggested that schools are not free agents able to adjust as educationists wish to what they see as changes in social need and demand. Schools have tended to lag behind social change largely because of the difficulty of reconciling divergent demands and because these demands have often been inappropriate to the nature of schooling. We shall say no more about these problems here, but turn immediately to the wide range of factors of institutional and systems inertia which would in any case make it difficult for schools to respond quickly.

We must first recognise the strength of historical factors. First, there is the fact that the perceptions of all concerned with education, parents, pupils, teachers, administrators and planners, have been moulded by what the school has been and done in the past. We find it very difficult to free ourselves of these blinkers and sometimes even to recognise that we are wearing them. Schools are places where certain activities go on and where certain consequences are achieved. So conventional is our thinking about these activities and outcomes that a teacher from one part of a country visiting a school in a totally different part of that country, or even in a different country altogether, will quickly feel at home in the new setting, and he will be disinclined even to consider whether this should be so, taking into account the very different social context in which the school is set. Of course we are all notionally committed to the principles of adapting schooling to individual and social differences and many of us to establishing distinctively national or regional patterns of schooling. In practice, however, we are more ready to recognise similarities between schools and to compare them only in such terms as the quality of buildings and amounts of teaching aids. We are far less ready to question differences in the basic function of schools or to analyse the factors which make it possible and desirable for certain activities to be pursued in the particular context of the school we are visiting, but which may not exist in our own schools where we may be seeking to promote similar activities.

These blinkers are particularly effective in inhibiting change when it is recognised that we cannot expect to be able to start afresh in constructing our school systems. For a variety of obvious reasons we must start with what we have and seek to build upon existing foundations. Those who advocate complete transform-ations of education systems, such as the de-schoolers who would abolish the school system altogether, are well aware of the problems of changing the basic and often unconscious assump-tions of those who operate within existing systems. Those of us who believe that such transformations are neither practicable nor necessarily desirable must be aware of our assumptions, and must further recognise that the process of grafting new ideas onto an old stock involves its own dangers. There is an old Turkish proverb which runs 'When the house is built, the man dies', which may be interpreted as meaning for us that when a school system has been brought into being, those who have built it from nothing lose the will, the energy and the imagination to rebuild it, being primarily concerned with maintaining it.

The house that we have built is, of course, a massive one which requires a great deal of maintaining. The education industry in our countries is probably the largest and most costly single enterprise that we possess. As it has grown it has become more complex, and the more complex and successful it has been, the more difficult it has become to make substantial changes in it.

Most of the resources allocated to education must be devoted to running it as it is. Although our countries are allocating quite enormous sums of money to education, the bulk of this goes simply to paying teachers' salaries and relatively little is available to finance innovation. Particularly where we are engaged in massive expansion of schooling, universal primary education programmes in several of our countries being a case in point, the demands upon existing resources of finance, expertise and effort are so great as to leave little available for serious questioning of whether this is the right kind of education, and for reorienting it. We try to do our best, particularly in terms of curriculum reform and the production of new materials for teaching, but our main concern is bound to be for building classrooms and training teachers to work in them as cheaply as possible. Consequently we are very likely to end up with more of that kind of schooling which we may have already criticised as inappropriate. The greater the expansion, whether lateral or vertical, the thinner must we spread our reserves of talent and experience, and the more resources must go into administration and keeping the system running. Our main concern under such circumstances tends to be to maintain the standards of the past rather than with changing them or seeking new ways of achieving desired quality.

Not only is education a massive and, commonly, an expanding enterprise, but it is a labour-intensive one. Essentially, as the situation stands, it comprises teachers, each working independently and in seclusion with a group of children or young people. Behind these teachers stands a great army of administrators, inspectors, teacher trainers and others whose sole justification is to make it possible for the teaching and learning process in the classroom to go on efficiently. Changes in formal education must in the end mean changes in what goes on 'in the classroom' or they mean nothing. But it is very difficult to change people, let alone change large numbers of people who are not subject to direct day-to-day control and supervision. We can change a factory fairly easily by removing obsolete machinery and replacing it, but people have to be convinced that they ought to change and shown how. We should not assume too readily that our teachers are easily to be convinced of the need to change or will be able and willing to make the changes even if we show them how.

One of the reasons why we may find it difficult to persuade teachers that the benefits to be derived from change are really worth all the bother of abandoning old familiar ways and struggling with the new is that these benefits are not easily demonstrated. In education we usually measure the quality of what we do by two means: by measuring the *inputs* into the process in terms of the number of trained teachers, their level of training and general education, the educational standard of the pupil intake, the number of books, the amount of equipment and plant and so on; or by measuring the *outputs* in terms of examination results. However we are increasingly recognising that beyond a fairly low threshold, the standard of the inputs into education does not guarantee high quality. We have known very poor graduate teachers, we have seen books and equipment not in fact used, or used badly, and whilst we all admire a fine laboratory, we recognise that much good science teaching can and should be undertaken in the natural environment of the school. We are also accustomed to arguing that examinations are very inadequate indicators of educational quality because they do not test many of the things such as attitudes and personality characteristics which education is supposed to be concerned with and because they do not necessarily test even the cognitive aspects of education particularly well. The fact is that the education profession has been unable to define in functional, measurable terms what good teaching is. In these circumstances it is not easy for an innovator to demonstrate to a teacher that what he proposes is necessarily better than what he wants to replace, let alone demonstrate to a reluctant treasury that the change should be financed unless, of course, there are savings to be made.

However the problem goes deeper than this. Some current proposals for change seem to assume that the teacher is some kind of universal man, the range of whose intellectual capacity is matched only by the diversity of his skills and the strength of his motivation. We must recognise that the average teacher is an average teacher not a superman, and we must note that, to the extent that the average teacher is modestly qualified, moderately well trained, activated by limited motivation, morale and status, he may well be inclined to view innovation with suspicion, to cling to the familiar ways which have seen him through his many difficulties, to resent any extra work which may be required of him, probably without extra remuneration, and to see proposals for change as a criticism of what he has been doing. Even if he has no alternative but to accept the change, and even if it is adequately explained to him and he is provided with any necessary training, he may still be inclined to return to his former practices with which he feels secure and in the course of time to modify the new practices in the light of those perceptions and habits which his previous experience has deeply implanted in him. In all this the teacher in Africa is not very different from teachers and other kinds of worker elsewhere in the world, though his problems may be greater than those of his counterparts in more fortunate countries. In suggesting here that the teaching forces in African countries may constitute a major inertial factor, we should remind ourselves that educational change must involve the teacher to be effective; indeed it will later be suggested that some of our best hopes for change lie in the teacher.

A number of structural issues must now be considered. What we refer to as a school system is made up of a number of interrelated sub-systems of which the most obvious are the primary schools, the secondary schools, the teacher training colleges, and various tertiary institutions including the universities. The product of one such sub-system constitutes the intake of another, thus primary schools feed secondary schools and teachers' colleges; secondary schools feed tertiary institutions and teachers' colleges; and in respect of teachers the universities and colleges will feed the secondary and primary schools. For the various sub-systems to operate efficiently therefore, they have to be kept in an appropriate balance with each other and some kinds of change may necessitate changing this balance. In consequence 'bottleneck' problems are likely to arise, commonly, as in the past, because secondary schools could not take up a sufficient proportion of the primary school output and could not provide sufficient entrants to the universities: the expansion of the secondary system to remove this bottleneck depended in part upon the capacity of universities and colleges to provide the necessary trained teachers. Change in one sub-system therefore may necessitate changes and often prior changes in other sub-systems and, in consequence, change may be a lengthy process.

Competition for resources between sub-systems may arise and lead to further delays. Universal Primary Education in Nigeria depends largely upon the production of a sufficient number of teachers from colleges of education. Such colleges have been increased in size and number and staffing for them has been drawn to some extent from the primary school system itself, and more largely from the secondary school system which already faces major difficulties of obtaining qualified and experienced staff, particularly in the science and mathematics areas. The inability of secondary schools to staff sixth forms efficiently was one reason why sixth forms have been abandoned and the universities required to provide preliminary studies and to extend programmes to four years, for which purposes they too must seek scarce staff.

Even more significant, however, has been the influence of the higher sub-systems upon the lower in terms of curriculum and methodology. University entrance requirements have been a major constraint upon the development of the secondary school curriculum whilst secondary school entrance examinations stressing the 'academic' and 'literary' skills have been the focus of primary school education, and have severely undermined attempts to diversify primary curricula and give practical and vocationally oriented studies the status they need if the needs of the majority of primary school leavers are to be met. In order to free the primary and secondary schools to develop more relevant curricula and to adopt the kinds of learning approaches which are commonly advocated, it may be that universities must first be persuaded to accept students with a very different educational background from that to which they are accustomed.

These constraints upon change operate largely through the examination system to which many teachers would point as being the major obstacle to change. Since large numbers of schools share a common allocative function, that is that their pupils are all competing for access to the next level of education, it has usually been found necessary to set a common external examination. Such an examination is likely to restrict severely the capacity of any particular school to develop individual approaches to study which it may consider more relevant to the needs of the majority of its pupils. At the same time the existing examination system places a premium upon the accumulation of knowledge, and does not encourage schools to teach their pupils how to use their knowledge other than in an examination. It may be argued that some of these problems could be reduced by reforming the examination system but such reforms as have been suggested may demand expertise in examining which is not necessarily available and the reformed system might not command the same degree of public confidence in its impartiality as the present system. We shall later examine some of the reforms which are being introduced.

Another kind of structural problem which impedes change is the fact that some kinds of change may involve and necessitate a ripple effect of further change even within the sub-system. We can recognise this most easily within a single school where to make a curricular or methodological change in one subject area may well affect other subject areas because of the demands it makes upon the timetable or upon the available staff and facilities. Teachers in the social studies area who wish to take their classes out of school to visit a museum or a post office, for instance, may not find it easy to persuade their colleagues to allocate a sufficient block of time on the timetable for this purpose or to give up their own claims on the school bus or lorry.

The problem is, of course, much wider than this. There is a complex relationship between the curriculum, the organisation of the school and the structure of the school system which may have to be taken into account. To achieve a change in one of these aspects, changes in all three areas may be necessary without which the purpose will not be served. Let us assume that a wholly new emphasis is to be put on producing in our pupils the much needed qualities of self-reliance and entrepreneurship, and to develop their skills of decision-making. Certain curricular changes may be necessary, not so much in terms of what is taught but more in terms of how it is to be taught, perhaps through independent discovery or resource-based approaches. But these measures are likely to be ineffective in a school which has a strongly hierarchical structure and authority-centred ethos. Pupils may best develop such skills through being given the opportunity within the school community to take their own decisions and work out what choices exist instead of having all decisions taken for them, and usually without consultation. Thus consideration may have to be given to how best the school may be reorganised to provide such opportunities and responsibilities. However neither curricular nor institutional changes are likely to succeed without changes in the wider educational system. Teachers will need to be trained both pre-service and in-service in these approaches and they will probably require support services, notably in the form of advisers to assist them in the early stages of making the change. Since the kinds of changes which they will need to make are unlikely to be clearly prescribed at the outset and they will have to learn largely from experience, some form of increased professional contact between teachers in a range of schools may be necessary. The implications of the approach for selection and certification will have to be worked out. Finally this kind of change is one which may cause concern to parents and the community, and some means whereby people outside the school can be consulted and informed may be necessary, perhaps through the schools themselves but possibly by other means.

One particular case is very much in point at the moment. In a number of African countries it is intended that all children will from an early date go on from primary school to junior secondary schools to receive pre-vocational education. We thus have not only a systems change involving the training of teachers with appropriate qualifications and the development of suitable syllabuses and teaching materials but also institutional change affecting not only plant and facilities but probably overall size, which will bring in train major changes in the amount and complexity of administrative and coordinating machinery required. We also have curricular change, demanding that teachers develop techniques for mixed-ability teaching which secondary school teachers have not faced before.

Clearly the introduction of changes of this kind are by no means simple, and demand considerable administrative and planning capacity and forethought. We therefore now turn to some general problems of educational management and ask whether current structures and procedures are likely to facilitate or impede change. Philip Coombs, among others, has attributed inertia largely to systems of management which are incapable of dealing with crises and new challenges, and has suggested that if we seek a revolution in education it is with education management that we need to begin.[2] Existing arrangements, he suggests, are archaic and anachronistic, reflecting historical factors and past circumstances rather than any coherent interpretation of the contemporary situation. Educational management lies in the hands of a diversity of groups and interests, including governments at both central and local level, churches and religious organisations, private individuals and organisations, and in certain respects even external aid agencies. There has, until recently, been a trend towards concentrating power and responsibility in the hands of the central government as, for example, in Nigeria where the federal government has steadily assumed greater responsibilities for the universities, for the inspection and even the management of schools, and a parallel trend towards reducing the traditional extensive involvement of the religious voluntary agencies and of private owners in school management. As we have noted earlier such trends do not necessarily make the management system more ready to accommodate and encourage change since within ministries of education responsibility for the various sectors of the education system is usually highly compartmentalised from a very high level in the administrative hierarchy in a manner which renders co-ordinated development less easy than it might be. Ministerial structures and administrative hierarchies are in any case often better suited to maintaining and running the system along routine lines than to bringing about changes. Even planning units are usually limited in their function to servicing existing systems rather than to reforming them. In Nigeria the feeling has been expressed for a number of years that there is something wrong with a structure which tends to isolate senior professional educationists from the political decision makers, and in which ministers and permanent secretaries are less and less likely to have been professional educationists.

The hierarchical systems which have come into existence are designed essentially to facilitate downwards communication of information and instructions. Indeed they may well give prior place to considerations of administrative convenience as opposed to educational desirability, for administrators, like teachers, often tend to prefer well-trodden paths and to resist change and fresh ideas as disturbing their accustomed patterns of work. They are less well adapted to encouraging an upward flow of ideas and suggestions from those whose work at the chalk face (as it is sometimes called) gives them a unique understanding of many practical problems and opportunity to analyse current problems and practice. We have noted the importance of this in connection with participative planning. Later we shall be looking at this question again and considering the importance of promoting a two-way exchange of thinking, of finding means of facilitating consultation and of encouraging the participation in analysis and decision-making of all levels of the education hierarchy. It will be suggested that whilst the centralisation of authority can in theory be a powerful instrument for bringing about change, in practice a top-down communication system has very definite limitations and is likely to inhibit desirable innovation from below.

Another aspect of educational management which tends to stand in the way of change is the way in which we recruit, train and utilise our professional staff. The process by which we recruit our teachers direct from the schools, provide them with further education and training in yet more school-type institutions, and then certify them as capable of returning to the schools from which they originally came, constitutes a closed cycle more suited to the perpetuation of existing practice than to changing it. Our teachers, we say, are responsible for preparing young people for life and for employment in the increasingly demanding and more complex society outside the schools, yet their own experience tends very largely to be confined to the society of the school. They may teach about urban living without having lived in a town, about manufacturing processes without having seen a factory, about the way government works without ever having experienced government except at the most local levels. And having no experience of a way of life other than that of the community in which they were brought up and in which they are often to teach, they cannot readily understand or appreciate the distinctive nature of that community, its potential for change and its relevance to the national community. Their knowledge being largely derived from books, how can we complain when their teaching is based upon books? Teachers in more developed countries, and perhaps in more advanced areas of a developing country, have the advantage of wider first-hand experience and of more diverse forms of vicarious experience; through television and a greater flow of published materials they can acquire a fuller understanding of the world around them. But many of our teachers have very few such resources to call upon and must depend very largely upon what they themselves have learned in the classrooms of their youth.

This is, of course, an immensely difficult problem to solve. We may encourage mature age entry into the teaching profession but must nevertheless accept that the great majority of our teachers will never leave the school–college–school cycle. In consequence we must pin our hopes of breaking out of this inbred situation upon the teacher training college. In the colleges we hope to train a new generation of teachers with new ideas and techniques at their disposal. Through them a breath of fresh air will be blown into the education system. But does it work out this way? Experience tells us that it does not. Newly certificated teachers moving back into the school system, it appears, readily fall into the pattern of working of their older serving colleagues, the pattern which they themselves experienced as pupils and from which their college experience has failed to wean them. Why should this be so? Partly it is a consequence of the fact that new young teachers do not possess the authority or the confidence to change their colleagues' way of working and in any case face a considerable struggle for survival in schools which may be very different from those situations described in their foundation and methodology lectures at college. The demand of the clientele that schooling focuses upon the prescribed syllabus and the examination, the high value placed upon the book and upon knowledge accumulation, and traditions of respect for authority are powerful constraints upon the young teacher who is quick to recognise that his own status will depend upon the numbers of passes his pupils achieve in examinations.

Often it is partly a consequence of the lack of motivation of the teacher himself. Many young people, as we know, enter teacher training not because they particularly wish to teach but because they have failed to achieve selection for a further stage of formal education. Teacher education is second best but at least it offers some further personal education and teaching may keep body and soul together until an opportunity arises of some other more desirable and better rewarded form of occupation. Consequently not only is the actual process of teacher education often distorted by a clientele placing greater value upon the study of academic subjects than upon the development of professional expertise, but there is less likelihood of the newly trained teacher persevering with the more demanding new methodology which the college has sought to encourage.

But it is also partly a consequence of the kind of teacher education we conventionally provide. Because our students often arrive with inadequate standards of general education we find we must use a good deal of their time for academic studies. In consequence the college curriculum often becomes overcrowded and professional studies must compete for the time and attention of the students with the more prestigious academic studies. Moreover among the professional studies the highest status is often given to the more theoretical and academically respectable studies of psychology, philosophy and sociology, and a correspondingly low status given to practical studies of methodology and classroom practice. However, even more important than these factors, which tend to reduce the professional value of the training programme, is the fact that the general ethos of many colleges is that of a secondary school. Far from learning to exercise responsibility through practice of it, students in many colleges are expected to behave like secondary school pupils, leaving decisions to their tutors, being subjected to a code of rules which may be so detailed as to suggest that these future teachers cannot be trusted to make wise decisions or to behave responsibly without such constraints. They may even be required to wear uniforms, though this practice, like the others just mentioned, is gradually disappearing. In general teachers learn the theory of school management without having any share in the management of the college in which they are learning the theory, and study the professional responsibilities of teachers whilst being treated as irresponsible schoolboys. When the final day of his training dawns the college will bestow upon the student a certificate which will magically transform him from pupil to colleague, from student to teacher, and from adolescent into adult.

However, even if our colleges were able to focus upon professional development and gear both the formal curriculum and the general life of the institution to producing responsible, enthusiastic and well equipped teachers – and for this they would require a more highly qualified and specially trained staff of tutors and greater teaching and learning resources than many of them have at the present – there would remain a further deficiency in our training patterns. This lies in the general assumption that once a teacher has been trained and has received his certificate he is thereby equipped sufficiently for a lifetime in teaching – even though during the coming forty years we might hope for major changes in the school system many of which we cannot anticipate during his training programme. For many years it has been argued that initial training can hope to do little more than to equip a teacher to start out on his career. Whether or not major changes in the schools render his training out of date he will require from time to time opportunities to recharge his batteries, to up-date his knowledge and to sharpen his skills if he is not to succumb to habit, routine and staleness. Where changes of methodology, syllabus or school organisation are intended he will be particularly in need of further training and if his career prospers and he moves from the classroom to become a headmaster, an inspector, a tutor in a teachers' college, a curriculum developer, an administrator or a planner, he will probably need specialist training. But in practice such opportunities have been sadly under-provided. We have attempted to compensate for the dearth of in-service training opportunities by packing some extra elements into the initial training package, such as school administration or curriculum theory, but we should recognise that the proper time to provide such studies is when they are relevant to the immediate needs of the teacher, when his motivation for study is high and when theory can be translated into practice immediately. Many of us would argue that even many of the standard components of initial training cannot be effectively provided until the teacher has gained some first-hand experience of his work: at this stage he may recognise the full relevance of what he is to study and be able to bring to it the lessons of his own personal experience.

The case for far more coherent and extensive provision of in-service training has been acknowledged for many years. It should embrace refresher programmes for serving teachers, upgrading programmes for teachers who are underqualified or whose qualification has become obsolete, and re-training programmes for those who will be moving into new kinds of post for which their previous training and experience have not adequately prepared them. Little, however, has been achieved. A good deal of in-service training is, of course, currently being provided but all too often on a random and occasional, unsystematic and uncoordinated basis, and it tends to attract those teachers who need it least. As a means of facilitating change and qualitative improvement in school systems its efficiency is low. A survey conducted in 1967–8 of in-service training in thirteen African countries reported that 'nowhere is there evidence of a clearly defined policy being systematically pursued'.[3] Whilst major developments in other areas of education have taken place since that date, there are many countries of which the same report would have to be made today. The basic reason is, of course, that to provide an adequate system of in-service training would demand an enormous allocation of resources, possibly at the expense of other sectors of the education system, and few governments have possessed the necessary conviction and determination to do this. Partial exceptions to the rule may exist where the introduction of distance training techniques has facilitated national in-service training programmes as in the case of the National Teachers Institute at Kaduna in Nigeria or in Lesotho. Most in-service training, however, remains conventional, involving expensive residential courses which, as we shall argue, are often ill-adapted to the real need both in terms of scale and nature.

There remains the matter of how we make use of our trained staff. Here two allied issues in particular concern us; the ways in which we encourage teachers to give of their best and to improve the quality of their work; and the vexed question of the career structure of the teaching profession. At the moment, with the exception of Ghana to which we will turn in a moment, we have usually not one teaching service but several. Not only do we often have distinct teaching services for government and for voluntary agency schools but also in effect for primary and secondary education, and within each there are a number of distinct grades. These grades, which carry different salary scales, are based essentially upon the initial qualification of the teacher and for sound historical reasons we have a variety of initial qualifications considerably wider than is found in more developed countries. In the early stages of development of a school system teachers are recruited with minimal general education and provided with a modest programme of training: as soon as possible we raise the entry requirement for teaching and provide programmes of training which build upon the higher level of general education; thereafter from time to time we again raise our entry requirements and modify the training programmes. The teachers produced from these various programmes, which may well overlap in time, will be awarded different certificates and placed on different salary scales. In consequence at any one time our school systems may be manned by a mixture of differently certificated and remunerated teachers, many of whom will in fact be doing the same job as teachers in a different category. Where upgrading facilities are limited, the consequences for morale and happy co-operative working cannot be favourable.

Equally serious, however, is the situation in which we place equally qualified teachers. The committed, enthusiastic and able teacher who constantly seeks means of improving his teaching, finds himself year by year on the same salary scale as the discontented, idle and inefficient teacher who is more concerned with his out-of-school money-earning activities. The system does not encourage the poor teacher to improve his work, and actively discourages the good teacher from working to the maximum of his capacity. Recognition may be given to the good teacher in the form of promotion, perhaps to a headship or to a post in some other branch of the education system, but there is commonly no way in which we can give effective recognition to good quality work without taking the teacher out of the classroom. Yet quality in the classroom is what we are primarily concerned with. There is something absurd about a system which can only encourage a teacher to improve the quality of his work by offering the inducement that at some stage he may be able to leave the classroom where he has proved his quality and be given a position for which he has not been trained, for which his talents may not be suited and which he might not otherwise wish to take. Not only does this system downgrade the status of the most important element in our education systems by implying that people with real ability should not stay in the classroom and by removing the best teachers from the classroom, but it gives an undue status to non-teaching posts in the education service and allocates these posts according to inappropriate as well as dysfunctional criteria. Of course administrators, inspectors and others are needed, and of course we should wish to see men of proved teaching ability in some of them, though we might well ask that they should be properly trained for the posts. But the basic problem is that such posts constitute the sole means whereby an able man may obtain the financial and status rewards which he will naturally seek, and the sole means at our disposal for encouraging teachers to work hard, other than punitive measures when they fall below a very modest minimum standard. In any case this incentive to work well may be very limited since conventionally promotions are made on the basis of the level of qualification of the teacher and his length of service. The actual quality of his work may be less significant. Consequently an under-qualified teacher may not be encouraged to work hard in the classroom since he sees that he will not be considered eligible for promotion until he has gained seniority or improved his own qualifications. Consequently he may devote his efforts to studying for external examinations instead of teaching his pupils. In so far as quality of work is taken into account this is likely to be on the basis of an inspector's report: the sensible teacher will therefore seek to please the inspector, to do as he suggests, to portray himself to the inspector as a teacher who has no problems, rather than to think for himself, to suggest ideas to the inspector, to ask the inspector for help with his problems.

The situation is not without its absurdity but these are indeed very difficult problems to resolve. A move towards a smaller number of grades of teacher through provision of upgrading opportunities or recognition of meritorious service may be one course of action. But the creation of a career structure which encourages teachers to improve their work and to remain where they are needed in the classrooms is more difficult. The use of promotion bars on the salary scale has not in the past proved effective since they have been used to hold back the very bad teacher rather than to recognise the very good teacher, and since the ways in which we may measure the quality of a teacher are likely to be suspect and unacceptable to many teachers. There may be some possibility of creating new kinds of promotion posts within the school – posts of special responsibility which will carry financial rewards – but there are fewer possibilities of providing such posts in smaller schools than in larger. Nevertheless the problem of the career structure of the teacher is one which must be solved if a system which currently encourages conformity and the minimum of effort is to be transformed into one which actively promotes steady improvement in the quality of education.

The establishment in March 1974 of the Ghana Education Service is worth mention in this context. In 1956 Ghana had abolished the distinction previously existing between government and voluntary agency teachers, and the key feature of the new service was the merger of the (non-graduate) teaching service and the education branch of the civil service consisting of education officers serving either in the administration or as graduate teachers in secondary schools and colleges. In addition all those employed by the Ministry of Education in accounting, secretarial and general administrative roles, and all supporting staff paid from public funds, including managers of voluntary agency schools, are now members of the new unified service. The service is governed by a council including representatives of the Public Services Commission and religious bodies as well as leading citizens and educationists. The purposes of the change were three. It was felt desirable, first, to offer to all teachers the same conditions of service and a common pattern of opportunities for professional advancement and, secondly, to facilitate the interchange of staff between administrative and teaching posts. Thirdly, it was intended to give educationists a greater measure of autonomy in the management of their profession. The establishment of the service did not alone solve the problems to which we have drawn attention but it created a framework which offers greater hope that they can be solved.

To this point we have been considering some of the factors which limit the capacity of school systems as currently organised to change rapidly and to respond promptly to new demands. We now turn to look at some factors which exist in the societal context of the school.

## Characteristics of the Social Context

Much has already been said about the strength of societal factors in determining what the schools do and how they do it. We have noted that education systems are not the sole determinants of the outcomes of education. Societies, whether traditional, transitional or modern, are not passive receivers of educational stimuli but have both an immense capacity for absorbing and for manipulating these stimuli. In consequence, through their response to education many societies have encouraged the development of formal schools and discouraged non-formal alternatives; have encouraged the perpetuation of bookish and knowledge-accumulating studies and discouraged the development of practical and knowledge-applying studies; have encouraged the rapid expansion of existing provision at the expense of controlled diversification and modification of that provision.

We have noted that because schooling is closely tied through certification to the existing employment structures and structures of privilege, it tends both to reinforce and legitimate those structures and in turn to be severely constrained by those structures from reforming itself in ways which may appear to threaten the structures.

We have noted that certain developments in educational practice designed to produce a more self-reliant and independent-minded individual have run counter to social expectations of the way in which an individual should behave, and that certain child-rearing and socialisation practices in the home and community have had a carry-over effect upon the school through the attitudes and habits of teachers and pupils. The prevalence of rote learning, dependence upon the authority of the book and the teacher are not simple hangovers from an out-of-date educational tradition but have roots in the society which are not easily to be affected by devising new school syllabuses, techniques of instruction and improved training for teachers.

We have also noted how children's capacity to succeed at school in mastering fundamental concepts and skills may be adversely affected by limited intellectual stimulation in the home, by the capacity of the mother tongue to deal in abstractions, by deficiencies in traditional concepts of number and of time. Insofar as such problems exist they may themselves suggest the forms innovation may need to take, but at the same time limit the range of innovation which may be effective. We are further aware of health and nutritional problems among our school children which must be dealt with before certain kinds of innovation can succeed.

There is great need for research into factors such as those mentioned. At this time our understanding of them is so limited that here we are compelled simply to hypothesise and draw

tentative conclusions. These conclusions would include the
following: that innovation should be cautiously undertaken and
after careful study of the societal and cultural context of the
school; that action may need to be taken to deal with external
factors before we seek to change the school; that in the final resort
in order to succeed innovations must present themselves at the
bar of public opinion. If it is vital that we carry teachers with us in
our innovation, it is equally vital to carry the public with us, and
for this a concomitant programme of consulting and informing
parents, employers and other members of the local and national
community may be necessary.

## The Characteristics of the Innovation

We must now turn to examine how the characteristics of
innovation, both the nature of the particular innovation intended and the process by which that innovation is to be
introduced, may affect the ease and success with which the change
takes place. Since the range of possible innovations is very great,
and these may range from small to large and sweeping changes, it
is not possible here to consider the full implications of particular
innovations. However some general considerations may be of
value.

We must begin by reflecting upon what has been said earlier
about the prevalence of unclear, confused and sometimes
conflicting aims and objectives in education. If an innovation is
to be successful its objectives must be clear, and where multiple
objectives are aimed at these must be in harmony with each other
and there should be clear understanding of the relative priority of
these objectives. A high degree of clarity is necessary for the
efficient designing of the innovation. It is also necessary that the
objectives be clear to those who are to carry out the innovation
and highly desirable that they be clear to those who are to be
affected by the change. Clarity alone will not be sufficient of
course. An innovation must not only be understood by teachers
and administrators and the clientele of the schools, but it must to
a crucial degree be acceptable to them and be supported by
them. Finally, of course, the objectives must be within the
capacity of the school system to implement.

It has been argued above that such conditions, though

logically necessary, are not always present and that we cannot expect completely satisfactory statements of the goals we should be aiming at. Assuming, however, that we have arrived at a clear, widely understood set of objectives for innovation, what other pre-conditions are likely to facilitate success in introducing and maintaining the change envisaged?

There are first of all a number of factors which relate to the acceptability of the innovation. An innovation which clearly offers advantages over current procedures and other alternatives is more likely to win support than one which does not. We have already commented on the difficulties which often exist in demonstrating the advantage of the new over the old and must note in addition that to be more acceptable changes must offer significant and not merely marginal advantages. A further problem here lies in the fact that we are discussing acceptability not simply to one group, for example the teachers, but to other groups including the administrators of the school system, the decision-makers within the system and the clientele of the system. What may be acceptable to one group may well not be acceptable to another – for instance the development of in-service training by distance techniques may be acceptable to teachers who might find it more welcome to pursue such training without having to leave their schools, homes and families, but might be less acceptable to hard-pressed administrators whose responsibilities might be enlarged to include distribution of materials, provision of facilities such as transport for itinerant tutors, and other support services. It is possible that a particular innovation may be acceptable to two or more groups but for different reasons, and so lead to tensions at the implementation stage which may distort the innovation or lead to rejection by one group at a later stage – for instance an extension of junior secondary education might be welcomed by parents who see wider opportunities for access to higher education opening up for their children only for them to find that the teachers have welcomed the change as a means of introducing a more practical work-oriented curriculum to a mature group of pupils and not simply as a means of providing the conventional general education desired by parents.

Such problems are more likely to arise where the nature of the innovation and its wider implications have not been fully and clearly explained, and it may be concluded that a second factor conducive to successful innovation is the simplicity with which it may be explained. The introduction of a more highly qualified class of teachers into the primary school system, for instance, is simple to explain and its potential advantages may be readily understood. On the other hand, the introduction of an environmental study approach to the teaching of science or geography, or activity and discovery-based learning approaches more generally, are less easy to explain and the balance of advantage is less clear.

Thirdly, of course, the acceptability of a particular proposal to those who are to implement it will largely depend upon the simplicity with which it may be implemented. We are not speaking here of ease of operation only, and whether it will mean extra work for someone, important though this may be. We are here thinking of complex changes which, for instance, may not mean that any given individuals or groups will have to work very much harder, but may mean that many different individuals and groups will be affected, and in various ways, with the consequence that the success of the innovation will depend upon all of them playing their parts, at the right time, in the right place and to the full extent. An innovation which has implications for a wide range of groups, each with its own interests to protect and promote, may well be less acceptable than one which affects only a few.

The more complex the innovation, of course, the more difficult it is not only to explain and gain acceptance for, but to implement, and we must recognise that many of the changes we wish to make are surprisingly complex. To be effective, curriculum change requires not merely that new syllabuses be produced, perhaps by a curriculum development team, and distributed by the administration to the schools, but often that new teaching materials have to be produced by a number of independent individuals and teams, printed and published by perhaps a number of publishing houses, and again distributed to schools by the administration. Examinations may need to be changed not merely in content but perhaps also in more fundamental ways if the syllabuses are to be taught by the methods thought appropriate to the aims, and this may pose further problems of administering examinations, providing materials and facilities to examination centres, collecting and distributing to markers new kinds of evidence for assessment. The need for training is likely to be extensive, in the first instance for curriculum developers and textbook writers, then for serving teachers and examiners, and then for the initial training of teachers and examiners – requiring possibly a further curriculum development exercise in respect of this training. Finally changes in the organisation of schools and in the administrative and support structure may be necessary.

All of this represents considerable cost, both financial and in terms of effort required. Oddly enough, in countries which are often extremely short of such resources, it is rare to find an innovation proposed which will reduce costs and demands upon available expertise. It seems an almost invariable rule that an innovation should demand greater outlay in these respects than what it replaces. In any case the very process of devising and introducing a change involves costs which may often be intolerably heavy. The simple conclusion that the lower these costs, the more likely an innovation is to be acceptable and feasible should not obscure the fact that it is often very difficult to estimate or to calculate the costs of particular changes since we are not thinking simply of the new materials or the new equipment and facilities which may be required but also of the costs of opportunities foregone, of the time and effort required by serving officers who might otherwise have devoted their time and effort to something else, possibly no less essential.

Nor should we forget that some kinds of innovation represent a major investment over a considerable period of time. A reorientation of the primary school curriculum may well require a stage by stage introduction of new syllabuses over several years since courses of study on which children have already embarked cannot readily be disrupted without penalising those children. When the time needed for initial research and design, and possibly for pilot testing and redesign, is taken into account the length of time over which an innovation may have to be consistently pursued may be surprisingly long. Its value will depend upon the success with which the designers have been able to forecast changes which may take place during the implementation period. Such changes may be in the extent of the need which demanded the innovation in the first place, in the priority given to other and perhaps new needs, and the availability of resources throughout and following the implementation period. The longer this period the more likely it is that changes will be needed in the innovation itself, and the greater the possibility that political, personnel and other changes may make consistent promotion of the innovation impossible. To be effective long-term innovation needs not merely careful planning and forecasting in the initial stages, but concurrent evaluation to permit appropriate adjustment and to enlist ongoing support for the project. It may be argued, therefore, that long-term innovation has clear disadvantages in terms of feasibility over short-term innovation, and that a longer-term innovation which has built in concurrent or formative evaluation has advantages over similar innovation which does not. We would recognise, of course, a basic problem here in that often it is not possible fully to evaluate an innovation for many years after it has been fully implemented – for example, efforts to develop the capacity of young people for self-employment can only be tested when the products of the school have had time to demonstrate their capacity in the employment field. This has implications not only for gaining acceptance for the innovation in the first place but also for its prospects of being given sufficient time to demonstrate its value.

The sad fact is that we are often so much in a hurry to reform education systems that we are tempted to load change upon change and to abandon developments before they have had time to prove their worth, so that our process of innovation becomes piecemeal and sporadic and consequently less likely to solve the basic problems we face.

It should be noted that some of the factors discussed above will have a less constraining effect to the extent that our school systems are ready for the particular change we have in mind. Readiness in this sense means not merely that plant and equipment is available which may be adapted to new purposes but far more importantly that the personnel who must carry out the changes possess the skills, the motivation and the awareness of the need for change which will enable them to respond flexibly to changing demands upon them. The importance of an appropriate climate for innovation cannot be overstressed and, as has been suggested earlier, this climate by and large does not exist at the moment. It will be suggested later that for education to be able to respond flexibly to the needs of development, efforts must be made to create both the climate and an internal capacity for change. It will be argued that innovation cannot be conducted simply through occasional major and external thrusts; in large measure it must be ongoing, small-scale and internally generated. For this to happen the schools cannot be expected to cope with innovation without adequate support services, such as advisory teams, resource centres, and professional organisations.

It must, however, be accepted that even school systems with highly professional staff, high standards of equipment and facilities and well organised support services, can be flexible and adaptable only up to a point. There are limits to the demands which may be made upon even the best qualified and progressive teacher. Teacher competence, existing facilities and current patterns of support service are closely related to the existing mode of operation, purposes and functions of the institutions. Consequently they may well possess only limited flexibility to accommodate proposed changes which really require new skills, facilities and forms of support. In general, therefore, it may be argued that an innovation which is readily compatible with the existing system may more easily and successfully be adopted than one which is less so. This factor may be used as an argument for incremental change and against radical change. But again we have to be aware of the limitations and dangers of incremental change in which changes may be partial and piecemeal, whereby old and new may lie uncomfortably side by side, and whereby the new, on adoption, may become resistant to further modification or change.

In this chapter we have been concerned with exploring the difficulties of innovation and with attempting to understand the factors which will largely determine its success and failure. Many of these factors are by no means disreputable. We may wish that they did not exist but must recognise that they do, and often for very good reason. We will end this chapter, therefore, with two further reflections which arise from this.

The first relates to the nature of the innovator. Huberman cites studies which suggest that pressure for change often comes from a class of people who are alienated from the existing system, who tend to place themselves outside it and to rebel against it.[4]

Often they are impatient and sometimes excessively idealistic, and this leads them to regard resistance to change as blind conservatism or even wilful obstructionism. Such people have often failed to understand the context within which they wish to introduce change and this may lead them to adopt ideas and methods which, whilst containing something of value, are unlikely to succeed. One reason for this is, of course, that they are liable to create resentment and resistance among the people whose work they are seeking to modify.

This brings us to the question of research. There is much that we do not understand about the nature of the innovation process and much that we do not understand about the interaction between various sectors of the education system and between the education system and its societal context. It is sad, therefore, to note that currently investment in research into these questions, and indeed into education generally, is deplorably low, despite the growing numbers of universities and other bodies with research responsibilities. It may be that consequent upon the recognition of the importance of such research by Ministers of Education at their conference in Lagos in 1976 there will be a progressive stepping up of research activity. However, there remain two kinds of danger which face us in establishing a knowledge base sufficient for our purposes. The first is the emphasis currently being placed on action research by official bodies, that is to say research into specific problems with a view to finding solutions to be applied in practice. It is not argued that such research is wrong – far from it, for we have long suffered from the lack of purposive research – but that there may be major disadvantage if fundamental research is neglected in favour of action research. By fundamental research here is meant studies, often long term, which are devoted to understanding broad and basic questions rather than to finding speedy answers to usually more limited questions. Without ongoing fundamental research, action research will be deprived of many of the basic inputs which will determine its direction, provide its tools and furnish a substantial proportion of its material. An appropriate balance between the two kinds of research activity is necessary, and there may be some danger at the present of the latter proving too attractive to government funding agencies.

Secondly, however, and this may help to explain why our

knowledge is so deficient as well as why governments are considering sponsoring their own research efforts, there are major deficiencies in the way research has been conducted in the universities. To a very considerable extent (and almost exclusively in the sphere of education) what research has been conducted has been undertaken by individuals, usually for purposes of achieving higher degrees, following up individual interests often with little regard to the broad conspectus of research needs and priorities, and frequently in ignorance of what other researchers were also doing in that field. The bulk of this research is not published or effectively disseminated to educationists and where it is there is a further problem in that published research is often incomprehensible to the people who need to make use of it. The kinds of research needs which have been identified in this chapter tend to demand interdisciplinary approaches, conducted on a team basis, with clear provision for disseminating the results of the research to the people who need to know in a form they can readily understand.

## References

1. R. G. Havelock and A. M. Huberman, *Solving Educational Problems, the Theory and Reality of Innovation in Developing Countries*, a study prepared for the International Bureau of Education (Paris: UNESCO, 1977) p. 15.
2. P. H. Coombs, *The World Educational Crisis, a Systems Analysis* (New York: Oxford University Press, 1968) pp. 120–1.
3. G. A. Trevaskis, *Inservice Teacher Training in English-Speaking Africa*, a report prepared for the Afro-Anglo-American Programme in Teacher Education (New York, 1969) p. 151.
4. A. M. Huberman, *Understanding Change in Education: An Introduction* (Paris: UNESCO/IBE, 1973) pp. 51–4.

# 7

# Management of Educational Reform

In addition to studying the factors which may inhibit educational change and the pre-conditions for successful change, scholars in many parts of the world have been increasingly concerned in recent years with the ways in which the desired changes may be introduced and managed. However reformers in Africa, it is probably true to say, have been naturally pre-occupied with the kinds of changes which they believe will achieve the results being sought but have been far less concerned with the question of how to manage the change in the context of the inertial factors which we have described. Indeed the necessity of doing so has not been widely understood until quite recently. Some years ago a major research study was undertaken with the intention of generating case study materials about how innovators in Africa have gone about their work, and how their ways of working have influenced the success of their innovation.[1] Case studies of innovations in countries were commissioned and the materials submitted were considered at an international symposium held in Addis Ababa in September 1971. It was found that although the case studies had been written up with the aid of quite explicit guidelines, they were inadequate for the intended purpose. Indeed in some of the case studies it was difficult to find any data at all about the strategy which had been pursued. Consequently the symposium, like many other conferences and working groups before and since, found itself concentrating simply upon what innovations were thought desirable. Havelock and Huberman, in surveying the theory and the reality of innovation in developing countries, have noted the tendency for educational reform to involve ambitious 'major system transformation' with what they describe as 'very rapid movement through the problem solving cycle, from the initial assessment of the need for change to the design of a solution and the implementation of that solution'.[2] Disregard for careful study and planning of the process of innovation has contributed to the 'rather dismal picture of international and national efforts to innovate, repetitions of obvious mistakes or omissions'.[3] They conclude that the practice of innovating requires drastic improvement.

In this short section it is suggested that the way in which we go about introducing changes may have a major determining influence upon the success of those changes and an attempt will be made to define some of the main kinds of strategy for change before examining in more detail in later chapters some of the lessons of African experience in this field.

Whilst scholars inevitably vary in their analytical approaches, it may be suggested that there are broadly three major strategies of innovation in operation around the world and in Africa. These have been labelled the power–coercive, the rational–empirical, and the normative–re-educative strategies.[4] Before we examine each of these in turn it should be clearly understood that these are not necessarily alternatives; in studying any given innovation we are likely to find elements of all three strategies involved. However, it may help to clarify our minds if we begin by considering them separately.

The *power–coercive strategy* is the way of introducing changes which is usual in highly centralised education systems, particularly those committed to planned approaches to educational development. A decision taken by a central authority at high level is communicated downwards through the bureaucratic hierarchy to those whose responsibility it becomes to carry the decision into effect. These people, who may be teachers or administrators, have in theory no choice in the matter. They are employees, in a civil servant capacity, and must do as they are told. The central authority has the capacity to compel them to do so through its possession of a range of powerful sanctions such as contracts of employment, control of and capacity to manipulate the career structure, and power to regulate the flow of financial support, together with an administrative, supervisory and evaluative structure to keep a fairly close eye on those who carry decisions into effect. These are extremely powerful instruments in theory, and their use is sanctioned by custom and by the general acceptance of the necessity of planning educational development to achieve national goals. Indeed the power–coercive strategy appears both simple and rational to the extent that its appropriateness in practice tends rarely to be questioned. Where changes are introduced by these means only to fail, or perhaps only partially or slowly to succeed, it is usual to assume that this is the consequence of simple inefficiency and that the solution is to make the bureaucratic machine more efficient.

However, the widespread failure of such strategies to bring about the kinds and degree of reform which we have been seeking over a long period of years suggests that questions need to be asked about the nature of the basic strategy as well as about the efficiency with which it may be pursued. We readily recognise that decision-makers at the top of the system are often remote from, and therefore may be relatively insensitive to, some of the realities of the local school and classroom situation. Their day-to-day concerns make them familiar with problems of scale and of structure which may well be appropriately dealt with at least in part through centralised initiatives. However in such areas as curricular and methodological change upon which much demand for reform has centred, they are less at home and their occasional forays into this field often betray a lack of understanding. Instances of this might be the introduction of productive work into schools in Zambia, or the abandonment of modern mathematics in Nigeria and Malawi by decree, actions which took educators by surprise and have been categorised as instances of 'management by crisis'. By their very nature top-down, power–coercive approaches to change tend to take the form of occasional acts of major surgery, which may sometimes be necessary but are less well suited to the steady and sustained process of modification and improvement through which most qualitative change must be achieved, and which must complement major surgery if the patient is to be restored to health.

The importance in Africa of such approaches to innovation should nevertheless not be underestimated. In particular Havelock and Huberman have stressed the crucial importance of leadership support for innovation at the highest level, support which should be more than formal or legal but must be active. However they argue also that there must be active participation from below.[5]

In the previous section we have noted a wide range of factors with which this or any other strategy must contend and in particular we need here to remind ourselves of the human factor in systems management. Bureaucracies, like teaching forces, are not impersonal machines but consist of people with their own personal and group interests and with their own capacities to interpret the instructions passed down through them. Indeed they have the responsibility of interpreting these instructions since they must work out the details of the implementation, and to some degree adapt it to practical situations and problems of which they are aware, and which their supervisors cannot be expected to have taken fully into account. The degree of freedom they possess to interpret and modify the instructions will be greater where the original instruction is less clear and prescriptive. As the Director of the UNESCO Regional Office for Education in Asia has put it:

> Administration affects reform positively or negatively. Positively it will make the intended goals of the reform an integral part of the day to day business of education . . . Negatively, an administration which is unprepared to handle a reform, changes the reform into what it can handle.[6]

An administration may be unprepared both for reasons of capacity and for reasons of willingness. The outcome may be a reform which as it is transmitted down through the bureaucratic hierarchy and outwards into more geographically remote branches is steadily modified into something less threatening to the people who operate it and, in the absence of will on their part to change their ways, more like what is already being done. This is the process of 'reversion' described by Havelock and Huberman by which,

> for example, an innovative rural education project tends to get smaller and more like the primary schools it was meant to replace as the project moves from the planning stage to the network of experimental schools. New types of entrepreneurial training programmes come to resemble the conventional in-school curriculum or the traditional apprenticeship schemes.[7]

Decision-makers do not usually seek simply to transmit instructions. Increasingly they have attempted to deal with the situation outlined above by explaining more fully the reasons for the decision so that implementors have a more complete understanding of what is proposed. Increasingly also, in recent years, they have tended to make their proposals known and to invite discussion and comment before the proposals are carried out. However, this does not overcome some of the basic problems in that those operating lower down the hierarchy are often unwilling to risk displeasing their superiors by criticising their suggestions and the superiors in turn tend to assume too readily that their proposals are accepted and that those below them are committed to implementing them through having been 'involved' in the making of the decision. Nor does the machinery necessarily exist whereby such discussion can effectively take place outside the formal bureaucratic hierarchy. Attempts have been made to make such discussion effective as in the instances mentioned earlier. Procedures, such as national debates and seminars, have their value, particularly in terms of making the policy more widely known and better understood, but they are essentially occasional and are often confined to broad principles. The carrying out of educational innovation is a matter of detail and depends upon more frequent initiatives. In general, even such consultative measures still assume that initiatives will come from the top and that the responsibility of other participants is simply to react to these initiatives.

The second broad strategy, the *rational–empirical strategy*, is based upon rather different assumptions: that the capacity for introducing changes is present at all levels of the education system and that for many purposes we require ongoing and regular change and adaptation in the light of changing needs and differing circumstances. It assumes that men are rational and will act in accordance with self-interest provided that they can be shown that there are benefits to be gained from particular courses of action. Consequently they will take up certain innovations which others may urge upon them when they are fully informed about them, and preferably when they can see examples of the innovation in action.

In such a strategy the function of controlling authorities, whether central or local, may be defined in three ways – to allow and indeed encourage creative groups and individuals to try out their own ideas and develop pilot projects; to establish groups and organisations specifically to undertake research, develop ways of applying the research and to disseminate their findings to the people who may wish to use them; and finally to find ways of encouraging and facilitating communication both vertically and horizontally, both within and outside the system, so that ideas can be widely discussed, information communicated, and experience studied and evaluated.

Havelock and Huberman suggest that such strategies have been little used as conscious means of inducing change in developing countries,[8] although there has undoubtedly been growing interest in particular in the Research, Development and Dissemination (R, D and D) model which has been in vogue for some time in Western countries, notably in respect of curriculum development. In this model, conventionally, centres of research and development, such as were involved in the Nuffield Foundation and Schools Council projects in Britain, are charged with conducting necessary research, designing an innovation and disseminating it to the schools through a planned process which may involve demonstrating its value and publicising and making available the associated materials. In the Nigeria Educational Research Council, the University of Zambia Educational Research and Curriculum Development Unit, and the variety of other curriculum development centres which have been established in Africa, we see elements of this approach, although often these are combined with the power-coercive approach since schools are usually given no choice in the matter of adopting the new curriculum approaches. However in the African Mathematics Programme, the Science Education Programme for Africa, and the African Social Studies Programme, all originating in the African Education Programme of the American Education Development Center, we have processes which may perhaps be viewed as R, D and D in action. The success of these approaches has been less than overwhelming even in Western countries where schools are more free to decide what they will teach because, although well researched and tested, the new materials have not sufficiently involved teachers in preparing them and it has been found that teachers, for reasons similar to those discussed above, have not been ready to change their patterns of work. It has been found too that teachers who have taken up the new materials have tended to incorporate them into their former teaching approaches, modifying them to enable them to fit in more easily and consequently destroying their innovative character.

Difficulties have been experienced with pilot projects also. All too often in Africa the sense of urgency has been so great that sweeping changes have been sought speedily with little trial and experiment beforehand. But where pilot projects have been introduced they have tended to remain such and have not been extended to the wider system largely because of the resistance which has built up against this. Schramm, describing the Niger pilot project for instructional television, suggests that passive resistance from the educational establishment to an imported project, conducted separately from the Ministry of Education, and not geared to the existing school curriculum, largely accounted for its failure to catch on.[9]

Efforts to promote the communication of new ideas have tended to be confined to the use of inspectorates (whose power-coercive functions have tended to prevent their becoming effective agents for this purpose) and to programmes of in-service training, which again have tended to function in a top-down manner, conveying information to teachers but guaranteeing neither acceptance nor support for new ideas.

There appear to be clear limits to the effectiveness of such a strategy even in more developed countries where teaching and administrative roles are played by highly qualified and often highly professional people, where support services for teachers are highly developed and where the resources of the mass media are available for dissemination of ideas, where professional organisation provides a valuable forum for discussion, and a decentralised system encourages local initiative and experiment. If, as many would argue, the extent to which individuals and groups have been innovative, adaptive and responsive has been disappointing even in such circumstances, what can we expect in Africa where many of these conditions exist to a much lesser extent. It is, furthermore, doubtful how far controlling auth-orities in Africa would be willing to move in the direction of this strategy because of their desire to direct changes in accordance with established goals, because of the danger that the extent to which the system can be controlled may be reduced, because of the widespread belief that staff at the lower levels of the hierarchy are not yet ready for such a degree of freedom and responsibility, and because administrators tend to prefer tidy overall patterns of education and institutionalised patterns of change.

The basic weakness of this strategy is its belief that educationists will respond positively to change because they are rational and can perceive the advantages to themselves of the innovation proposed. However, innovations rarely involve advantage only and one man's advantage may well appear to be another's disadvantage. Almost inevitably innovation will create some degree of dissonance in schools and administrations, upsetting established structures, procedures, roles and relationships. We should not be surprised when teachers, who gain much of their job satisfaction from the smooth accomplishment of routine activities according to accustomed patterns, balance the potential good of a proposed innovation against the uncertainties and possible disruption of these patterns. We should not assume that the problem is simply one of overcoming the initial resistance of teachers and others to change by convincing them intellectually. The real problem arises when we seek to carry the innovation into practice and ongoing consequential changes are demanded. These changes in the way men go about their work are not simple changes in their individual understandings but changes in the culture of the school. We may well need to change the attitudes and values on which this culture is based; these, in turn, are not necessarily based upon pure reason.

The *normative–re-educative strategy* recognises these facts and, whilst appealing to the reasonableness of those who must carry out an innovation, seeks also to take positive action to change habits and values through direct intervention in respect of those factors which affect the way in which the target system currently works. It is assumed that the capacity to respond positively to changing needs and demands exists among administrators and teachers at all levels but that this capacity may be dormant and constrained, that it must be liberated if innovations directed from above are to be successfully taken up and if ongoing processes of adaptation and improvement at the grassroots level are to take place.

For this to happen will involve first of all the re-education of staff through training procedures. Modifications may be made in the pre-service training of teachers and, in particular, more attention will be paid to in-service training and re-training to prepare serving staff for new syllabuses, new methodologies and new roles and relationships in schools and school systems. It must be said, however, that a good deal of training, as it is currently provided, is relatively inefficient in achieving the kind of re-education we need because it is not seen as part of a broader strategy. One way of describing this broad strategy is that it is concerned with creating a truly professional education service, that is one in which individuals wish to improve the quality of their own work, possess the capacity to do so and consequently are regularly engaged in a process of self-examination and self-improvement. Professional educators are not therefore mechanics, doing as they are told and dependent upon others to tell them what to do, but responsible men and women who, whilst being responsive to the views of others, are able to initiate, carry through and evaluate qualitative changes on their own account. Hoyle has distinguished between two types of teacher professionalism

> restricted professionalism (not using that term pejoratively) which refers to a high level of classroom competence, teaching skill and good relationships with pupils; and extended professionalism which embraces restricted professionalism but additionally embraces other attributes of a teacher. These include seeing his work in the wider context of community and society; ensuring that his work is informed by theory, research and current examples of good practice; being willing to collaborate with other teachers in teaching, curriculum development and the formulation of school policy; and having a commitment to keeping himself professionally informed.[10]

We are here clearly referring to extended professionalism.

The creation of a professional teaching force requires three kinds of action – action to improve their skills and knowledge so that they may understand the situation in which they are working and the potential of certain kinds of change in the ways in which they work; action to improve their motivation so that they will seek in practice to make use of the skills and knowledge they possess; and action to ensure that they have genuine opportunity to do so. Conventional approaches to re-education tend to concentrate upon inculcating skills and knowledge, assume that adequate motivation exists and neglect to provide the kind of opportunity which even the most highly skilled and motivated teacher needs. Perhaps if we reverse the order of these requirements we may be able to see more clearly the implications of this approach. Let us therefore begin with opportunity.

If we are to provide teachers with real opportunity to respond positively to change and to develop their capacity to initiate certain kinds of ongoing innovation and qualitative improvement, several things may be required. Most obvious of these are the various kinds of support service – access to resources such as teaching materials, not simply the materials they will need in the classroom to make their teaching effective, though there are many cases where a lack of such basic material has made it impossible for teachers to adopt a new approach or teach a new syllabus, but also the materials they will need to extend their own knowledge beyond the range of the class textbook and to enliven and diversify their teaching. Clearly resource centres from which books, pictures and teaching aids of all kinds may be borrowed would have an important function here. But ideally the opportunity must extend beyond such things. There is great need for teachers and other education staff to be able to share experience, to study common problems together and, in cooperation, work out ways of solving them. The professional isolation of many schools and many teachers effectively deprives them of opportunity to act professionally, and it may be that to some degree solutions may be found in teachers' centres and various forms of professional associations. But, possibly most important of all, teachers must be freed from the constraints of fear. If their response is to be imaginative, constructive and not merely mechanical obedience, they should not be unduly constrained by fear of displeasing a superior or of making a mistake. If they are to behave in a professional manner, if they are to accept responsibility for making innovations work and for initiating the important though often small-scale adaptations necessary for this, then they must be treated as professionals and this may imply that they should be given specific responsibilities for determining their own actions. We have suggested that already teachers have a substantial degree of freedom of action which arises from the inadequacy and ineffectiveness of supervisory procedures, but this is a negative residual freedom which usually tends to operate against change. What may be necessary is more positive freedom which will encourage change by giving teachers not merely the right but the responsibility of making change.

This is not to suggest that African countries should forthwith adopt the pattern of devolution of responsibility to schools which characterises the British system, for example. Devolution of this kind and to this extent might well be unacceptable at the present stage of professional development in many African countries, and might also be inappropriate to education systems which are seen as crucial investments in national development and which therefore require careful planning. It may be possible, however, to allocate particular kinds and degrees of responsibility more specifically to subordinate level staff – to give teachers, for example, greater responsibility for such matters as materials production, teaching methodology, syllabus design and student assessment. Indeed in a later chapter we shall see that action of this kind is already being taken in a number of African countries, though not necessarily for the reasons advanced here. In general the suggestion here is that, wherever possible, decisions should be taken at a level as close to the point where they will be implemented as feasible. We seek to modify the bureaucratic procedures, all too common at present, which insist that all decisions of substance be reserved for the most senior man in the hierarchy.

It may, of course, be argued that it would be dangerous to grant such responsibility if those who are to exercise it do not possess the necessary competencies or are of low morale and motivation. To do so would be unrealistic and counterproductive. Indeed many teachers and administrators might well interpret such a move as an indication that their superiors were abdicating their leadership role and were therefore not interested in what actually happens in the schools.

However the counter-argument would be that by providing this opportunity, by allocating responsibility and by treating teachers in a more professional way, a significant contribution might well be made to their self-respect and morale, and that this would tend to motivate them to behave more professionally. Certainly it would be unrealistic to expect them to develop professional characteristics where they are not accorded professional esteem by their superiors. But clearly other actions must be undertaken to reinforce what might otherwise remain an empty gesture. Professional attitudes are unlikely to be generated within a career structure which allocates rewards on the basis of length of service, entering qualifications, conformity and obedience to superiors, and fails adequately to take into account quality of performance. If teachers are to be encouraged to respond with enthusiasm to external initiatives and to develop willingness to make them work through adaptation, there must be some recognition accorded to their efforts, and not of a form which would reward the most professional and innovative teachers by removing them from the classroom. It may be that in some degree job satisfaction will constitute a reward, that the respect of colleagues and personal status within the group will encourage more professional conduct, and there may be other ways in which authority can provide recognition through praise and through using the good teacher as a model for others, though there are dangers here. But it is probably realistic to suggest that to be effectively motivated teachers must be accorded recognition in the form of career and salary progression.

Other developments may, however, play an increasingly important part. The formation of professional associations and groups is likely to be particularly significant, not merely in giving good teachers an opportunity to make a contribution to improving educational quality, but in improving their self-confidence, mutual respect and pride in their work, all factors which contribute to good morale and which further motivate the teacher to move ahead. Of particular value in these respects would be local or regional teachers' associations seeking to bring together all teachers irrespective of subject specialism, level of school or career grade, to devise and carry out programmes of activities which will generate fellings of belonging and shared professionality. But participation in problem solving activities may well do more than this – it may assist teachers to develop the skills they need in order to fulfil their professional responsibilities.

What is particularly significant about this approach to skills development is that skills may be sought when the teacher is conscious that he needs them and may be acquired when he is able to put them to immediate practical use. How different this is from many training procedures which obtain at present, which involve taking teachers away from the places where they work, providing them with training which the instructors think is relevant, assuming that the teachers also think it relevant, and finally assuming that at some time in the future the teacher will actually use what he has learned. It must be recognised, however, that administratively the latter arrangement is a good deal more simple and that to provide teachers with the opportunities to acquire skills on demand, as it were, is much less easy.

However we should reflect a little further on the kinds of skills we are discussing before we consider how best to make training available. To use the current term, we are envisaging the development of 'problem-solving schools', the staff of which are not content simply to do as they have always done or to react briefly to the occasional visit of an inspector, but who are concerned to seek ways of improving the quality of what they do. This may imply that they need to be able to identify the problems they face and the deficiencies in what they do, to diagnose the reasons for the existence of these problems and deficiencies, to investigate ways of dealing with the situation and to try out possible solutions and finally to evaluate the results of their efforts. We are not, therefore, talking about the conventional skills of teaching, important though they may be, but about a range of professional skills for which existing patterns of training provide little or no preparation. Such skills probably cannot effectively be taught although many of the theoretical underpinnings may be taught in, for example, studies of philosophy, psychology and sociology. However, the application of this body of theory can probably best be learned in a problem-solving situation and it may well be that the theory itself may best be learned in the process of problem solving. Since the problems manifest themselves in schools, and since colleges or other training centres find it very difficult to provide other than fairly artificial problem-solving contexts, the case for developing the relevant skills in the school context is a strong one provided that it is administratively feasible.

Here we may refer to one of the more influential ideas current in management of innovation studies – the use of change agents. Change agents may of course operate within any one of the three strategies we have been examining. Within the power–coercive strategy their role would be to direct change and ensure compliance with directives and within the rational–empirical strategy it would be to convey information and link schools with resource centres, pilot projects and each other. Within the normative–re-educative strategy however their role becomes considerably more significant and demanding. The school system, we have suggested, suffers from inertial forces largely resulting from the vicious circle whereby the products of the system become the staff of the system. 'New' education, it has been argued, needs 'new' teachers, which requires 'new' education'. Somehow, therefore, we need to break into this circle, to intervene directly through introducing a group of highly able and committed people to serve as agents of change. Their responsibilities would be threefold – to serve as catalysts encouraging and stimulating staff to re-examine their work and to devise means for its improvement, as trainers helping staff to develop the skills they need to perform this task largely through the informal process of working together, and as link agents seeking to bring staff together and to put them in contact with resources which exist elsewhere. This is not the place for an extended discussion of how such a system of change agents would operate but a number of things are clear.

First, the intervention of change agents is only one of several steps which may need to be taken and which have been discussed above. Secondly, no rapid transformation in staff attitudes and practices should be anticipated – the process of professional growth will inevitably be a slow and difficult one to which there will be resistance and suspicion which can only be overcome by a high degree of skill. Thirdly, therefore, such change agents cannot be inspectors, reporting to authority and largely responsible for the allocation of rewards and punishments, for these functions would destroy the kinds of personal relationships with staff upon which their success depends. Fourthly, their involvement in schools and departments cannot simply be occasional but must be regular and frequent, not an 'occasion' but a normal feature of the life of the institution. And, finally, the task of these people is not to design and introduce change but to encourage and assist the staff to do it for themselves; their intervention will be subtle and not crude so that responsibility remains with the staff.

The recruitment, training, deployment and coordination of such change agents clearly presents many problems. It would, furthermore, be vital that they possess the full support and confidence of the central authorities. Nevertheless some such role may be a vital part of normative–re-educative strategies of innovation in Africa and fully merits further thought and study.

Having briefly examined these three broad strategies we need to remind ourselves that these are not to be regarded as alternatives but that they are complementary to each other. In most African countries, it has been argued, there will be a continuing need for centralised initiatives of a kind which have been termed power–coercive, and there will also be an important place for modes of operation we have classified as rational–empirical. However, without changes in the culture of the school and of the education system as a whole such as are envisaged in the normative–re-educative approach, their effectiveness appears likely to be very limited. The management of innovation should perhaps be viewed therefore less as a matter of devising techniques for bringing about change in an institutional context permanently characterised by inertia, and more as a process of transforming that context into one characterised by active quality seeking.

However, in practice, there are many ways in which conflicts between the three strategies may arise where insufficient thought has been given to the elimination of discordant elements. These conflicts commonly arise where an instrument or technique designed for use in one strategic context is utilised in another. A teachers' centre, for example, set in a power-coercive context is likely to function very differently from one set in a normative–re-educative context, and a supervisory service established to serve in one of these contexts may well prove unsuitable for use in another. Before we select our techniques, instruments and agencies we need to make some very difficult decisions about what mix of strategies will best serve our particular purposes in our specific circumstances.

From this analysis of problems and theories of educational

reform we now turn to examine some of the major current trends of reform in Africa. The foregoing discussion will illuminate some of these trends and the extent to which they may be succeeding or failing, and help us in passing judgments upon their potential.

## References

1. J. Ponsioen (ed.), *Educational Innovations in Africa: Policies and Administration* (The Hague: Institute of Social Studies, 1972).
2. R. G. Havelock and A. M. Huberman, *Solving Educational Problems, the Theory and Reality of Innovation in Developing Countries*, a study prepared for the International Bureau of Education (Paris: UNESCO 1977) p. 15.
3. *Ibid.*, p. 19.
4. See R. Chin and K. D. Benne, 'General Strategies for Effecting Change in Human Systems', in W. G. Bennis, K. D. Benne, R. Chin and K. E. Corey (eds), *The Planning of Change* (3rd edition) (New York: Holt, Rinehart & Winston, 1976) pp. 22–45.
5. Havelock and Huberman, *Solving Educational Problems*, p. 16.
6. Raja Roy Singh, 'Statement to the Inaugural Session', in R. F. Lyons, *Administrative Support for Educational Reform*, final report of an IIEP/ROEA Seminar held in Bangkok 21–25 February 1977 (Paris: IIEP, 1977) pp. 9–10.
7. Havelock and Huberman, *Solving Educational Problems*, p. 72.
8. *Ibid.*, p. 18.
9. W. Schramm, *Big Media, Little Media* (Washington, DC: Academy for Educational Development, 1973) p. 145.
10. E. Hoyle, 'Strategies of Curriculum Change' in R. Watkins (ed.), *Inservice Training: Structure and Content* (London: Ward Lock 1973) pp. 97–8.

# Part IV

# Current Trends of Educational Reform in Africa

# 8

# The Climate of Opinion

Growing understanding of the many problems involved in stimulating and co-ordinating development of a kind which will more genuinely meet the aspirations and needs of African peoples as a whole has led to what the Director General of UNESCO has described as 'an entirely new idea of development' and one which carries with it profound implications for education:

> development can only come from within. It must be endogenous, thought out by people for themselves, springing from the soil on which they live and attuned to their aspirations, the conditions of their natural environment, the resources at their disposal and the particular genius of their culture . . . Education should accordingly contribute to the promotion of such endogenous development.[1]

For education systems to make this contribution, he argued, implied democratisation involving continuing quantitative expansion but also a restructuring of the systems in such a way as to provide educational opportunities to match the characteristics and needs of all groups within the population.

Such a view of development should be taken to imply not 'a selfish attempt by each country to exist for itself alone' but international co-operation perhaps within the framework of a new economic order. It must also involve mobilising the capacity of sub-groups within the population of a nation to contribute to their own development through self-help within a framework of national unity and equity. Schooling, it may be argued, has been dominated by the need to perform its selection and certification functions, and consequently has to this time essentially formed part of the urban and modern-sector directed strategies of development which are now to be substantially modified. Schools have neither served the needs of the whole population nor even the needs of a large proportion of those fortunate enough to be admitted. Whilst overloading the school with tasks beyond its capacity we have neglected alternative ways of meeting these learning needs. Consequently, it may be suggested, we now face the task of seeking out these alternatives and of building up national education systems which may be better able to meet the diversity of our needs through employing a diversity of means.

In the process of re-thinking educational strategies, a number of new concepts have been formulated and a number of new terms such as basic, lifelong, recurrent or continuing education have entered the educationists' vocabulary, somewhat confusingly alongside other terms such as mass, adult or fundamental education which have been in use for some time. We shall seek in this chapter to clarify some of these terms though it must be accepted that many of them will continue to be used to carry a variety of meanings.

Mass education, as the term was used in the 1940s, and fundamental education which largely replaced it in the 1950s and 1960s, referred to kinds of non-schooling provision made in parallel to formal school systems as a form of social service to those unable to gain places in the latter. Basic education, as the term has been generally used in recent years refers not to an alternative system but to an approach to education which may take place either within or outside the formal school system, which seeks to some extent to integrate the two, and which is more closely geared to nation building and development than simply to social welfare.[2] Whilst in some quarters the idea of basic education has been associated with efforts to provide for at least the minimum learning needs of youth and young adults, it has perhaps more generally been associated with the idea that we should not confine ourselves to young people but seek to provide some form of education, as and when appropriate, to meet the needs which arise throughout the life of every individual. Basic education has therefore been thought of as providing by various means an educational base which will enable people to take full advantage of later opportunities to learn skills, acquire knowledge or otherwise develop their potential. Basic education and lifelong or recurrent education are thus closely associated concepts. As the African Ministers of Education meeting in Lagos in 1976 agreed:

> Although [basic education] may represent the maximum which governments can offer to all at a given time, it should not be seen as an inferior substitute with which the greater number will have to be contented, but as an initial phase in the perspective of life-long education.[3]

This concern that basic education should not be seen as separate from and inferior to formal schooling stems from experience such as that of the Ivory Coast which, in the 1960s, sought to limit the expansion of primary schooling to the numbers needed to supply secondary schools, and through them provide the economy with only the amounts of high-level manpower it was capable of absorbing. Rural Education Centres were introduced as a means whereby the majority of the population might receive three years of basic education in literacy, numeracy and agriculture commencing at age fourteen. In practice only a limited development of Rural Education Centres was achieved whilst primary schooling continued to expand rapidly largely because of resistance from their clienteles, the majority of whom found themselves cut off from the kind of educational opportunity they most wanted and consigned to a parallel and clearly restricted system.[4] This was very similar to the experience with Rural Education Centres in Upper Volta, the lesson of which, according to Grabe, is that 'a rural education programme cannot be effective as long as it stands as a symbol of discrimination and fails to get the acceptance of the rural people.' In consequence after ten years and the establishment of over 700 centres the programme is still officially 'experimental' and in practice stagnating.[5]

A long, often heated, debate has taken place in recent years about how this problem may be avoided and how just and fair systems of basic and lifelong education may be created in face of such resistance stemming from the position of prestige and popularity in which the formal school system has been entrenched. The debate continues and is far from being concluded. Before we begin to look at some of the proposals which are being implemented and in order that we may examine them more critically we need to look briefly at some of the main arguments which have been put forward in the debate.

As will be apparent from the earlier chapters in this book, the demand for the reform of school systems has long been with us. Admittedly a good deal of this demand has tended to stem from concern about the internal inefficiency of schools, the proportions of untrained teachers, the size of classes, the amounts of equipment, facilities and supervisory services, the high wastage and repetition rates, and poor examination performance. Consequently many of the reforms which have been attempted have not affected the real function of the schools or the socio-economic framework within which they operate, other than to strengthen them. The current demand for reform is, however, of a very different character and seeks, in theory at least, substantial structural change and the creation of a 'new', and not merely an improved, school.

It has furthermore been argued above that efforts to reform existing school systems are likely to continue to be impeded by the very fact that modern sectors exist within our national societies, that these sectors are essential to further national development, and that they consequently need to be manned by personnel of the highest quality. The school, we have noted, has been firmly entrenched as the most efficient, convenient and generally acceptable means both for training and for selecting this personnel. Since the rewards, whether of money, status or power, received by this personnel are a natural focus for the aspirations of ordinary people, efforts to provide more 'relevant' education within the school for the many who will be rejected by the selection process and to enable the school to perform other socially desirable functions tend to be thrust aside by its dominant function.

Some educationists have consequently formed the opinion that efforts to reform school systems are futile and that we need to make a completely fresh start. This view, forcefully expressed by Illich, Reimer and Freire at the level of intellectual speculation, has been reinforced significantly by recent studies of attempts during the last decade or more to reform education systems in more highly developed countries in order to achieve social changes, notably in respect of greater equity. Many of these studies are, however, open to the criticism that, whilst arguing that school systems essentially reflect the established social order, reinforcing and legitimating it, and that educational change is dependent upon preceding social change rather than the reverse, they have not seriously attempted to explore whether and to what extent there exists within school systems a capacity to operate independently and to bring pressure upon the social order.

An external advisory panel on education, reporting to the World Bank in 1978, stated:

> We do not accept the view, which seems to us too simple, that in the absence of radical social change, education serves only as an instrument for social control by the ruling elites. On the contrary, we consider that educational activities may be one of the means for modifying a structural situation. Education may equip disadvantaged youngsters to break through traditional barriers. Educational activities may contribute to the organisation of the unorganised as a means for community change.[6]

In the preceding chapters the argument of this book has been that schools do bring pressures for change to bear upon our societies but not necessarily of a kind which can be accurately anticipated or planned for, and schools are better suited to reinforcing changes which are already beginning to take place in the social order. The functions which are currently being imposed upon the school, notably by the recruitment, promotion and remuneration practices of the labour market, are equally likely to be imposed upon an alternative education system, which might well meet these demands in a less fair way even than present school systems, unless educational change is accompanied by changes in the labour market.

The influential report of the International Commission on the Development of Education published in 1972 argued that

> Education, being a sub-system of society, necessarily reflects the main features of that society. It would be vain to hope for a rational, humane education in an unjust society. A bureaucratic system, habitually estranged from life, finds it hard to entertain the idea that schools are made for children instead of children being made for schools. Regimes based upon auth-

ority from the top and obedience from the bottom cannot develop an education for freedom. It is difficult to imagine school imparting a taste for creative work in socio-economic conditions in which work is generally an alienation. And how can one imagine a society woven out of privileges and discrimination developing a democratic education system?[7]

The Commission concluded that it is almost impossible to break out of the vicious circle of underdevelopment and of inequality of educational provision without an attempt to deal both with the reform of social and economic structures and with the renewal of education systems. This argument is now widely accepted in African countries, as several submissions to the Conference of African Ministers of Education held in Lagos in 1976 demonstrate. The national programme for building the new school in Benin argued that 'there is no schooling problem to be solved in isolation, the problem is one of development of which the schooling problem is an important element'[8] and the Tanzanian Ministry of Education argued that 'To achieve any meaningful success, any educational reform must take place concurrently with the reform of the society'.[9] In Togo 'the main concern is no longer with reforming the content of education but with the whole system. The reform concerns not only the school but society as a whole'.[10]

However, as the International Commission also argued:

It by no means follows that for lack of being able to modify and correct social conditions by itself that education must remain their passive offshoot. The subordinate relationship of education to the socio-economic system is not such as to make it impossible to act, if not upon the entire complex, at least on this or that important element . . . it is hard to conceive of a society developing without a renewal in education.[11]

This argument implies that we should seek to identify more realistically the role which education may play and accept that it may well be more limited than we have tended to suppose in the past. However, as the earlier chapters in the book have also argued, we are only beginning to understand what that role may be and what the specific role of the school may be within that broader role. One of the Commissions at Lagos called for detailed study to determine the exact nature of the relationship between education and society in order that education might become a driving force in the process of social transformation.[12] Without greater understanding we may well be in danger of repeating the errors of the past. However such is the urgency of our need for development that our countries feel it necessary to take action quickly and it is not surprising in consequence that educationists are divided about the way in which we should approach educational reform.

On the one hand there is the school of thought, perhaps best represented in the International Commission, which demanded that the old linear expansion strategies should be replaced by transformational approaches based upon an overall conception of educational goals and systems and a rejection of piecemeal modification. As the Chairman of the Commission, Edgar Faure, argued

> Traditional formulae and partial reforms cannot meet the unprecedented demand for education arising out of the new tasks and functions to be fulfilled. We accordingly rejected timid half measures which are, in fact, costly because of their very inefficiency.[13]

This point of view has the considerable merit of intellectual clarity. We should not tinker with separate elements within the education system but approach its reform from a broad and comprehensive viewpoint, embracing all forms of educational provision and seeking to integrate them in a bold attack upon those elements in the socio-economic system which are susceptible of being changed in this way.

On the other hand many educationists have misgivings about this view, feeling that its apparent simplicity is deceptive. The transformation of education systems demands considerable political courage and the existence of the will to sustain the lengthy process of implementation in the face of the resistance, often subtle but no less powerful, which such changes would (as in the past) inevitably generate. Similar qualities will be required in even greater measure to implement the parallel attack upon unjust and strongly entrenched social structures without which it would be difficult to sustain and make effective even the more limited pressures for change which education systems are now thought to be capable of applying. Even the logical process of arriving at an overall conception of development strategy, of formulating an agreed set of priorities and thereafter of deciding on the appropriate educational measures, is one which is fraught with difficulties and uncertainties arising largely from the necessity of reconciling the many diverse interests and viewpoints which exist in our societies. The reform of education in more developed countries during the last half century, it may be argued, has been achieved not by transformational approaches but through piecemeal change. Yet it has often been remarkably speedy. Societies themselves tend naturally to change through a steady process of adjustment even where there is commitment to speedy and planned change, and it may be that the main concern of educationists should be to ensure that the education systems are sufficiently responsive to be able to change in an ongoing process rather than to subject the system to the massive stress of a transformational adjustment to the circumstances existing at one particular time. Consequently there are many who would see the steady flow of improvements, both large and small, in educational systems as both a more practicable and more desirable course of action.

In the light of these unresolved considerations we must now turn to the task of examining some of the trends which may perhaps be identified in the ways in which African countries have sought (and are seeking) to restructure and reform their education systems. We shall first examine non-formal education to explore its potential for contributing to the solution of our problems. We shall then turn to the formal system since, clearly, so long as it remains in its present state it is likely to be inadequate in important respects in serving its own clienteles and, moreover, may damage the capacity of non-formal approaches to serve their clienteles. Finally we shall examine ways in which formal and non-formal systems may be linked or even integrated into coherent, nationwide learning systems.

There are, however, fundamental difficulties in doing so. Whilst the flow of published material relating to educational innovations, notably in the non-formal sector, has increased considerably of late, this material contains major deficiencies.

Rarely do case studies provide full and accurate information about particular innovations, but more seriously they tend not to provide the kind of information which those of us who wish to learn from them need.[14] Many studies are content to set out the rationale for a development and to express the hopes and beliefs of the innovators: those which attempt some evaluation of progress rarely go beyond general assessment of success in terms of reaching set goals and do not seek to analyse in any detail the nature of the problem in its particular context or to examine the actual management of the innovation. This is hardly surprising since many of the developments which have been recorded are too recent to permit effective evaluation. Even where this is not so, the projects commonly, for reasons of expense or other practical difficulties, did not provide for evaluation other than of a crude summative kind.

## References

1. Amadou-Mahtar M'Bow, 'Address to the 36th Session of the International Conference on Education', Geneva, August–September 1977, *Final Report* (Paris: UNESCO International Bureau of Education, 1977) p. 35.
2. See C. Bonanni, in Unit for Cooperation with UNESCO, UNICEF, *Notes, Comments* no. 14, (Paris: UNESCO, October 1977).
3. Conference of Ministers of Education of African Member States, Lagos, 27 January–4 February 1976, *Final Report* (Paris: UNESCO 1976) p. 14.
4. See C. Coleclough, and J. Hallak, 'Some Issues in Rural Education – Equity, Efficiency and Employment', Discussion Paper no. 89, Institute of Development Studies, Sussex University.
5. S. Grabe, quoted by the editors, in M. Ahmed and P. H. Coombs, *Education for Rural Development, Case Studies for Planners*, (New York: Praeger, 1975) p. 361.
6. D. E. Bell (Chairman), *Report of the External Advisory Panel on Education to the World Bank, 31 October 1978* (Washington, DC: World Bank, 1978) p. 8.
7. E. Faure *et al.*, *Learning To Be, the World of Education Today and Tomorrow* (Paris: UNESCO, 1972) p. 60.
8. UNESCO, *Educational Reforms and Innovations in Africa* (Paris: UNESCO, 1978) p. 31.
9. *Ibid.*, p. 26.
10. *Ibid.*, p. 38
11. Faure, *Learning To Be*, pp. 60–1.
12. Conference of Ministers of Education, *Final Report*, p. 21.
13. Faure, *Learning To Be*, p. vi.
14. See M. Debeauvais, 'The Popularity of the Idea of Innovation: A Tentative Interpretation of the Texts', *Innotech Journal*, vol. 1 no. 2 (July 1977) for

further discussion. Debeauvais sets out a list of key questions which should be asked in analysing the communication value of monographs on innovation. These are worthy of consideration by any researcher proposing to study an innovation.

# 9

# Non-formal Education

Africa has a substantial history of non-formal educational activity, but has perhaps only in recent years sought to relate in any coherent way the various strands of which this activity was composed. Adult education, it has been observed, tended in Africa to develop around the two very different poles of university extra-mural studies and mass education. The extra-mural tradition, which was introduced to Africa with the new university colleges established in the post war years, reflected the strength of the British and notably the Oxford tradition in the establishment by these colleges of institutes of adult education. These institutes were not intended as instruments of mass education but as means whereby a relatively small number of local men and women might be trained to assume positions of leadership in their communities. This 'elitist' approach was roundly criticised when, following the achievement of independence, national leaders proclaimed their commitment to making education more widely available to the masses, yet it made a useful if modest contribution to equipping the countries concerned for self-government.

Mass education, on the other hand, embraced perhaps three main elements. The first of these was mass literacy programmes to which attention will be paid later. The second was the tradition of community development, starting with the Jeanes Schools in East and Central Africa between the wars, and evolving into broader programmes associating education with other community development activities, though still with a strong emphasis on leadership training. The third was agricultural extension to which again we shall return.

In addition to these main elements there was a range of other activities run by government departments or by voluntary agencies. These included what has been called fundamental education to provide instruction in better ways of living, improved techniques of farming, food storage, nutrition, child care, hygiene and health, as well as more developed skill-training designed to improve the vocational competence of workers in commerce, industry and government employment as well as those privately engaged in agriculture. The work of institutes of adult education in providing second chance substitutes for formal education, courses following the same syllabuses and leading to the same examinations as the formal school, was supplemented by a very considerable growth in popularity of correspondence courses commonly provided by international commercial firms.

In these various ways a good deal was done and often with some success. However these activities were characterised by an almost total lack of co-ordination for many years. Many different forms of action were undertaken by many different organisations, both official and voluntary, and under many different titles without full consciousness of what others were doing in similar fields. Overlapping and even competition was inevitable though the scale of the need and the fact that many activities were purely local in their effect meant that this was often thought of as unimportant. However what was serious was that a great deal of effort was being expended without effective evaluation and without opportunities effectively to learn from the experience of others. Kenya provided a notable initiative in seeking to introduce order into a very confused situation when in 1965 it set up a Board of Adult Education representing all major providing agencies and with a permanent secretariat to survey and coordinate adult education activities both at central and local level.

Coombs and Ahmed point to the basic underlying weakness of some of the major approaches when in classifying non-formal activities in rural areas they draw a clear distinction between those which they see as expressing the extension approach and those which comprise the training approach.[1] Although in practice overlapping to some degree, each possesses a narrow and self-contained view of the appropriate strategy for development. The traditional extension approach, admittedly much modified in recent years, was based upon the conviction that an extension service, bringing trained workers into face-to-face contact with individual farmers, enabling the former to observe what the latter actually did and the latter to see improved practice demonstrated, had the capacity by itself to bring about major changes in the economic system and way of life of the clientele. Whilst the extension approach stressed the communication of information about better farming practice, the training approach stressed the need for systematic learning of the basic skills and of the reasons for their use. Often the techniques of the formal system were employed, withdrawing clients into a training centre for a set period to follow a planned study programme. The basic premise was that knowledge and skills by themselves could precipitate the process of development. In practice the basic premise of both approaches was that knowledge and skills needed to be injected into rural communities, the extension approach stressing the physical presence of the external expert and the training approach often assuming that its products would provide the necessary catalytic presence.

The disconnected nature of non-formal activities, stemming partly from administrative weaknesses, was perhaps primarily an inevitable consequence of the manner in which they developed – to meet particular needs in particular places at particular times. This, we should note, was a process which was by no means without its advantages. Nevertheless, the full significance of these activities was unlikely to be realised until they were placed in a clearer conceptual framework demonstrating their relationship to each other and to the overall task of development. Until this began to happen adult education had to remain a cinderella service operating very much in the shadow of the formal school system and receiving wholly inadequate support in the form of funds and staffing from governments which could not see clearly how resources should be allocated and remained uncertain about the degree of commitment the enterprise merited. Two things more than any others contributed to change in this not very encouraging picture in the early 1970s. The first was growing recognition of the fact that formal education was not adequately serving the bulk of the population, particularly in the rural areas, and the second was the new consciousness of the need for greater equity, for enabling the masses to have greater opportunity to share in the benefits of development. It was clear that rates of economic growth would not for long support the wider extension of formal education upon which hopes had been primarily been placed. The significance of adult education and of non-formal activities, not merely as a supplement to formal education but as a vital contributor to development in its own right was perhaps most clearly recognised in Tanzania where President Nyerere declared that the year 1970 would be devoted to adult education to achieve three objectives: 'To shake ourselves out of a resignation to the kind of life Tanzanian people have lived for centuries past; To learn how to improve our lives; To understand our national policies of socialism and self-reliance.'[2]

This development in thinking together with the somewhat limited success achieved by many of the programmes of extension, training and community development which had been pursued for many years led to the emergence of what Coombs and Ahmed have categorised as co-operative self-help approaches, based upon the belief that national development involved rural transformation which must begin with fundamental changes in the attitudes and aspirations of rural peoples themselves. As we have seen, it was asserted that rural people must emerge from traditions of dependence, must become full partners in the process of development building upon their own capacity to improve their own lives independent of that of government bodies. As Nyerere was to point out, the first task of adult education was

> to inspire both a desire for change and an understanding that change is possible. For a belief that poverty or suffering is 'the will of God' and that man's only task is to endure, is the most fundamental of all the enemies of freedom. Yet dissatisfaction with what *is* must be combined with a conviction that it can be changed: otherwise it is simply destructive.[3]

The second stage of adult education would build upon this first stage, helping the people to work out what kind of change they want and how to create it, an activity which in Nyerere's view had not normally been regarded as adult education.

The call for greater self-reliance which might be stimulated by appropriate adult education was most powerfully expressed in the ujamaa movement in Tanzania from the late 1960s and spread rapidly, taking different forms in other African countries.

However as the idea took hold and practical men began to examine how best to put it into effect, thinking took a further step forward. It became quite rapidly recognised that there were dangers in over-emphasising the capacity of groups and communities within the population to help themselves, to pull themselves up by their own bootstraps, that whilst these groups undoubtedly could contribute a great deal provided that they could be educated into greater belief in themselves, they would only be able to do so and to channel their new aspirations into productive channels if sufficient external assistance were available to help break down some of the fundamental obstacles which faced them, particularly in the early stages. Self-help demanded a new kind of partnership with central authorities without which the frustration feared by Nyerere would become a counter developmental force. But this partnership should not confirm the old habits of dependence. It would be necessary to abandon traditional approaches to community development based upon concepts of inducing psychological change and promoting independent and self-sufficient development activities and to adopt what Coombs and Ahmed have termed 'the integrated development approach' in which all forms of development activity, including all forms of education, would be coordinated under a single 'management system', providing a more supportive context to satisfy aspirations once they were aroused.

In these ways a variety of concepts of adult and mass education have tended to converge towards concepts of nationwide learning systems providing each section of the population with the skills and understandings it needs to contribute to the improvement of its way of life. In this wider integrated development context non-formal education and training for adult men and women and for out-of-school youth assumed a new significance.

Non-formal education has been defined as: 'any organized, systematic, educational activity carried on outside the framework of the formal system to provide selected types of learning to particular subgroups in the population, adults as well as children'.[4] This definition deserves further examination. Of particular interest is the idea that, instead of seeking to provide a broad, multi-purpose and common form of education to the population as a whole, we are here concerned with identifying different groups of people, diagnosing the specific learning needs of each group, and then of seeking the most appropriate means whereby these needs may be catered for. Whereas formal approaches to education have tended to begin with the school as the virtually unchallenged tool and have then asked how that tool may be used to provide for the wide range of learning needs of a particular age range within the population, non-formal approaches drawing upon a different set of traditions more logically begin with people and their needs and with the assumption that no single tool or technique will serve all purposes.

This approach will lead us to the kind of conclusion reached by Coombs and Ahmed when they suggest that there are four main kinds of learning need and three main groups of people who must be considered in the rural areas with which they were concerned.[5] The learning needs they identified included:

*General or basic education*, including such elements as literacy, numeracy and understanding of one's society and environment. Some educationists would include liberal and cultural studies in this category. Other than literacy campaigns and second chance programmes for school leavers, Coombs and Ahmed found relatively few examples of non-formal programmes of this kind.

*Family improvement education* to develop the knowledge, skills and attitudes which would help people to raise their standards of health, nutrition, homemaking, child-care, family planning, home construction and repair, in order to improve the quality of their domestic lives.

*Community improvement education*, to provide for the strengthening of local and national institutions and organisations, to enable people to participate more effectively in civic affairs, in the management of co-operatives, credit banks, associations and clubs, and in undertaking community improvement projects. A wide range of both family and community education projects existed but these were thought to be generally over-fragmented, limited in scale and relatively inefficient.

*Occupational education*, to assist people to make a better living for themselves and to contribute more effectively to the economic development of their communities and countries. The bulk of existing non-formal provision fell into this category.

The three main rural clienteles identified were:

*Persons directly engaged in agriculture* – farmers, herders, fishermen and so on, groups which would vary in their activities and needs according to the areas in which they lived. Account would have to be taken of the different circumstances of, for example, commercial farmers, subsistence and semi-subsistence farmers, and landless labourers.

*Persons engaged in off-farm commercial activities*, such as traders, large and small, repair and maintenance workers, construction and transport workers, manufacturers, including the small roadside producers of domestic implements and tools as well as tailors and dressmakers, and all those engaged in service activities.

*General service personnel*, including local civic leaders and planners, administrators and managers responsible at various levels for the provision of public services such as schools, clinics, transport and supply, storage and marketing, the running of co-operatives, farmers associations and community organisations.

It is not here suggested that these are the only or necessarily the best ways of categorising subgroups and learning needs but simply that they may illustrate how we may begin to analyse what kinds of education we may need to provide in order to lead us to consider the most appropriate means of providing them. If, for example, we take subsistence farmers in a particular area as the subgroup which we wish to assist, we may begin by asking what their needs are in terms, first, of general education – do they need to be literate, what kind of literacy is appropriate, at what times of the day and of the year are they available for instruction, what kinds of material do they need to study, to what learning situation and kind of instructor are they most likely to respond, and so on? In respect of family and community improvement education, what are the particular problems faced by this group of people in their particular environment, what solutions are within their capacity, what kinds of external assistance may be necessary, and how best can they be informed about and encouraged to adopt appropriate solutions? In terms of occupational education, what are the present problems and deficiencies of their production techniques, what possibilities exist to improve or modify these and how best may they be communicated – through training courses, through demonstration units, through encouraging more progressive farmers to experiment or by other means or combinations of means?

In examining the learning needs and the specific situations of each group we can seek to place their various needs in order of priority, or group them in a coherent strategy so that one activity may lead into and underpin the next. We can take account of existing motivation and seek to develop new motivations: for instance we may believe that the first priority is to communicate new production techniques, to encourage diversification of crops perhaps, but we may find that what the group wants is something else, literacy perhaps. In this case we have to begin by asking ourselves whether we should not begin with what is most demanded and build from this. If literacy is demanded, we may seek to instruct the farmers in new production techniques or the possibilities of new crops through the actual literature we use, in other words we may develop work-oriented literacy materials, and we may take advantage of the fact that a group of farmers has come together for literacy classes to involve them in discussion of other needs and activities in which they might engage. And by adopting this more focussed approach we may be able to assess more clearly to what extent the educational input needs to be matched by other inputs and facilities to give practical expression to the interest, understanding and skills which education may generate.

Above all, perhaps, we shall be able to see the full range of learning and other needs of a particular subgroup, or a particular community, to see these in relation to each other, and to develop flexibility of response, not relying upon standardised program- mes and institutions. Though the above examples have been drawn from rural areas, the same approach may be equally valuable in looking at the problems and potentiality of other communities – rural market towns, the shanty suburbs of major cities and inner-city areas. By looking at specific groups and specific circumstances we shall, in conjunction with local people themselves, begin to devise measures appropriate to their needs and encourage their further initiative in assessing what needs to be done.

In particular, we shall perhaps be able to think more clearly about which needs may be met more effectively, whether in the short or longer term, by non-formal education and which by formal schooling, perhaps taking away from the school some of the unrealistic and impractical responsibilities which we have been inclined to allocate to it in the past in the absence of any apparent alternative.

This then, briefly summarised, is the approach which is being suggested. Clearly it raises many questions. If we were to follow this line of action, the educational scene would be a confusing one, very different from the clean and tidy system of schooling with which we are familiar. A wide variety of techniques may be employed to meet a wide range of needs and situations, even within a single community, and a large number of agencies may be involved, both governmental and, since we are concerned with self-help, voluntary and community-based. To some, non-formal education appears to be a ragbag of agencies, techniques, clienteles and objectives, between which co-ordination and synthesis may in practice be impossible. To others the concept of co-ordination raises the fear of bureaucratic controls and inefficiency, and practices antipathetic to the promotion of community-based self-help activities. This is a genuine problem, since if we wish to see greater resources allocated to non-formal education, we must be concerned about the means whereby decisions will be taken about their allocation and distribution. It is widely admitted that the problem has nowhere been satisfactorily solved.

Confusion may also arise from the use of the term 'non-formal' education, since for many purposes such as training a pattern of organisation may be used which appears very formal. Is a literacy class with its syllabus arranged in a sequence of steps, with specially designed materials, with courses taught by an appointed teacher, lasting for a predetermined period of time, and taking place perhaps in a primary school classroom, not really formal education? Is a farmers' training centre providing residential courses again of planned and sequential learning experiences not more formal than non-formal? The conclusion which we must draw is that there is indeed considerable overlap in respect of techniques between formal and non-formal education but that there is little to be gained from seeking to draw too precise a dividing line between them. Indeed, as we shall see, there are conscious efforts being made to build effective bridges between the two. For those with tidy minds, the term 'out-of-school education' has its attractions as an alternative to 'non-formal education', but it may be argued that in addition to building bridges we are in some cases seeking to achieve a more complete merging of the two.

It may also be asked whether many of the activities we are discussing should not more appropriately be termed informal since they have much in common with those traditional means whereby a mother instructs her daughter in homemaking and a father teaches his son how to farm and to build. There is no assumption that these kinds of education will be replaced by the systematic and organised activities of non-formal education but it is clearly envisaged that to some extent informal education will take over where non-formal education stops and will be much strengthened if those who are providing the informal education have themselves had the opportunity to improve their own skills and understanding through systematic instruction.

Although pursuit of precise definitions may not be particularly rewarding, a number of writers have found it helpful in analysing the potential strengths of non-formal approaches to compare and contrast these with the formal school system. In the earlier chapters of this book we examined some of the basic weaknesses and disabilities of the school in serving some of the needs of our societies. Analysis of the ways in which non-formal education may differ from schooling may indicate how the two forms of education may complement each other.

The most fundamental distinction to be drawn is in respect of purpose. Whereas schooling is intended to provide the knowledge and skills a pupil will need for all aspects of his whole life, non-formal education seeks to provide for a client's specific and immediate need. Consequently, whilst schooling must therefore deal with generally valid packages of knowledge, must to a considerable extent standardise its content and, in order to make it both comprehensive and intensive, must deal largely with theoretical and abstract knowledge, non-formal education may be focussed on the specific task or skill which is needed, and will be able to deal with modular units of learning derived not from some accepted concept of the way knowledge is structured but from the problem which is being faced.

Consequently, in terms of methodology, whilst schooling must be largely vicarious, relying heavily upon the second-hand experience derived from the teacher or the book, non-formal education may be essentially practical, a process of learning by doing. Whilst schooling provides indirect learning experience which requires mastery in some degree of the symbolic language of the book, non-formal education may be a direct learning experience adopting whatever methodologies may be suited to the client as he is, whether literate or not.

Whilst formal education is relatively inflexible, requiring full-time attendance over long periods of time at a particular place, non-formal education is likely to be more flexible since it will normally be available on a part-time and spare-time basis as and when the clientele is available, and for as long and as often as may be required or possible. Many non-formal activities may be located close to the life and work of the clientele whereas schooling tends to withdraw people from their normal life context and to isolate them in specially designed institutions. As a result the education provided will be closely related to the home or to the workplace, will not be so much a preparation for doing something at some time in the future but for applying the learning experience as it is learned.

The close relationship which non-formal education at least promises between learning and application has further significance. We have argued that training in skills is insufficient in itself and needs to be matched by motivation both to learn and to apply the skills and by the opportunity to put skills into practice. Whilst formal education may communicate certain skills, it commonly finds that the motivation of its pupils, whilst strong, is not of the kind which the teachers and the curriculum developers prefer. Pupils may be highly motivated to learn but in order not so much to apply the skills as to achieve a certificate, and consequently the manner in which they learn, whilst perhaps effective for examination purposes, may not be such as to enable them actually to use the knowledge they have gained. Moreover, as we have seen, schools are not concerned with providing opportunities for pupils to practice and apply their skills once they have left school. There is thus disjunction between skills, motivation and opportunity in the context of formal education. This is far less likely to be the case in non-formal education, where it is possible to bring these three elements into close relationship. The skills which are learned will be selected according to their immediate applicability in the daily life and circumstances of the client, there will be opportunity to assess the value of the skills in some tangible form almost immediately, and where, as is commonly intended, the educational process is linked with some other development activity in that particular area there is greater likelihood that the necessary support services will be available. If opportunity to use certain skills does not exist then it is unlikely that they will be taught, and if the motivation to learn the skills in the first place does not exist, this need will be approached by building onto an activity for which the motivation does exist.

Whilst formal education is available only to the young and even then is selective, depending upon the attainments of the child, non-formal education is geared not to attainment and qualification but to need and is therefore open to all. Whilst schooling withdraws a person from participation in production, non-formal education may be made available without disrupting the client's life.

This does not mean that he will not be required to make some sacrifices in order to participate in non-formal education. One of the strongest arguments in favour of non-formal education is that whilst schooling is heavily state subsidised (even though fees and other costs may be paid), many forms of non-formal education can be entirely paid for by the participants, firms, groups and individuals who will benefit from it, and it may be argued that where they pay a good proportion of the costs they are likely to value the learning experience more highly. Moreover since existing local resources will be widely used it may be argued that some forms of non-formal education will be relatively cheap by comparison with formal schooling which demands very considerable extra resources of plant and equipment and may often actually duplicate resources which are available in the local community – by establishing a school farm or workshop for instance. Equally important, perhaps, in the non-formal activities there will be careful consideration of cost/benefit ratios: it is unlikely that organisers and participants will engage in activities for which they must pay without being fairly sure that the expenditure will be worthwhile, and since these activities are practical and specific it is likely to be a good deal easier to make an assessment of that benefit. Schooling, on the other hand, as well as being costly is conventionally less concerned with cost/benefit ratios and the benefits are less easily measurable.

On the other hand we must not simply assume that all non-formal education will necessarily be cheaper than formal provision. The latter affords opportunities for economies of scale which may be denied to non-formal activities, mounted as a whole range of small-scale activities each affecting relatively small numbers of people.

These, then, are some of the considerations which have been advanced in arguing for greater provision of non-formal education. Later in this chapter we shall be looking at the formal school and examining some of the ways in which it is thought we may be able to reform it and to counter some of the criticisms presented in analyses of the above kind. At this point we shall remind ourselves that we are not simply concerned with formal *or* non-formal education. The kinds of activities which have been mentioned as being non-formal in character do not make up the whole of the learning needs of our societies. Perhaps, as has been argued, they are likely to be better than schools for bringing about immediate and practical changes in the way of life of our peoples and perhaps they will reinforce efforts to promote self development. But our societies will continue to need people with knowledge both broader and deeper, as well as of a different kind, from that needed in our day-to-day lives in order to deal with affairs at a national level and to lead the way in bringing about longer term change.

Later we shall be looking again at the question of the relationship between formal and non-formal education. At this point, however, we must turn our attention to the practice of non-formal education to assess the validity of some of the claims which have been made on its behalf. Although the non-formal education scene is too complex to be studied comprehensively and in detail here, we need to examine briefly what has been done, and what is being done, in some of the major sectors of activity.

## Literacy Programmes

Efforts to reduce rates of adult illiteracy which run at between 80 per cent and 90 per cent over much of Africa have a substantial history. In part these have been motivated by the belief that literacy is a human right and illiteracy a source of shame, but in part also by the growing recognition that, whatever its value in its own right, literacy is a tool for promoting national development in all spheres. An illiterate population, it has been argued, may be condemned to continuing the modes of production of its ancestors. Literacy would act as the bridge between fatalistic passivity and uncomprehending acceptance, which has been thought of as characterising many rural peoples, and real participation both in promoting and in determining the nature of the social transformation thought to be necessary. It would act in this way by facilitating a flow of vital ideas and information to the masses, increasing their awareness of the situation in which they live, and of the possibilities and choices before them. It would motivate them to increase their efforts to break out of the poverty cycle, to adopt more advantageous modes of production and distribution, stimulating the desire for skill training, without which such training had been shown to be largely ineffective; it would enable them to participate in civic affairs, both local and national, and reduce those kinds of injustice which stem from ignorance; it would make it possible for them to learn rapidly and cheaply ways of improving the quality of their domestic lives.

The outcome of such thinking was the development in the 1950s and 1960s of large-scale mass literacy campaigns, similar in nature to earlier pioneering efforts in that the aim was to provide rudimentary general literacy to the whole adult population of particular areas. Such programmes were often greeted with considerable enthusiasm in those areas, and in some of the more successful campaigns the teaching of literacy was accompanied by elementary numeracy and led directly into the formation of groups and clubs in which other instruction such as in hygiene, nutrition and child care were taught, and into other community development activities. On the whole, however, the results of such campaigns proved disappointing. Enrolment rates were often high initially but dropout rates were also high. This was sometimes attributed to poor teaching by ill-trained instructors and to the use of materials and methods designed for use by young children, sometimes to the excessive demands upon the time and energy of participants, taking them away from their normal farming and domestic responsibilities, and sometimes to sociological problems involved in teaching mixed classes of men and women, young and old, and high and low status. Often, also, wastage was attributable to the fact that the real motivation for participation was largely confined to considerations of status – a man might pride himself on being able to write his name but the benefits of more advanced literacy were often less apparent. Indeed a fundamental difficulty in encouraging people to persevere with what is, after all, a demanding activity was that very rarely did general literacy of this kind lead immediately to practical benefit, higher production or increased incomes. Furthermore rates of relapse into illiteracy among those who did persevere and were awarded certificates of achievement proved generally excessive, mainly perhaps because of the dearth of suitable follow-up literature, the production and distribution of which proved more laborious and expensive than had often been anticipated.

Although there were examples of more successful mass literacy campaigns, their impact was at this time insufficiently wide-spread to make significant inroads into rates of illiteracy among Africa's rapidly growing populations. There was general reluctance to make available the resources necessary for the creation of the large corps of skilled teachers and community development workers which would have been needed, and for proper analysis of the effects of pilot campaigns. Most of the funds expended on adult education were devoted to the extension programmes of natural resources departments. Education departments tended to concern themselves almost exclusively with the formal school systems, which consumed the lion's share of whatever resources could be assembled for educational purposes. Indeed in the financial situation of the time the massive investment in adult education which had been called for since the 1920s could only have been made at the expense of the formal system. Yet all the arguments in favour of eradicating adult illiteracy could equally well be used to justify the further extension of primary education to cut off illiteracy at its roots. By comparison with full-time education over a period of years, according to a carefully structured and broad curriculum, adult literacy programmes appeared at best very makeshift substitutes, even to the adults they were intended to serve.

Moreover those concerned with extension work among rural

populations were by no means always convinced of the fundamental significance of literacy. They were inclined to argue that
the best way of communicating with a farmer in order to
persuade him to make significant changes in his modes of
production and way of life was unlikely to be through written
advice and instructions despatched from a distance. Was it not
clearly better to maintain direct and personal contact, combining discussion with demonstration and taking into account the
individual personality and circumstances of the farmer? At a
later stage, perhaps, when the farmer was already committed to
new methods and regular reinforcement might be necessary,
written communication might well play a valuable role but in the
early stages expenditure on making him literate might drain
funds away from more fundamental undertakings.

Advocates of adult literacy programmes did not find it easy to
present a convincing case in face of these arguments. Their own
experience had been inconclusive and their own thinking was
sometimes unsatisfactorily vague and idealistic, and too little
concerned with cost effectiveness. Ahmed has pointed out that:

> far too many programmes have been spawned by nothing
> more than a well meaning faith in the virtues of literacy rather
> than being guided by a clear concept of the ways that, and the
> circumstances in which, literacy can help people and what is
> the best way of giving literacy to those who are under-
> privileged and deprived in many respects.[6]

Many of the assertions about the importance of literacy which
had been made, and which continue to be made today, are not
grounded in rigorous research and evaluation and the impact of
literacy is certainly more complex than was often supposed until
recently. Correlation studies of groups of rich and poor countries
might well demonstrate that literacy is commonly associated
with prosperity but do not indicate which is cause and which
consequence. Whilst it might be argued that no major industrial
nation has ever achieved steady economic growth with a literacy
rate of below 40 per cent, it could also be argued that countries
exist which possess higher literacy rates yet which have remained
poor. Blaug argued that literacy alone was not a sufficient
condition for economic progress and was not of high value in a

subsistence economy though it might well become more important with the emergence of exchange economies.[7] A good deal, he pointed out, might be achieved by illiterate people even then, and he noted that the markets of West Africa and some quite large trading enterprises have long been successfully managed by illiterate market women and entrepreneurs.

Clearly, it was being argued in the 1960s, not all production functions demand literacy, and in the transitional state of most African economies it might be that groups of producers are capable of quite rapid progress so long as they include in their number a sufficient proportion of literates, the effect of whose presence would spill over to their neighbours. What this proportion might be was in some doubt and would inevitably vary from situation to situation. However Indian experience was suggesting that there were dangers in relying upon too small a proportion of literates since these were likely to include the more progressive farmers who might seek to take advantage of their opportunities at the expense of their less progressive and less fortunate neighbours. Moreover the absence of widespread literacy was likely to reduce 'second generation' effects whereby the surrounding groups and communities have an opportunity indirectly to benefit from the progress made in certain key areas. We were also being reminded that we should not be concerned solely with the economic arguments, that perhaps the earlier social welfare and civic concerns were tending to be lost sight of.

These arguments, together with the very limited degree of success of earlier mass literacy campaigns, led UNESCO to abandon its proposed world campaign for the eradication of mass illiteracy and to adopt in 1965 a new selective and intensive strategy of functional literacy on an experimental basis, associated with a deliberate attempt to evaluate the results and answer some of the questions which had been raised. A number of African nations including Algeria, Guinea, Malagasy, Ethiopia, Mali, Sudan and Tanzania participated in this programme. The intention was to relate literacy to the particular collective and individual needs and to the circumstances of specific target groups within the national populations. Not all groups had the same need for literacy and the intention was to provide differing tailor-made kinds of programmes linked to development needs, including preparing man for a social, civic and economic role that goes far beyond the limits of rudimentary literacy training. The very process of learning to read and write should be made an opportunity for acquiring information that can immediately be used to improve living standards; reading and writing should lead not only to elementary general knowledge but to training for work, increased productivity, a greater participation in civil life and a better understanding of the surrounding world, and should ultimately open the way to basic human culture.[8]

In practice, however, the programme tended to equate the concept of functional literacy to that of work-oriented literacy, equipping the learner not only to apply learning immediately in earning his living but preparing him to take advantage of other programmes of training which might be available. In practice too, in the cases of Guinea and Tanzania, there was noted a tendency to convert the selective approach into large-scale nationwide campaigns.

A critical study of these experimental programmes which commenced in 1967 has been made but unfortunately has yielded somewhat inconclusive results. Indeed attempts to measure the impact of literacy on development generally had largely to be abandoned. Studies of its impact upon the behaviour of individuals suggested that this was very limited:

> Relatively few (probably less than a third) of all socio-economic changes advocated in the various programmes were, in fact, ever adopted by participants. And these changes, on the whole, were those which were perceived by participants as having some immediate personal benefit and requiring little expenditure of time and resources to achieve. Thus, notwithstanding the high percentages of such modest changes which were regarded as 'positive' by the Evaluation Unit attached to UNESCO's Literacy Division, the fact is that these positive changes were very modest in nature and few in number.[9]

This result, however, contrasts with a number of studies drawn from various parts of the world by UNESCO in 1970. These found that in respect of increasing production and reducing family size literacy made a significant contribution which justified increased investment in literacy programmes.[10] Towards the end of the 1970s we find ourselves still without firm answers to many of the questions raised in the 1960s. It is being suggested that there should now be a return to simpler and potentially cheaper kinds of literacy programmes, possibly providing literacy training only when development activities and available literature have created both a real demand for literacy and genuine opportunities to apply it. It may be that we should not continue to rely upon conventional and labour-intensive techniques of training but look to the new technologies of mass communication to improve effectiveness and reduce costs. There is perhaps more general agreement with the notion that adult literacy should not stand alone but be more coherently linked with other forms of adult education and planned in support of other development activities.[11]

## Extension Services

Agricultural extension services, whilst varying considerably from country to country, have existed for many years in most African countries. Similar, though usually smaller-scale, extension services have been operated by other government departments independently, notably in respect of health and co-operatives. The agricultural extension services, which were often quite diverse within a single country, continue to be operated by agricultural departments and ministries and seek to persuade farmers to increase and diversify production through the introduction of new farming practices. Secondarily they may seek to persuade rural women to adopt new homecraft practices though commonly this tends to be left to a variety of other, often voluntary, agencies working in this field. Oddly, in view of the significant role of women in agriculture, extension programmes tended to focus primarily on the menfolk. Essentially they sought to bring farmers into personal contact with advisers and demonstrators, and it was argued that through such means guidance could reach even the least educated and progressive farmers who might otherwise remain unaware of the potentiality of new crops and methods. In practice, however, because the resistance to change was greatest among those who were most dependent upon traditional practices and had the most to risk in changing them, extension agents commonly tended to concentrate upon the wealthier and more progressive farmers in the belief that these could serve as a model for their fellows. This ideal was rarely realised and the practice was also criticised by egalitarian thinkers such as Nyerere who saw the danger that his country was becoming 'a nation of individual peasant producers who are gradually adopting the incentives and ethics of the capitalist system'.[12] Consequently, in some socialist countries concerned with equalising opportunites and rewards as much as with increasing production, extension approaches were modified and absorbed into co-operative agriculture approaches.

In most African countries, Coombs and Ahmed point out,[13] the effort was not so much to produce a nationwide extension service to meet the needs of all kinds of farmers in all parts of the country, as to promote the production of certain kinds of cash crop for export (where circumstances favoured this) with a corresponding neglect of food crops and subsistence agriculture. Extension became concerned not simply with teaching new techniques of cultivation but part of a wider process involving the development and supply of new seeds, fertilisers and insecticides, and the collection, storage and marketing of produce, often through specially created marketing boards. The pressing need for increased production of major export crops tended to lead to authoritarian practices on the part of extension workers with compulsion not infrequently being applied. In consequence these workers sometimes became regarded by farmers less as allies and helpers than as inspectors whose motives were not clearly understood and whose advice might quietly be ignored where possible.

The efficiency of even the more enlightened extension services depended upon a number of factors of which the number and quality of the field workers was the most crucial. In Kenya and Zambia extension staff came to number approximately one to every 1000 farm holdings, a proportion recommended as a minimum by the UN Food and Agriculture Organisation but one which obviously made it impossible for them to meet the majority of their clientele on a regular and individual basis. Yet even this figure compares favourably with the situation of most other

African countries: Malawi, for instance, with one worker for every 1800 holdings; Senegal with one for every 2000 families and Mali with one for every 8500 families. The quality of the extension staff has also been criticised. They have sometimes possessed an inadequate amount of formal education and subsequent training, and their career patterns have encouraged the more able field officers to seek to move speedily into administrative posts carrying greater seniority. Morale has often been insufficient to sustain them through programmes involving extensive and arduous travel with inadequate transport and poor communications, and dealings with often suspicious local farmers with whose language and culture they were not necessarily familiar. Often field workers found themselves loaded with ancillary duties – the enforcement of regulations, the collection of data and the maintenance of records – and working to a considerable extent in isolation from other similar workers with minimal support and not even a coherent local development plan to direct their own activities. The tendency to concentrate upon particular clients and areas, and for advice and instruction to become stereotyped, was reinforced by these factors.

Extension services also depend upon the quality of the research upon which their guidance is based. However research findings need to be carefully interpreted in relation to particular geographical situations and, since extension workers were commonly trained to communicate information rather than to diagnose local needs, mistakes were not infrequently made which sometimes severely retarded growth of confidence in new ideas and techniques. Research centres have themselves been criticised for neglecting subsistence crops, and for concentrating too much on the production of crops and too little on vital matters of farm management, record keeping, accounting, use of credit facilities, crop storage and marketing. A common failing was the tendency to underestimate the amount of time and effort needed to convince farmers of benefits which seemed all too obvious to agricultural officers: technical research was rarely complemented by sociological research to guide dissemination practices because the need for this was not generally recognised.

As we have noted above, there has been growing consciousness that agricultural (and indeed other) extension services would benefit from being more closely associated with training approaches and from closer association in the field between different kinds of technical worker within coherently planned development programmes. Once again we should note that whilst the concept appears to have much to offer, it may not be an easy matter to apply in practical situations, certainly not without substantial qualitative improvements in the training and utilisation of staff. All of these things will cost money, and sadly the history of extension services like that of many other non-formal education programmes has been one of inadequate finance.

## Animation Rurale

An alternative approach to mobilising the rural masses and one which sought to combine extension with training activities was developed in some French-speaking countries. *Animation Rurale* is a technique which was first developed in Morocco in the 1950s and taken up notably in Senegal after 1960 and by Mali more recently. The following brief discussion is based upon the experience of Senegal.

As with community development programmes in other African countries, *animation rurale* is concerned with harnessing the energy and resources of local communities in their own development. It is clearly understood not to be simply a process whereby the people may be re-educated and conditioned to accept those kinds of change which may be initiated by government agencies and through the use of national resources, but rather one which would reduce dependence upon these agencies and make unnecessary the deployment of large numbers of extension workers. One of its principal functions was to provide living links between the somewhat limited numbers of expert extension workers who were available and the local people. This was to be achieved by training some of the more progressive local people to serve as *animateurs*, catalysts of self-development at village level capable of identifying what might be done to improve production and of encouraging their fellow villagers to do it. At the same time the *animateurs* would provide a link with extension workers and be able to obtain their assistance. In this way the initiative for change would largely remain in the hands of the local people themselves.

The *animateurs* would in no sense become officials. They were to be volunteers, democratically selected by their fellows, who were and would remain farmers. Nor would they replace traditional leadership in their villages. Their role was to be based not upon authority or status but upon expertise and personality.

Training for *animateurs* was provided in stages. The first stage was an intensive course at Centres of Rural Animation consisting of two major elements, civics and understanding of the national and local development situation, and knowledge of the various techniques in agriculture and animal husbandry which might be appropriate in their area. The training was designed to be a process of participative practical experience and discussion rather than of formal teaching by experts, providing a model by which adults might learn how to deal with other adults more appropriately. A later second stage of training would more specifically be concerned with the technical skills of production and management, providing opportunities for working relationships between *animateurs* and technical extension workers to be developed.

The *animateurs* would, after training, be introduced to their own community and their role explained by the Centre Director. Thereafter they would seek to work with *animateurs* in neighbouring villages to provide a mutually supportive cell developing their activities cooperatively over the wider area. By 1967 some 7000 animateurs had been trained in more than 50 centres and approximately 20 per cent of the local communities in Senegal were being served. A range of complementary and support services and organisation was also brought into being including Rural Expansion Centres to provide technical support and a strong thrust was being made in the direction of encouraging co-operative societies.

However this latter development was in part a recognition of the fact that 'animation' alone was not enough, that to encourage a desire for change and progress was capable of breeding frustration if the community did not possess some crucial kinds of capacity to bring about the changes. The movement suffered from too much stress upon self-help and too little upon providing the material and technical assistance inputs which were necessary to make the efforts and skills of the people themselves effective. Other difficulties were also experienced arising from the fact that the role of *animateur* is an extremely sophisticated and difficult one. Frictions arose between the *animateurs* and traditional leadership, despite the provision of training sessions for village chiefs, and between *animateurs* and other extension workers. It appears that a substantial measure of success was nevertheless achieved by these workers, more especially in those areas where parallel extension services were strong. The main value of rural animation may have been in respect of paving the way for these services and enabling them to be more effective than in promoting grass roots self-help development activities. Unfortunately the extension services were themselves insufficiently developed to take advantage of the situation and after 1967 when new recognition was given to the importance of technical services, their development tended to replace rather than build upon the network of rural *animateurs*. In 1970 *animation rurale* was reorganised, its production-oriented activities were taken away, and it became a cultural and social organisation concerned principally with rural youth.

## Training Programmes

A high proportion of non-formal education projects in Africa in recent years have been concerned with skill training. Whilst the range and variety of these programmes is very great, there are perhaps three main categories of activity which we should note. These are pre-employment training programmes for mainly urban industry, skill-upgrading programmes for industry, and training programmes for farmers and craftsmen in rural areas.

Pre-employment training programmes for industry mainly focussed on school leavers both because of the need to supplement what education they had received with vocational training and because of a generally held belief that for skilled occupations in the modern sector, training could best be built onto a foundation of general education which had not merely improved the potential trainee's communication skills but prepared him for the higher degree of discipline, timekeeping and application demanded by modern-sector employment. Whilst government departments had for many years provided training schools for their own apprentices, and other government programmes had come into being to serve industry generally, these had tended to be extensions of the formal school system, often taking the form of trade schools run by ministries of education with access being based on selection from formal schooling. However a number of specialist training programmes less clearly articulated with the formal education system, such as the centres for training motor vehicle mechanics in Nigeria and the Ivory Coast, had also come into being. Many pre-employment programmes have been developed by non-government agencies such as the Young Women's Christian Association which operated training workshops in Kenya, Tanzania and Zambia, and examples existed of community-based training centres such as that at Luanshya in Zambia which sought to finance themselves through undertaking contract work. Some of these, like the privately run Opportunities Industrialization Centres brought into being in six African countries on an American model and intended to provide school leavers with both vocational training and job placement, received financial aid from overseas donors.

Skill-upgrading programmes mainly providing on-the-job training for employees are largely sponsored by governments, as are the National Vocational Training Institute in Ghana, the Industrial Development Centres at Zaria and Owerri, Nigeria, started in 1964 to assist local entrepreneurs through advice and training in order to stimulate growth of small-scale industry, and the particularly interesting Vocational Improvement Centres established from 1965 in six northern Nigerian States. These centres, though usually run by ministries of education, apply no minimum education entry requirements and are open to people without formal education providing they have worked at their trade for at least two years, even though their training programmes are directed towards government trade tests. They operate part-time, normally in the evenings, and possess no physical facilities of their own, making use of local government and school workshops available in the town on which they are based. Similarly, they employ only a relatively small number of permanent staff and make extensive use of lowly paid instructors drawn from local industry, government employment and technical schools. Consequently their average per capita cost has been only about one-ninth of that of a conventional trade school.

Operating on this basis the centres are able to charge no fees and have proved popular. Each centre is likely to be training about a hundred workers, mainly in the fields of furniture making, building and carpentry, motor vehicle maintenance and repair, and electrical installation. Since a principal objective of the centres is to encourage the growth of small scale industries and it is intended that successful trainees may set up in business on their own, elements of general education and business management are also included. Although drop-out rates are high and pass rates in the trade tests are fairly low, it must be remembered that the centres are attempting with very modest trainees to provide the equivalent of a three-year, full-time course in a government trade school in one year of evening instruction, and it must be assumed that even those who complete a substantial part of the course will gain additional skill which they may make use of in their existing employment. It is not yet, however, evident that the training offered by the centres is making much contribution to the growth of local industry and generating additional employment and demand for training. This may partly be due to the fact that more than half of their intake is drawn from government departments and large firms probably motivated by the possibility of a salary increment, relatively few being already self-employed.

A number of programmes, however, are operated by larger firms. In Zambia, for instance, which is well provided with industrial training institutions, a high proportion are provided by private firms. The structure of industry in many parts of Africa, however, inhibits such provision. A very high proportion of firms are extremely small and unable to provide more than very informal on-the-job training for their employees, whilst major firms may be reluctant to invest heavily in training for their own employees if these are later lured away by other firms. The efforts of the Kenya Government to encourage firms to undertake industrial training through the introduction of a compulsory levy used to support those firms which do so are worthy of note. The national industrial training scheme based upon such levies supports two polytechnics and two national industrial training centres, responsible respectively for more than 60 per cent of higher technician level training and 40 per cent of intermediate level skill training. Since most courses are open only to employer-sponsored trainees, the training provided is economically related to effective demand. In 1973 the Tanzania Government directed all employers and also all government departments and parastatal organisations to provide one hour of work time per day for the further education and training of their employees and to appoint workers' education officers to organise programmes including literacy, production skills and political education.

Farmer training and associated programmes have been widely provided, notably in eastern and central Africa. Often they take the form of farmers training centres, many of which are long established and which provide short residential courses in improved agricultural practice to the farmers. Their wives, who may accompany them, receive instruction in various aspects of home economics. These centres are often run by ministries of agriculture in association with their extension services and a number are run also by churches. The costs of such centres may be defrayed by sale of produce from centre farms.

Possibly the best known examples of such centres are the farmer training centres of Kenya which were established from 1954 onwards drawing upon the successful experience of the Jeanes School at Kabete which remained in operation from 1934 to 1961. By 1971 there were twenty-seven such centres each with its own farm. Whereas originally one-year courses had been provided, the centres have more recently mainly provided short courses in very specific skills often lasting only a week. Some difficulty was experienced in recruiting and retaining staff for whom no adequate training in adult education methods was provided and whose career structure did not encourage them to remain in the centres. In more recent years the centres also suffered from a severe decline in popularity amongst farmers and they were increasingly used for other kinds of training. What evaluation of their work has been done suggests that the products of the centres were more likely than other farmers to adopt improved farming methods although it has also been suggested that this may be attributable less to the training provided than to the fact that those farmers who attended courses were themselves more innovative than their fellows.

The approach adopted in the Rural Training Centres of Senegal was somewhat different since it sought to provide training for farmers and other workers in the rural areas of a kind which would be successful without the ongoing support of an agricultural extension service such as was assumed in the Kenya situation. The aim was to produce a cadre of progressive farmers through intensive and systematic vocational training. This programme, which was begun in 1960, differs considerably from the *animation rurale* approach which was being developed in Senegal at the same time, in that it emphasised the capacity of progressive farmers to influence their fellows not through teaching or advising but through the example of their prosperity. In this sense it is closer to the thinking about agricultural development current in the interwar years. It seems that whilst many of the highly trained farmers produced by the centres were able to increase their production very considerably, others found the absence of support services too great a handicap, and their neighbours tended to resent them rather than seeking to emulate them.

These rural training centres were, however, seen as only one part of a broader programme of providing intensive institutional-ised training for rural workers in Senegal. An associated programme of rural artisan training offered young artisans a structured sandwich programme in metalwork, carpentry or building, consisting of three periods of training, each of three months and separated by three months back at work. The programmes were carefully designed to relate to local conditions and to avoid developing the kind of urban skills and certification which would encourage the artisan to migrate to the towns. By 1971 eight centres were in operation, three for farmers, four for artisans and one for women. Permanent facilities and full-time specialist staff were employed, involving high costs in view of the fact that each centre could accommodate only 36 trainees at a time. In practice, however, the artisan training centres have been unable to attract sufficient artisans to fill even the limited number of places available even though a tracer study suggests that a significant number of trainees had been able to utilise the skills taught and in certain trades at least had been able to increase their income. It is possible, though not certain, that the cost of leaving one's trade to attend training programmes of this length was too great.

In its Rural Reconstruction Programme, Zambia provides an example of a not dissimilar programme for farmer training but one conceived of on a far larger scale, intended to reach a quarter of the total rural population of the country within five years and potentially capable of making significant inroads into the school leaver problem. The goal is to establish a Rural Reconstruction Centre in each district, each with a capacity to accommodate 800 trainees for two-year programmes of training following which the majority are expected to settle permanently around the centres and to provide an impetus for local development on the basis of collective farming. It is too early to assess the success of this ambitious programme.

## Brigades

The brigade pattern of non-formal training for out-of-school youth originated in Botswana in 1965 and has since been taken up in Ghana and Kenya though it is the Botswana model which has attracted most attention. In Botswana brigades were initially conceived of as a means of providing a more appropriate form of post-primary education and training than was afforded by conventional secondary school courses and were associated directly with the secondary schools at Serowe and Swaneng. More recently they have evolved independently of the formal school system whilst continuing to offer a balanced combination of general education and skill training. They seek to promote rural development both indirectly through training activities to produce young people with the skills needed in those areas and directly through undertaking contracts for government or for local people and organisations, and by involving local people in the management of their activities. Perhaps the main innovative feature of most, if not all, brigades is their attempt to develop more effective training procedures through associating training firmly with production and to cover recurrent costs through their own production activities. In this way brigades may be able to serve a number of functions within a relatively low cost framework.

Thirteen main centres have been established, together operating over 60 brigades with a total of about 2000 trainees in various fields including building, carpentry, agriculture, textiles, mechanics and handicrafts. The brigades today differ considerably in character, some providing training in modern-sector skills leading to government trade tests, some organised on a production workshop or farm basis, and some in the agricultural sector utilising the services of a small, mobile instructional unit. The earlier brigades were organised as relatively simple training operations extending over three years, following which the trainees were sent out to seek employment. However there was speedy recognition of the fact that training was of little value if jobs did not exist and concern was expressed that many trainees were unable to find employment of the kind for which they had been trained, many of them joining the drift to the towns where the prospects were brighter. Consequently, most recently established brigades, particularly in those fields where national demand is less certain than in the construction trades in which the earlier brigades specialised, have tended to offer what is termed *in situ* training, closely related to job creation. This has particularly applied in respect of farmer training in which efforts are now made to secure land upon which trainees may be settled before the training programme commences. Thereafter the training may be conducted both on the brigade farm and on the trainees' own farm settlements. A survey conducted in 1976 showed that 83 per cent of the trainees managed to find employment in their trade within three months of completing training. This is encouraging, though the relatively small numbers involved suggests that there is still cause for concern.

Experience has shown that management skills of a high order are necessary in the operation of brigades if they are to cope successfully with the problems presented by the often low standards of motivation possessed by trainees drawn from among the rejects of the formal school system. The balanced programme of general education and skill training is often difficult to maintain in face of pressures for courses of a secondary school nature opening up opportunities to gain conventional certification. The effective integration of training with production presents difficulties in the absence of sufficient highly skilled instructors. Indeed in 1973 a Brigade Survey Mission strongly criticised the brigade system on the grounds that the demands of training and of production were irreconcilable and in consequence neither was being adequately achieved. The mission proposed instead that conventional district trade schools be established but the Botswana government rejected this recommendation. There are also problems presented by weaknesses in the support, supply and communications services of the country. It has been suggested that the poor performance of some brigades may be attributed to management failure, and it is of interest that a Brigade Skills Development Centre to train managerial as well as instructional staff is now proposed.

However it is thought that the brigades have been successful in avoiding over-bureaucratic administrative procedures which might have constrained their development, largely because they have not been dependent upon the Botswana government for finance. They have been allowed to develop in different forms and under the auspices of various agencies though the three brigades operated directly by the government have perhaps been less successful because of management and financial rigidity. It has been clear, however, that some coordination with necessary government support services has to be maintained and there are obvious advantages in the brigades themselves making use of common services and rationalising their efforts, as in bulk purchasing for example, whilst retaining a high degree of self-sufficiency so as to retain flexibility and local relevance. The establishment in 1969 within the Ministry of Education of a National Brigade Coordinating Committee representative both of government and the brigades, together with the practice of developing clusters of brigades from a smaller number of brigade centres, each under a single authority, should greatly facilitate the maintenance of this balance. All brigades are now to be operated by independent trusts under the control of a board of local people, a development which may be of considerable importance in ensuring effective community involvement in order that *in situ* approaches may be developed and that training, production and employment activities may be successfully integrated in particular areas. The Botswana Government has begun to subsidise the brigades through paying a proportion of the salaries of instructors and making allowances available to trainees.

Among the recent achievements which have attracted attention have been the building of two hotels from local materials, which brigades now own, the development by a welding brigade of the Makgonatsotlhe tool carrier, an ox-drawn multi-purpose vehicle for ploughing, planting and towing which has been recommended by the government as a cheap and effective substitute for imported equipment, and the recent opening of the first bicycle plant in Botswana by another brigade. The introduction at Serowe in 1975 of a bridging course designed to recruit primary school leavers too young to enter the brigades directly has attracted interest. The course consists of half general education and half training in a variety of production activities, and lasts for three years. The problem of financing such courses unable to pay for themselves from production has led to the suggestion in the 1977 Report of the National Commission on Education that the Ministry of Education should consider supporting such courses nationally as a skill-based, post-primary programme alternative to lower secondary education.

Whilst a substantial degree of success has been claimed for the brigades, and the self-financing capacity claimed by many of them suggests that the approach may be more widely extended, a number of reservations remain. Aid from international development agencies and private donors has played a significant part in establishing many brigades. The extension of brigade activities is likely to involve the Botswana government in increasing financial commitments. Many trainees continue to migrate to seek modern-sector employment in the urban and mining areas. Relatively few seek to work in the rural areas, which, whilst needing certain kinds of skill for their development, cannot readily or immediately offer the trainee the opportunities he is seeking. The direct contribution of the brigades to local development through undertaking projects and stimulating the local community to take advantage of their services has not been as great as it might possibly have been because of the tendency to locate brigades too far away from the communities they might serve. 'Brigades as presently organised, do not need the villages and the villages have little to offer them, though brigades could be instrumental in raising the living standards of the villages'.[14] However it may be that community participation in management and the *in situ* policy can help to overcome these problems. It must, however, be recognised that the capacity of brigades to finance their own activities must depend to a significant extent upon there being local demand for what they produce, and that those areas which are most in need of development may be those least able to support brigade activities. The problem of staffing and the excessive dependence of the brigades upon expatriate staff willing to work for modest salaries must also be overcome.

The most critical question, however, is the extent to which the brigade system is capable of contributing to the solution of the problems of a country like Botswana. Considered as a solution to the school leaver problem it is clear that the contribution must be modest until brigades are greatly increased in number, and this must be dependent upon the capacity of the country to employ their graduates and purchase their production. A policy of cautious expansion and diversification appears to be indicated at this time together with careful monitoring of the effects of the new policies. Considered however as an economic means of providing some of the intermediate level skills needed by the national economy, brigades may well have a good deal to offer, though once again their activities must be matched with absorptive capacity. Considered as a multi-purpose tool for promoting rural development, brigades may, if more consciously organised to avoid past deficiencies, be capable of making a useful contribution both in stimulating and in supporting local self-help activities. However they must principally be considered training institutions and, if their expansion is to be geared to employment opportunities, their overall contribution to the rural areas is likely to be modest.

It has been suggested that brigades might well be most valuable in areas which possess a strong local market but it would be unfortunate if brigades were merely to confirm the relative advantage already possessed by these areas. The possibility of a number of poor communities pooling resources in support of a brigade programme may well offer some hope.

## Village Polytechnics

Village polytechnics as developed in Kenya are another way of attacking the problems described. They originated in 1966 at the instance of the National Christian Council of Kenya (NCCK). The number of polytechnics grew rapidly and by 1978 there were over 170.

The activities of the village polytechnics are focussed on primary school leavers. The farmer training centres and rural industrial training centres which were providing some training opportunities for adults were thought too expensive to cope with the large number of school leavers, approaching 70 000 in 1966, who would not be able to find employment, further training or education and a cheaper alternative was sought which would at the same time be more closely related to the needs and absorption capacity of rural villages. Village polytechnics were therefore conceived of as small, non-residential, centres, providing not the specialised skills offered in trade schools but generalisable skills associated with the farming activities of the neighbourhood. Whilst a general education component would be included, as in the case of the brigades, in order to promote among trainees an awareness and understanding of their situation, no effort was to be made to replicate formal schooling. The products would become or remain self-employed in the agricultural areas. A deliberate effort was made to avoid over-elaborate and expensive buildings and plant, and staffing support was received from overseas voluntary and official bodies.

Originally the main financial support of the polytechnics was the NCCK with additional funds coming from the local community and churches. Whilst some support is received from sale of products and the undertaking of contracts by some polytechnics, self-financing is a far less prominent feature than in the brigade system. Nor has training been so closely related to production. From 1971 the Ministry of Co-operatives and Social Services began to convert its youth centres into village polytechnics, to provide financial assistance to others, and gradually to assume responsibility for co-ordination. Fears have been expressed that this may lead to increasing formalisation and systematisation within a nationally organised programme and so reduce the responsiveness of polytechnics to local situations.

Initially the village polytechnics tended to adopt relatively formal and centralised operating procedures with students following prescribed courses within the institution; however less formal procedures with much of the instruction taking place on the student's own farm or workplace were evolved in many of them. There has also been a change in the nature of the curriculum followed. By 1970 the strongly agricultural focus of the programmes had been modified by the inclusion of more technical skills including trades training, though at a relatively modest level, but with a heavy emphasis on traditional building, carpentry and tailoring. This was partly in response to the hostile reactions of polytechnic students to the informal, agriculturally oriented programmes but partly also a consequence of the negative response of the Ministry of Agriculture which discouraged extension workers from spending time on village polytechnics instead of concentrating on production activities.

The outcome has been a relatively cheap form of provision with costs per student running at about half that of non-residential secondary education. Most courses run for between six months and two years. Whilst in the early years it was estimated that about half the trainees were able to find employment in which to use their skills, about one-third moved away from their home areas and of these a high proportion sought other work, further training or education, and it seems likely that with the spread of village polytechnics and the limited absorptive capacity of the poorer areas, this proportion is likely to increase. A number of observers have commented that village polytechnics have not received the kind of enthusiastic support from local communities which has been given to schools built and managed by many such communities in Kenya, independently of the government school system, on the 'harambee' or 'pull together' principle. Harambee schools are of course more conventional educational institutions offering greater promise of modern-sector employment.

The crucial problems of improving the employment opportunities and prospects of the rural areas in order to create a real and extensive demand for the kinds of skill the village polytechnics offer, of encouraging the growth of the movement without stifling local initiative and without losing that capacity to respond to often quite small-scale skill needs of local communities, may still remain. Clearly, as in the case of brigades, whilst the village polytechnics may well have an important contribution to make to absorbing school leavers and promoting rural development, this contribution will be small in relation to the scale of the problem, since only about 5 per cent of school leavers can be accommodated even in the increased number of polytechnics envisaged. Both institutions need to be developed within the context of rural development generally, and may need to keep in step with, rather than move ahead of, that development.

## National Youth Services

Several African countries have established national youth services following the introduction of the Ghana Young Pioneers in 1955 with the benefit of Israeli experience in this field. Their purposes have generally been to mobilise unemployed youth not for military purposes, although military patterns of organisation and uniform are commonly employed, but for undertaking project work in the cause of national development. In the course of doing so a contribution may be made to relieving immediate unemployment pressures, though the numbers involved have made little significant impact on this problem. They also provide vocational training and the opportunity to accumulate a little capital to enable 'graduates' to find appropriate employment. A further major emphasis, particularly important in the National Youth Service Corps of Nigeria, has often been to inculcate through common participation in the programme and through appropriate education and deployment programmes those attitudes which are believed to be desirable for the promotion of national unity, the work ethic and a spirit of service. In part this emphasis has been concerned with remedying the dysfunctional attitudes and inappropriate levels and kinds of skills with which young people leave formal schooling. Their purpose therefore is largely an educational and training one, the cost of which may partly be borne from the contributions received from project work.

Basic training, consisting of physical training and the inculcation of corporate discipline, is usually followed by an educational programme including both elements of general education and of skill training. Deliberate efforts are made to avoid programmes which duplicate formal schooling in order that they may be both immediately practical and avoid encouraging aspirations for further education and employment of a kind other than that to which the vocational training component is itself directed. Ministries of education are not responsible for the operation of the schemes.

The nature of the training programmes and of subsequent projects varies though in the Malawi Young Pioneers and more recently in the Kenya and Tanzania national youth services the emphasis has been on rural development. Experience on a co-operative farm prepares the participants for later involvement in land settlement schemes. In the Kenya scheme a three-month vocational training course may be provided in masonry, carpentry, motor vehicle maintenance or electrical installation and repair. This training has been provided in a special training unit in Mombasa but it should be noted that in several countries there has been a trend away from such centres (which have proved expensive) towards training in the field.

The popularity of such programmes is attested to by the fact that applicants substantially exceed in number those who can be accepted, by low drop-out rates and generally satisfactory performance reported in the field. However the scale of the services is small, generally between one and three thousand, and is reported to be declining. The reason for this is their cost. Although difficult to assess because of support received from outside agencies and because of expenses absorbed in other ways, costs clearly vary considerably. By comparison with formal education it would appear that on average the cost of national service is very close to that of an equivalent period of secondary education. In Malawi, which has not made use of expensive training camps and centres, the cost has been calculated to be a little over half of this but in Zambia, which has used such facilities, costs are about three times that of a secondary boarding education. Costs constitute the main constraint upon the expansion of national youth services. Moreover whilst some services claim considerable success in placing their products in appropriate employment, a major question exists as to whether this would be so if numbers were substantially increased. Nor is it clear that external financing would be available to support this expansion. It may well be argued that alternative patterns of non-formal education may achieve the goal of skill training more cheaply and expeditiously though possibly at the expense of the attitudinal goals.

## Self-development Programmes in Tanzania

A number of the programmes described above, whether they are regarded as mainly mass general education, extension or training, also contain a substantial component of local leadership development and seek to promote the capacity for self-development of local communities. The long-standing community development tradition, *animation rurale* and some of the training programmes for farmers and other workers fall into this category. However there are other programmes which are more specifically concerned with leadership training mainly directed towards the strengthening of local institutions which are central to self-development. This is a particularly important characteristic of the Tanzanian approach to non-formal education. Some of the Tanzanian programmes came into being prior to the inception of the ujamaa village strategy but a diverse range of programmes is now being developed which are clearly seen as being the means to produce the various kinds of community leadership needed if ujamaa villages are genuinely to become socialist self-sufficient communities in the years ahead. These programmes are an interesting blend of formal institutionalised procedures and less conventional educational methods.

The nationwide learning system to which Tanzania is committed is rooted in a network of adult education classes built up by the Ministry of National Education from 1970. These classes, which may take place in homes, village schools or anywhere a group of people may be conveniently collected together, are intended to be essentially self-directed with the members deciding for themselves what they want to learn and where and when they want to learn it. Their activities will be facilitated by ward and divisional co-ordinators working with adult education committees at each level, and may include learning new farming or craft techniques, home improvement and health practices, literacy and general education subjects, as well as discussion of political affairs and local issues. This network of autonomous classes provides a basic framework through which other specialised leadership training programmes may extend their influence to a wider number of people and enrolments totalling several million people are now claimed.

Courses of study for higher levels of political leadership have for many years been provided at Kivukoni College in Dar es Salaam and, notably through studies in political theory, economics, sociology and history, have contributed a great deal to the ideological unity and commitment of the ruling party, the Tanganyika African National Union, now the *Chama cha Mapinduzi* or Party of the Revolution.

More recently a number of local centres providing this kind of training for local party leadership has been brought into being, linked with Kivukoni College, which has become a higher level institution for those who have completed courses at local centres. The programmes of short courses and seminars continue to emphasise studies relevant to Tanzania's chosen pattern of development but also include training in the techniques of disseminating the principles of ujamaa. The products of these programmes will be able to participate more effectively in the nation-wide network of adult education classes, which lay considerable stress on understanding of the national ideology and policies.

The Rural Training Centres, which were run by the Rural Development Division of the Prime Minister's Office and which it was intended to establish in each district, were intended to provide for a variety of production skills but also for political education. In 1978 the centres were transferred to the Ministry of National Education to be remodelled as Folk Development Colleges to provide improved facilities for a wider variety of courses for local leadership cadres. Participants on the short courses offered by these centres are selected by their fellow villagers and are expected to communicate what they have learned to their fellows on return to the village, and to play a leading role in applying this knowledge.

A further area of interest is the well-developed programme of training offered by the Rural Development and Co-operative Division for the members and staff of co-operatives. The co-operative movement has a long history in Tanzania but with the adoption of the ujamaa strategy it was called upon to play an even more central role in promoting the establishment and strengthening the operation of ujamaa villages. Production and marketing on a co-operative basis had to replace private trading at all levels in the economy, production had to be stepped up, a stronger domestic market generated, local savings and investment encouraged and credit facilities to support these activities made more readily available to communities. All this required not merely the creation of a network of primary societies to produce the crops and regional co-operative unions to market them under the guidance of the national Co-operative Union but an extensive training structure to ensure efficiency and to allow development to take place whilst retaining a strong emphasis on the autonomy of local societies consonant with the principle of self-reliance.

The Co-operative Education Centre at Moshi provides, through its system of regional centres, study groups and seminars for local committee men and members but extends its outreach through correspondence courses and radio programmes. Those who successfully complete programmes on this basis may then attend residential courses organised at the associated Co-operative College at Moshi for periods ranging between two weeks and several months. The Co-operative College also provides training for the smaller numbers of full time staff of the co-operatives in, for example, accountancy, bookkeeping, management and administration. By these means relevant training is provided to all levels of leadership in the co-operative movement, whilst through national campaigns organised by the Co-operative Education Centres efforts are made to inform and interest the general public in the functioning of their co-operatives.

The problems faced in providing this wide range of programmes for diverse clienteles have been considerable, notably those of maintaining a sufficient number of qualified and efficient education officers to staff them, and high wastage rates, particularly in the correspondence programmes. Nevertheless this imaginative and comprehensive approach to the production of local leadership for the co-operative movement offers a most interesting model of non-formal educational activity geared to community self-development.

## Multi-purpose Centres

The bulk of the projects thus far examined have been single-purpose projects. We conclude this brief survey with some account of multi-purpose agencies which appear to offer promise of providing more effective linking of activities with saving of scarce resources. As yet these are far fewer than the specialised projects and are in the early stages of development, consequently it is with their *potential* that we are concerned.

Kenya offers the best example. In 1969 the country found itself with a substantial network of Farmer Training Centres and a diversity of other single-purpose centres run by ministries, local government and voluntary agencies. The distribution of these activities was uneven and some were operating at below capacity. In other cases the back-up resources were not available for proper functioning and development. The government allocated to the recently established Board of Adult Education responsibility for consolidating these various centres into District Development Centres, commencing with two experimental centres. Each centre, with its own Director and staff, will be responsible for determining local priorities in consultation with the local community and co-ordinating the services to be provided, with sharing of facilities and staffing. The various ministries involved would establish training wings at each centre which would therefore have capacity in respect of many aspects of rural development – agriculture, community development, health, skill training for trades, co-operatives. This arrangement would introduce a much needed degree of flexibility enabling the centre to operate at fuller capacity by responding to local needs as they arose, and drawing together the activities of the various sectors. The Centres would also be associated with field operation through the establishment of administrative offices for district operation by the various ministries at the centre and through support for local non-residential training centres in the district.

The particular significance of this approach is that rural development is no longer conceived of as merely implying increases in production but is a multi-faceted process to which a wide range of activities may make their contribution. Development will take place through the interaction between these activities and whilst there should be room for a diversity of patterns according to the resources and situation of particular districts, some means needs to be sought whereby their co-ordination may be better planned and implemented. That this should be achieved without laying on the process what Coombs and Ahmed have called the 'deadening hand of traditionalism and uniformity',[15] which they see as heaviest where central bureaucracy assumes control, is attested by experience in a number of countries. For example in Tanzania it is reported that the new Folk Development Colleges, which are multi-purpose institutions, have lost much of their practical focus in their evolution from rural training centres, and that as a result of poor utilisation of staff and facilities they have become about two-and-a-half times as expensive as secondary boarding schools.[16] That

co-ordination should be achieved without reducing the involvement of local people in decision-making which affects their lives is
suggested perhaps less by experience as by theoretical considerations based upon the necessity for balancing external inputs
with self-help, and here it is clear that it is a balance which should
be sought. Too much responsibility for their own development
cannot be thrown onto the shoulders of poor communities at this
stage. The Kenya model which seeks co-ordination through
largely autonomous local institutions rather than central
bureaucracy may be a model worthy of replication.

## Conclusions

A number of general conclusions about the current operation of
non-formal education approaches in Africa may be drawn,
although the enormous diversity of these programmes and the
dearth of useful information about many of them make these
conclusions tentative at best.

It is readily apparent that non-formal education in Africa is
not a novelty. Many of the activities which have been mentioned
have a substantial history although others are comparatively
recent and cannot yet be conclusively evaluated. Many problems
have been identified and much experience has been gained in
dealing with them. The fact that these problems are being
experienced should not be a cause for despondency but rather a
reason for taking project evaluation and the sharing of experience more seriously, and for undertaking intensive preliminary investigation of local and national situations before
undertaking particular projects or proposing extension and
replication of projects which appear to have achieved some
success. It should be clear that non-formal education in all its
various manifestations is of itself no easy and complete solution to
our educational and developmental problems, but this awareness
should encourage us to approach it in a constructively critical
manner and to examine to what extent, in what ways and under
what conditions one or other kind of non-formal education may
contribute to the solution of these problems.

At this time we remain ignorant even of the total scale of non-
formal educational activities in our countries let alone of their
cost and cost-effectiveness. In their survey of some 75 program-

mes in 15 countries conducted in 1971 Sheffield and Diejomaoh drew some conclusions which in all probability remain valid today.[17] They believed that the financial basis on which many programmes were operating was extremely shaky. In a number of cases there was excessive dependence upon external aid, even in theoretically self-financing projects, with the consequent danger of programmes contracting or collapsing with the eventual phasing out or withdrawal of this aid. The natural reluctance of donors to finance recurrent costs was throwing a heavy burden upon local agencies and national governments but the ongoing success of a programme, let alone its successful extension, must inevitably depend upon their ability to carry it for a substantial period of time. This fact is sometimes overlooked in the euphoria evoked by advocates of self-financing programmes. The extent to which self-financing is possible even for certain limited kinds of programme such as the brigade system has yet to be clearly established. The possibility of undesirable side-effects, such as the limitation of training in range and depth by the need to concentrate upon production activities or where the training institution enters into direct competition with local producers and indeed its own graduates for the sale of its produce, must also be taken into account. The belief that non-formal education is likely to be largely paid for by its clientele may well have some justification but if expensive training involves the payment of high fees there is the danger of excluding from training programmes those who are in most need of them. The tendency to adopt 'formal' training procedures and to institutionalise non-formal education, which is quite pronounced, may well render invalid some of the claims that non-formal education will be cheaper than formal schooling. And if we are going to claim that the more formal approaches are justified because of their greater efficiency, we shall need more rigorous cost-effectiveness information than we currently appear to possess. We face a fundamental difficulty here that it is rarely possible to make such comparisons between formal and non-formal education or between various kinds of non-formal education because of the considerable differences between them in terms of goals and clienteles.

We cannot therefore simply assume that non-formal alternatives will be cheaper than formal education, though under certain circumstances and for certain purposes some of them may be. In any case it seems extremely probable that any major extension of non-formal education will demand substantially higher financial commitments by governments, both to prime the pump and to meet at least a proportion of recurrent costs, than they have often been willing to accept in the past. Sheffield and Diejomaoh concluded that the overall national commitment to non-formal education, both in the public and private sectors, had been grossly inadequate in view of the scale and importance of the task. Although a number of countries have increased their financial allocations to non-formal education since this report, their general conclusion may still have some validity.

This raises a further consideration: that in consequence of their financial commitment, but also because of the need for some degree of planning and co-ordination in relation to clearly perceived priorities, governments will need to involve themselves more effectively than has often been the case in the past. Non-formal education is not at present a system and possibly it never can be in the sense that all activities can be interlocked tidily within a single coherent conceptual and administrative framework, but without some planning and some means of ensuring that non-formal activities are not competing with each other for scarce resources or creating demands for support services which cannot be met, there is some danger that proliferation of small projects may create confusion and waste. Yet it may be that government involvement should be directed towards ensuring that there is effective co-ordination rather than necessarily implying government management of provision. A high proportion of the cases of non-formal activity was being undertaken and managed by non-official bodies each with its own resources of expertise and finance, of which perhaps fuller use should be made. It is also interesting that Sheffield and Diejomaoh noted that whilst governments were sponsoring a considerable number of activities, few of these appeared to be working as efficiently as privately managed projects. They offered no explanation for this but it may well be that voluntary bodies have of necessity to work more closely with the people in order to obtain their support and consent than officialdom may be inclined, or feel it is necessary, to do, and are therefore more strongly community-based than larger scale and remotely directed government programmes. In any event the kind of private and personal initiative which has resulted in the village poly-technics of Kenya and the brigades of Botswana, as well as in countless other examples of less well publicised activities, must surely be encouraged.

As has been noted at several points above, fears have often been expressed that centralised control and direction may bring with it not merely the 'deadening hand of traditionalism and uniformity', which may reduce the degree of necessary flexibility in projects which seek to meet the particular needs of one target group and to adapt in the light of experience and changing needs, but also undermine efforts to transfer to local people themselves responsibility for decision-making as a means of encouraging self-development. Admittedly, in few instances at present are local communities contributing significantly to the design and management of programmes affecting them but, it may be argued, this should be encouraged through deliberate decentralisation of management responsibility. Clearly, therefore, a balance should be sought between official and non-official involvement and between central and local management.

The planning techniques which are being applied to the formal school system are not, in any case, suitable for non-formal education. Each non-formal programme may require separate planning in relation to its own objectives, clientele and resources, taking into account other development activities in the area which it may support or draw upon. Therefore non-formal education planning must be decentralised, a process which will facilitate the involvement of local people in the process and discourage the tendency which afflicts centralised planning of regarding non-formal education in isolation. Whilst centralised planning would seek to bring various non-formal programmes into effective relationship with each other, local planning is more likely to bring individual programmes into effective relationship with what is actually happening within a particular community and with development activity generally.

Yet there will clearly remain need for planning above the local level in order to ensure support services are available both to stimulate activity and to sustain and develop it, and in order to focus scarce resources on agreed priority projects. For this purpose some form of regional planning network such as is emerging in a number of countries may meet the need, being able to view non-formal and other educational activity alongside other aspects of development. This form of regional planning may be preferable to regional planning of non-formal education as an independent activity for a further reason. As we have argued above, there has been a natural tendency among educationists to regard education as always of central importance to development; the fact is that often it is not and advocates of non-formal education must themselves be protected from the dangers of overvaluing their activities by being required to argue their case in a forum more widely representative of development specialists.

It is also apparent that most of the non-formal programmes which have been studied are very small in scale, the average enrolment in training projects ranging from 10 to 60 participants per year in most cases, whilst even extension programmes appear to reach only a small proportion of the populations which might benefit from them. Sheffield and Diejomaoh described the situation as being one of 'micro-solutions to macro-problems'. Yet major question marks hang over the potential for replication and extension of many of these projects, particularly in the skill training field. Whilst certain approaches such as the vocational improvement centres of Nigeria might be expanded substantially because of the limited costs involved and the considerable take-up capacity of at least the urban centres for the kinds of skill upgrading they offer, other approaches might involve high costs often because of the 'formal' procedures being used but also because their production might easily exceed the demand for particular skills in particular areas. The more successful of the skill-focussed schemes were those which were taking greatest account of the need for placing participants in jobs on completion of training. In the Bako project in Ethiopia it was found, for instance, that even well-trained youths might be unable to apply their farming skills because of their inability to obtain land and starting capital. On the other hand the Farm Institutes of Kano State in Nigeria and the Botswana Brigades were seeking to obtain a commitment from local communities that relevant local opportunities would be available before commencing a training programme. The matching of training activities with criteria for the granting of loans, as in some programmes in Nigeria, Kenya and the Cameroons, might provide a model for other areas where such loans are available.

The evidence that skill training should be associated with some degree of management training, whether for the rural or for the urban sectors, also appears clear particularly where, as is increasingly the case, the thrust of much non-formal activity is directed towards self-employment.

Certainly the conclusion must be that the business of skill creation, whether by formal or non-formal means, cannot be treated in isolation from the general problem of creating opportunities, and no amount of advocacy of training directed to 'self-employment' can disguise the fact. The underlying major question in regard to the expansion of non-formal training is, in fact, not how much will it cost but will the larger number of graduates emerging from these programmes be able to apply their skills, either in the rural areas for which they may have been trained or in the urban areas to which they will look in the absence of adequate opportunities nearer home. The experience of even the small-scale training programmes which exist at the present time suggests that there is need to pay much greater attention to assessing the absorptive capacity of local economies, an endeavour which has been largely neglected largely because provision for training has in fact been on such a small scale to date. The need for training activities to be effectively complemented by follow-up and support services, and for expert advice and encouragement to be available, along with credit, supply and marketing infrastructures is also clear, notably from Senegalese experience.

Sheffield and Diejomaoh concluded their survey with a very appropriate word of caution: 'Non-formal education programmes, no matter how well designed and funded, cannot by themselves solve the related problems of employment generation and rural development'. On the other hand: 'Research and development in these areas, however, must pay greater attention to the variety of opportunities for upgrading human resources outside the formal school systems'.

A further conclusion to be drawn is the need for dedicated, able and enthusiastic leadership in non-formal education projects. Such qualities are always in short supply and this fact might suggest that the growth of non-formal education should be undertaken cautiously with the maximum encouragement given to the development of leadership capacity. Mention has been made of the particular need to increase the capacity of local people to play leadership roles but it is quite clear that in the majority of situations, and notably in the early stages, a great deal will depend upon the quality of the field staff of government departments or non-official agencies. Experience suggests that there is need to pay greater attention to the selection and training of field officers for their role is one of unusual difficulty. No longer are they to be merely the transmitters of centrally-designed packages of knowledge or exponents of certain narrow skills: rather they are being called upon to act as *animateurs*, working with and not merely for the local community. Their sensitivity and responsiveness will be crucially important. Consequently we must recognise that there is a need to transform the attitudes of field staff as great as the need to change those of target groups. The need for field staff of different specialisms to work more closely together in the field may suggest that there is value in the approach pioneered notably at Kabete in Kenya and Tengeru in Tanzania many years ago of linking a range of staff training programmes within a single training institution rather than persevering with separate training programmes. Yet selection and training alone are insufficient. If morale is to be maintained, career structures must be evolved which encourage men and women of proven ability to continue in the field in which they have demonstrated their value. Once again the expansion of non-formal services may afford opportunities for creating such career structures but this is less likely to be effective where there is overmuch dependence upon central and regional bureaucratic hierarchies which may withdraw experienced staff from the point of contact with local people.

More attention should be directed towards improving the technologies of non-formal education. As Coombs and Ahmed have argued, non-formal education has, on the whole, tended to cling to costly, traditional and often formal modes of operation and, particularly, labour-intensive face-to-face techniques.[18] Non-formal education, it is argued, has a very considerable capacity for using a variety of technologies and if the scale of activity is to be stepped up to the extent which appears necessary there must be more intensive search for methods which are both educationally effective and of low cost. This does not mean in their view the adoption of advanced technologies such as computerised instruction and television via satellites which are likely to be beyond the capacity of many countries in the foreseeable future but the development and utilisation of existing technologies which have already proved their worth. As long ago as the mid 1950s the campaign against cocoa blight in Ghana demonstrated how an appropriate combination of techniques including literature, posters, radio recordings of a specially written 'jingle', and dramatised demonstrations conducted by specially trained field teams may achieve success. The remarkable achievement of the African Institute for Economic and Social Development (INADES) founded in the Ivory Coast in 1963 to provide instruction in farming, business management and home improvement through the use of correspondence and other distance learning techniques, and which now reaches out to fifteen other African countries, mainly French speaking, must be well worth careful examination. The use of radio study groups and notably of the *Mtu ni Afya* (Man is Health) radio campaign against common diseases which began in 1973 and is estimated to have reached a million people in Tanzania has taught many lessons as to their potential and the means of making them effective.

Whilst distance teaching techniques offer relatively cheap and flexible means of reaching the people over considerable distances and without withdrawing them from their work spaces, and whilst radio, television and film can cross the literacy gap, the value of combining these with some form of face-to-face and two-way communication has been demonstrated. The ambitious television project introduced by the Ivory Coast in 1967, which in addition to serving primary schools was to provide out of school education for adults in both urban and rural areas, was adjudged to have resulted in no significant behavioural change among the adults served and to require more direct follow-up action. Judicially used such media can help to stimulate rural activity and win support for the activities of other development agencies working in particular areas. We should also, however, note the lesson of Senegal's *Radio Educative Rurale*, a pilot project initiated in 1973 which succeeded in evoking considerable community response but found the government unable to provide the support necessary for the projects which radio and also television was intended to promote. For certain purposes correspondence courses as developed in the Institute of Adult Studies at the University of Nairobi have demonstrated their value, provided that the student is strongly motivated and the problems of student isolation from instructor, fellow students and library resources can be overcome. The Mauritius College of the Air, the Botswana Extension College and the Lesotho Distance Teaching Centre have pioneered the way in major developments of multi-technique distance teaching, with the support of the International Extension College in Cambridge. Up to the present such programmes have concentrated upon the schooled population but their experience may have much to offer in approaches to non-schooled populations.

However the need, as Coombs and Ahmed have argued, is to identify first the learning needs of particular groups, to assess what stimuli they are most likely to respond to, to take account of constraints which exist in respect of particular groups, and only then to decide what techniques or combinations of techniques are appropriate. This approach may be common sense, but, they argue, has rarely been followed.

Up to the present time, and in the great majority of cases, non-formal programmes are not seen as alternatives to formal education but as complementary provision. Indeed a high proportion, particularly of training projects, require some degree of formal education as a condition of entry and certainly of effective performance in training. There is a general belief among employers that nonformal training is more effective when it is based upon a sound formal education. If this complimentarity between formal and non-formal education is to be worked out in ways which do not undermine one or the other, it would appear that careful consideration should be given to the question of which forms of non-formal activity really require a basis of formal education, and what kind of formal education may best contribute to successful involvement in later, non-formal programmes. At this point we turn to examine some of the current trends in the reform of formal schooling.

# References

1. P. H. Coombs, with M. Ahmed, *Attacking Rural Poverty, How Nonformal Education Can Help*, a research report for the World Bank prepared by the International Council for Educational Development (Baltimore: Johns Hopkins University Press, 1974) pp. 24–5.
2. J. K. Nyerere, New Year's Eve Speech to the Nation, December 1969, quoted in B. L. Hall, 'The Structure of Adult Education and Rural Development in Tanzania', Discussion Paper no. 67, Institute of Development Studies, Sussex University, January 1975, p. 1.
3. J. K. Nyerere, Address to the International Adult Education Conference, Dar es Salaam, June 1976.
4. Coombs, *Attacking Rural Poverty*, p. 8.
5. *Ibid.*, pp. 24–6.
6. M. Ahmed, *The Economics of Nonformal Education*, (New York: Praeger, 1975) p. 91.
7. M. Blaug, 'Literacy and Economic Development', *The School Review*, Winter 1966, pp. 393–415.
8. UNESCO, *The Experimental World Literacy Programme: a Critical Assessment* (Paris: UNESCO and UNDP, 1976) p. 10.
9. *Ibid.*, p. 182.
10. H. M. Phillips, *Literacy and Development* (Paris: UNESCO, 1970).
11. See J. Bowers, 'Literacy and the Community: A Pan-African Perspective', in K. King (ed.) *Education and Community in Africa* (University of Edinburgh 1976) pp. 33–43.
12. J. K. Nyerere, 'Socialism and Rural Development', in *Ujamaa: Essays on Socialism* (Dar es Salaam: Oxford University Press, 1968).
13. Coombs, Attacking Rural Poverty, pp. 32–3.
14. NEIDA, *Inventory of Educational Innovations in Africa* (Dakar: UNESCO) p. 25.
15. Coombs, *Attacking Rural Poverty*, p. 146.
16. J. R. Sheffield, 'Basic Education for the Rural Poor, the Tanzanian Case', unpublished paper, 1979, pp. 7–8.
17. J. R. Sheffield and V. P. Diejomaoh, *Nonformal Education in African Development* (New York: African-American Institute, 1972) pp. 199–210.
18. Coombs, *Attacking Rural Poverty*, pp. 156–73. See also D. R. Evans, 'Technology in Nonformal Education, a Critical Appraisal', *Comparative Education Review*, no. 20 (1976) pp. 305–27.

# 10

# Re-schooling: Some Current Trends

In this survey of some of the more important recent trends in the reform of formal schooling in African countries some qualifications must be stated from the outset. We shall be discussing a number of key ideas currently very much in the forefront of educational thinking and referring to countries where attempts are being made to apply these ideas. However it would be wrong to assume that these ideas and practices are characteristic of schooling everywhere, even in the countries most committed to them. Indeed it could well be argued that the most pronounced trend is for existing patterns of schooling to be expanded without significant modification of their basic structures and functions. It cannot be assumed that even where a country has embarked upon a well-publicised process of reform it has necessarily been able to move very quickly. After ten years of applying a new educational policy the government of Mali ruefully concluded that 'it seems that the education system itself prohibits any fundamental ameliorations',[1] a statement we should find fully understandable in the light of our earlier discussions of the many powerful inertial forces at work in school and society alike. And again we note that many innovations have not been in existence for a sufficient length of time for worthwhile evaluation to have taken place.

We have discussed the widespread criticisms that schools create new elites and neglect the real needs of the majority of their pupils rejected by selection mechanisms, that they divorce pupils from their cultures and render them both unfit and unwilling to contribute to the development of their own communities, that they impede the growth of integrated national societies and do not contribute sufficiently to the evolution of stable democratic systems of government, and that they provide an inadequate return even in economic terms for the enormous sums of money invested in them. We have suggested that some of these criticisms are unjustified in that the schools have been allocated tasks beyond their capacity and roles which are conflicting, and that the reasons for their apparent failure may have more to do with unrealistic expectations and with the societal context of schooling than with the schools themselves.

We have described the growing interest in alternative patterns of education and particularly in the capacity of non-formal approaches to solve our problems. Yet it remains true that even at a time when African countries are seeking to modify their development strategies and give priority to rural development, and are urging the virtues of self-reliance at local and national levels, schooling is still seen as the crucial means of providing the mass education needed for such strategies to succeed. As the Ministers of Education meeting in Lagos in 1976 pointed out 'school continues to be regarded by the majority of African countries as an essential educational agent although its functions and role should be redefined.'[2] The conference made its contribution to redefining the proper functions and role of the school by spelling out a number of key principles which we shall take as our themes for this chapter. The reform of schooling should seek to integrate the individual with his community and environment, to equip him for a productive life and for full participation in the progress of that community. To these ends three seminal ideas were advanced, reflecting what some member countries were already attempting but re-stating them as component parts of a coherent strategy. These ideas, which we shall examine in turn, were 'the linking of school and the community; the linking of school and working life; the strengthening of the African cultural identity.'[3]

## The Linking of School and the Community

The linking of the school with life, or the integration of the school with the environment, means trying to make the school a motive force in the grass-roots community. The school should not be a foreign body within the community but an emanation of it, organising itself steadily for the community's development.[4]

Much depends of course on how we interpret 'community'. It could well be argued that schools have indeed served their communities and served them well but that the natural focus of their activities was the national community and the regional community. All of us belong to a whole range of communities extending in a continuum from the most local and personal to national and international communities in each of which we play different roles, possibly in accordance with different value systems, and towards which we have different degrees of belonging identity. The school, it may be argued, has a responsibility to prepare its pupils for all of these roles and levels of operation, but that in the past it has got its priorities wrong and unjustifiably neglected the 'grass-roots community'. As we enter the era of mass education educationists must remedy this neglect particularly at those levels of education which are most clearly mass education. For the time being, at least, this may imply that we should seek a closer relationship between school and community, particularly at the first level of education which will be terminal for the majority of our pupils, where the schools are more likely to be physically a part of local communities and at the same time less tightly enmeshed with the modern-sector occupational structure than secondary schools.

It would be unwise, however, to draw too clear a distinction between primary schools with a local community orientation and secondary schools which might be regarded as more nationally oriented. Although in practice selective secondary institutions will continue to feed tertiary education and higher levels of employment, so long as lower schools serve as instruments for selection they will be impeded in performing their local functions. Consequently in some countries efforts are being made to extend the concept of the community school to the secondary stage. In Guinea, for instance, it is intended that every school, no matter what its level or the type of education it provides, will be a *Centre d'Éducation Révolutionnaire* (CER) which will take its place in the life of the local community. Consequently 'for each stage of education, there is a concrete form of corresponding CER activity, which dovetails into the life of the village, the ward, the region and the nation.'[5] In other countries the effort is being made to eliminate the present sharp cut-off point between primary and secondary education by extending the range of open education and of post-primary opportunities and to reduce the backwash effect of selection by using new assessment procedures and guidance techniques. We shall refer to these later. At this point, however, we should note that the local community orientation will be easier to sustain where the schooling provided is clearly terminal.

Even the use of the term 'community' begs many questions. Where communities exist which comprise small and homogeneous groups of people, living and working together in close proximity, knit together by inter-dependence, close personal relationships, common value systems and strong awareness of their distinct group identity, it is relatively easy to conceive of a school functioning in a closely linked manner within it. However such communities are far from universal over Africa. In many areas people are widely dispersed in extended family homesteads between which cultural and personal ties may be strong but not matched by organisational coherence. There are also the nomadic groups in which the sense of community is not associated with permanent settlement in a single location. Many common ideas about community-linked schools appear less meaningful in circumstances like these and it is interesting to note, in policies of population concentration such as in the ujamaa villages of Tanzania, the *aldeias communais* of Mozambique, and elsewhere, recognition of the desirability of creating village-type units in order to make social services, including education, more effective.

Even where population density is high, the sense of community may be absent. We are aware of urban areas which include large numbers of recently arrived and transient people who remain unassimilated into the group, and in which relationships may be very different from those of the archetypal village, cultural and organisational cohesion may be lacking, and belonging-identity may be weak. The nature of such communities may necessitate very different school-community links.

In surveying recent efforts to link school and community we shall be generalising a great deal and the reader must be prepared to consider how far the approaches and ideas presented here would apply to particular communities known to him.

In the following sections we shall be examining some of the main strands in recent attempts to link schools more closely and fundamentally with their communities. These strands take various forms in different parts of Africa and are combined in various ways. They fall into four main categories:

1. efforts to increase the 'relevance' of the education provided to the young, through environmentally related curriculum reform;
2. efforts to involve the community more effectively in the activities of the school in order that it may be the school *of* the community and not merely a school *for* the community;
3. efforts to serve the community directly and to meet the learning needs of all its members;
4. efforts to develop the school as a community, both as a microcosm of the external community and as a functioning part of that wider community.

As we shall see these categories are not independent of each other but are closely inter-related.

RELEVANCE IN THE CURRICULUM

Curriculum reform has long been the dominant feature of effort to achieve greater community relevance in schooling because of the belief that traditional 'imported' curricula tended to interpose a cultural barrier between the child and his community which meant that on leaving school he found it difficult to 'reintegrate' with the people among whom he was to spend his life. The process of decolonising syllabuses and textbooks has perhaps gone further in English-speaking than in French-speaking countries but is still continuing, hindered mainly perhaps by the costs and technical difficulties of materials production. It is doubtful if any country is now without its curriculum-development units or centres, usually based in universities or ministries of education, and international projects such as the Entebbe Mathematics Programme, the African Primary Science Programme and to a lesser extent the African Social Studies Programme have stimulated a flow of ideas into national projects.

It must be noted, however, that many of these innovations have been content merely to substitute local or African material for European material without significantly changing the structure or bias of the curriculum as a whole. Consequently, whilst pupils may have found their learning more meaningful, the reformed curriculum may have been no less 'academic' and functionally irrelevant than that which it replaced. It has been suggested that a truly community-oriented curriculum implies a changeover from one which is structured around the various disciplines of knowledge to one based upon an analysis of community learning needs, and that this might imply the use of short modules of instruction based upon practical activities.[6] However such a structure appears less suitable as a preparation for further education in which mastery of the disciplines may be more fundamentally important. Consequently it has rarely been tried out in formal schooling, though as we shall see various attempts at a compromise between the two are being made. Moreover much of curriculum development has been associated with the introduction of new methodologies, with the effort to move away from rote learning and teacher-centred procedures towards activity and discovery, child-centred procedures, and as such have been more an attempt to modernise education in terms of the best international practice than to make it relevant to the lives and needs of the child in his community. Many education-ists would argue that the adoption of methodologies which are likely to facilitate the understanding and application of know-ledge, to develop the skills of enquiry and problem solving, and to liberate the mind of the child are just as relevant to Africa as to any other part of the world, and certainly more relevant than the simple accumulation of factual knowledge. No doubt this is true but these new methodologies are essentially concerned with making the school more efficient in doing what it is already doing at a time when many people believe the school is doing the wrong thing. Such methods will again not significantly change the way in which the school functions in relation to the employment market and the local community and may indeed make it a more effective tool for cultural alienation, wherever such methodologies are themselves alien to local child-rearing practices as is the case in very many communities. For example it has been argued that the new primary approach in Kenya (now partially abandoned) stressing spontaneity, self-reliance and individualism is very much at odds with existing patterns of socialisation in that country which stress collectivism, submission, consultation and consensus.[7] There are as yet few studies of the ways in which African children learn and of the ways in which the fundamental culture of the school may differ from that of the home, and a good deal of the work which has been done has been concerned with ways in which the school may counteract the influence of the home regarding this as an important barrier to success in schooling. Consequently the child who succeeds in schooling is likely to be the one who has most effectively broken with the patterns of belief and thinking and modes of behaviour to be found in his community: society then rewards him with status and employment whilst deploring the fact that he, and even more his less successful classmate, appear to be no longer at home in their own communities. We must further ask whether in educating our children as best we can to develop in them the abilities needed for innovation in our local and national communities, we are not bound to encourage their tendency to look towards the towns since that is where these abilities will find a readier outlet. And of course, as we saw in an earlier chapter, we must ask ourselves whether schools should not seek to set a distance between the child and his local community if he is to be able to understand that community and play an effective role in helping it to change and adapt. Moreover the balance to be achieved between local and national community orientations is a matter which must be borne in mind throughout this discussion of community schooling.

The new school which we are seeking to build in some of our countries may well be totally different from that of Europe in function as well as form. The best international practice, therefore, may well be irrelevant. But at the same time as we develop a new school with new functions we must ask ourselves how the purposes served by the old functions, notably in respect of the production of leaders in the intellectual, political, technological and commercial life of our nations, may be met. Can we really hope to serve two such dissimilar sets of functions through one and the same educational institution? Hawes has commented that many of the larger-scale centralised curriculum development projects in Africa suffered other deficiencies in common – ambitious goals and policies, unrealistic time scales, high hopes and eventually very fragmentary success, even in terms of introducing the new methodologies and content into schools.[8] Whilst changes in the approaches to curriculum reform may be introduced, the fundamental question of possible conflict of objectives remains unresolved. Brief reference may be made to some of the efforts being made to innovate through the introduction of new subjects. These include the development of work-oriented studies to which special attention will be paid later. A common trend is the introduction of political education, often labelled civics but intended to do more than familiarise students with the structure of government and the operation of legislatures, judiciaries and the executive arms of government. In Botswana and Lesotho the secondary school curriculum now includes development studies, intended to incorporate this kind of civics teaching but in addition to introduce pupils to the social, economic and political problems of their countries. The intention is to develop commitment in the pupils but also to equip them with the knowledge and skill they will need if they themselves are to tackle the problems of development. Ideological bias is to be minimised and 'development practicals' outside the school are to be emphasised to give pupils a sense of real involvement. These practicals may include various production activities, farming, building and construction, repair and maintenance, both within and outside the schools.

In Tanzania and Zambia the aim may be defined as politicisation, the generation of awareness of national policies with a view to generating both understanding of and commitment to the policies of the government and the ideologies upon which they rest.

Whilst political education may produce better informed students, there is little evidence that it will bring about profound attitude change by itself or that the attitudes formed by students will be influenced in the particular direction desired by the syllabus writers. Moreover in so far as political education takes its place as a subject for study alongside other subjects in a conventional school, if it is examined it is likely to be taught and studied in a conventional way with the usual outcomes – a process of knowledge accumulation to meet examination needs; if it is not it will lack esteem and attract little in the way of effort. This same consideration applies to other curriculum innovations and that which can be most easily tested in the examinations may well prove to be that which is taught in the classroom. Hirji's criticism of political education in Tanzanian schools makes this point forcibly:

The contents are dominated by sloganeering and sycophancy, the emphasis being on forms, appearances, declarations rather than scientific understanding of social reality . . . Rather than permeating the entire curriculum and organisation of the school, political education has been relegated to the level of a compulsory examinable subject a pass in which is essential if one is to proceed to the next stage of education.[9]

Trends in the primary or first-level curriculum present a fairly similar appearance in a number of countries. There is commonly the attempt to compromise between the disciplines of knowledge and the desire to study the community as a whole by adopting a curriculum based on areas of study in which the community focus will be achieved through the integration of subjects and the introduction of practical activities. Unlike some of the earlier curricular innovations, new mathematics and new science, for instance, which were essentially importations of best international practice, these environmental approaches will, it is believed, through their focus on the local community rather than on bodies of knowledge, result in a more genuinely and uniquely African form of education.

The community schools evolving on the Kwamsisi model in Tanzania will have an experimental curriculum extending over four areas: literacy and numeracy, citizenship or political education, self-help and cultural activities, and environmental studies. These 'Mtuu' schools will however retain as subjects English, Swahili and mathematics upon which the selection examination at standard VIII is based. Since the number of classroom periods has been reduced from 40 to 27 to allow time for practical and skill activities, concern has been expressed that the pupils will suffer from being treated as guinea pigs whilst still having to compete on equal terms with children from other schools not yet part of the experiment. We note here the difficulties presented by new-type schools operating alongside more conventional schools, a situation characteristic of experimental or pilot developments. In Tanzania the problem is perhaps more apparent because the Mtuu programme is administered directly by the Ministry of National Education whereas elsewhere a process of decentralising responsibility is being pursued, and it has been suggested that stronger school-community links could be, and in fact are being, forged in the schools under local management.

The 'new school' in Benin will at this level offer three main areas of study: instrumental disciplines which in addition to literacy and numeracy are thought to include environmental and social sciences, practical activities appropriate to the transformation of the environment similar to Tanzania's self-help studies, and an introduction to political, civil, military, artistic, and physical education which will embrace Tanzania's political and cultural education. The Togo curriculum will be not dissimilar to that of Benin though here there is strong commitment both to lightening the curriculum (so much curriculum reform appears to involve levering in ever-larger packages of learning for children) and, interestingly, to 'the suppression of all that is purely academic, of all that is not immediately practical'[10] though this principle does not appear to extend so far as it might seem, since at lower levels literature will be retained as a subject and at higher levels the sciences, international languages and philosophy will appear. There is, however, a determination that all subjects will be studied as a means of understanding the problems, resources and potential that the country possesses.

The general approach of using the local environment as a laboratory is one which has long been commended by educationists in many parts of the world. There are strong reasons for adopting this approach in terms of making conventional learning more effective and meaningful which have little to do with generating concern for and ability to deal with the problems of the local community. In terms of this latter aim there are serious problems, notably of the capacity and willingness of the local community to allow itself to be studied on a continuous basis by generations of its children, but these are capable of being overcome through careful design based upon consultation. However the main problems of the approach are the extent to which the particular environment will support learning activities. Concern may be expressed that the child from a disadvantaged area may find much of his study circumscribed by the absence from that area of stimulating and fruitful kinds of study which are open to children in other areas. In the final resort a balanced education may demand that theory and the use of vicarious experience techniques retain a vital role in the educational process, and this will particularly be true as more advanced levels of education are reached.

Discussion of curriculum innovation must inevitably involve some mention of the procedures being adopted for the assessment of student progress and in particular for selection for those higher levels of education which will not be open to all. No matter how carefully we design our curriculum, reorientate our subject syllabuses, promote integration of studies and build from practice towards both theoretical understanding and skill for application, all may be undermined by the looming presence of examinations. Successful performance in these may be to a pupil the principal reason for being in school and so determine how he approaches various aspects of study, where he puts his effort and what kind of understanding and skill he seeks to develop. At the Lagos Conference the Director-General of UNESCO criticised examinations as being 'an element of rigidity and formalism which permeates the very spirit of the educational system, and takes no account of values, experience and skills which could well be used in many cases as criteria in assessing acquirements and aptitudes'.[11] The Zambian Draft Statement on Educational Reform published in 1976 suggested that there are four main lines of attack on the problem: to reduce the economic benefit to be gained by possession of higher educational qualifications, to eliminate selection within the school system by opening the system to all as far as possible, to separate selection from certification processes, and, lastly, thereby to free certification to represent attainment in all those aspects aimed at by the school and to free the school to promote and assess those aspects more effectively. Because the first line of attack is not within the power of educationists and the second only to a limited extent, the attention of reformers has focussed on the latter two.[12] The Lagos conference received a call from one of its commissions for examination reform to accompany reform of content in respect both of grade by grade promotion and terminal examinations. The commission however acknowledged the great difficulties involved. The community itself was often too accustomed to hierarchical structures based on academic achievement criteria to support reform which might reduce the emphasis on achievement tests and certification, and there were inherent difficulties in finding means of assessing a training system which is entirely new and unconventional – the difficulty of assessing practical activities, production, artistic creation, particularly when these are designed as co-operative activities, encouraging social values and attitudes, is very plain.[13] Yet some form of individual assessment is necessary wherever selection applies, and this alone is likely to undermine co-operative working and so distort objectives.

A survey of national primary leaving and secondary entrance examinations in 10 anglophone African countries in 1978 showed that in all except Ghana a single examination was used for both purposes though in Nigeria other selection examinations were used in addition.[14] In Ghana the examination was not used for primary leaving certification. All examinations were conducted in English, except in Tanzania where Swahili was used. All examinations were of the objective test or multiple choice type, except for language examinations in all except the east and central African countries where even language papers were of this type. Inevitably the selection function was viewed as more important than the certification function and often examinations were set with a view to what a secondary school entrant needed rather than what a primary school leaver should have achieved. The examinations were heavily weighted towards language proficiency and did not attempt to assess all aspects of the curriculum, notably practical, environmental and cultural subjects. Moreover the use of objective tests, because of the dearth of skilled examiners and the limited linguistic ability of the candidates, tested recall of facts virtually exclusively. Consequently their backwash effect upon the primary school has been greater than it might otherwise have been. Improvement in the quality of these examinations might have a beneficial impact upon the schools without perhaps ever reducing the tendency for pupils to learn in order to pass examinations rather than to apply skills in their lives.

In Tanzania, *Education for Self-Reliance* of 1967 called for formal examinations, which were then the sole mechanism for selection for entry to secondary school, sixth form and university, to be down-graded in importance. In 1974 the Musoma declaration still asked for greater weight to be given to school assessment made on a continuous basis. This is now to be implemented for entry to sixth forms (50 per cent weighting) and entry to university is now based upon recommendations from employers and the political party following a compulsory period of national service and work experience preceding university entrance, as well as form six examination results. In 1972 selection to secondary school had been based upon examination marks together with teachers' reports, but criticism of this system led to the adoption in 1973 of selection according to examinations plus cumulative records of performance maintained by the schools.

In Benin the diploma formerly awarded at the end of the primary course has been abolished and replaced in the new basic schools by continuous assessment. Pupils are 'guided' either to the polytechnic complex to learn a trade or to middle-level (secondary) education by advice from a guidance council. Similarly, in Togo continuous assessment is to be used together with continuous guidance to determine which of four kinds of second level school – general, technical, agricultural, or arts and crafts – a pupil will enter having completed six years of primary schooling and a two year observation stage. Admission to third-level senior secondary education in either general schools of the above four types or specialized training institutions is based on 'merit'.

There will be a great deal of attention paid to such developments as these. Time will tell whether 'community assessment' will outweigh academic attainment in Tanzania's selection but at present only about one in one thousand academically qualified applicants is turned down on grounds of inappropriate attitudes.[15] To the extent that academic achievement is still a central feature of the selection system it seems inherently unlikely that examination backwash effects on the school curriculum will be significantly reduced. The use of continuous assessment in place of examinations genuinely offers to open up a new degree of flexibility, able to take into account performance in a wider range of activities than an examination can test but much will depend upon those who are making the assessment in practice giving weight to other than the traditional academic achievements. The use of guidance may have an ameliorative effect if a child is made aware from an early stage whether or not his aspirations are realistic; he may during his course therefore be more willing to apply himself to those aspects of his education which will be relevant to the kind of further education or training he is likely to receive. It will not alone solve the problem of unrealistic aspirations however. Moreover the fairness of the procedure depends upon the skill with which counsellors work (and one notes the dearth which currently exists of diagnostic tests suitable for their use) whilst the acceptability of the process will depend upon its demonstrable fairness.

COMMUNITY INVOLVEMENT IN THE SCHOOL

The second major aspect of the efforts being made to link schools more closely with their communities is that of increasing the direct involvement of local people in the work of the school as teachers and resource personnel, as managers and as financiers. Again this is a theme which has a substantial history.

In part this was an extension of the idea that the community should be a laboratory for study in order that the content of the curriculum might be more relevant to the lives pupils led and would continue to lead in their community. Some of the earliest community schools in Africa recognised the need for their teaching staff to be augmented by local people possessing skills in craft and farming and also in traditional history and custom which the teachers, often drawn from distant communities, might well not possess. Also present was the idea that children should learn that not all the knowledge which was of value was to be found in textbooks but might also be learned from the storehouse of community experience. Malangali school in Tanganyika in the early 1930s perhaps took this idea furthest in its deliberate attempt to combine in the school the modern forms of knowledge of the outside world with the traditional knowledge of local tribes which was being conveyed to other young people outside the school. To this end the school appointed four Watambuli (elders with long experience in traditional education), one from each of the main local tribes, to come into residence in the school and to continue their teaching as part of the normal curriculum. In common with other similar experiments the practice was short-lived largely because of its artificiality in a context dominated by the prestige of modern knowledge and because of the departure of the education officer responsible for instigating the system.

Recent interest in the use of local people as teachers is not very different although in the current effort to introduce work experience into the curriculum the need to find instructors with relevant production skills has also been associated with the need to do so cheaply. The use of community personnel resources, as well as other resources such as farms and workshops, is increasingly being argued for on economic and not merely educational grounds. On the other hand teachers continue to be doubtful about the value of instruction provided by members of the community who may well be themselves 'uneducated' as well as unskilled in the art of teaching, pupils remain unwilling to give the respect due to such instructors, and the local instructors who have often found their work uncongenial have tended to be unreliable and to fall away. Moreover other members of the community have been doubtful about the importance being ascribed to practical work in the schools to which they send their children and whilst perhaps accepting the value of vocationally oriented courses have preferred these to be urban oriented. Why should the schools teach local production practices which they themselves could and did teach their children? And if these things were to be taught why should this be done by people no better qualified than themselves? They sent their children to school to learn what they themselves did not know: why did not the teachers allow the children to get ahead with preparing for their examinations which was the main job of the school? These are not trivial but, on the contrary, fundamental questions relating to the function of the school, and that they are asked by parents is important because of the influence they have on the success or failure of innovations.

A second important aspect of community involvement is the current trend towards the devolution of responsibility for managing schools and school systems to local people. Again in some measure this represents a return to the thinking of the interwar years in some countries. At that time, for example, encouragement was given to Native Authorities in Tanganyika to develop their own schools largely independently of government and to promote in these schools a 'tribal' character and orientation. The slightly later attempt by the then Director of Education to hand over to Native Authorities responsibility for the administration of the whole primary school system failed because the missions and the British government did not feel the Authorities to be ready to assume financial responsibility. In other countries community involvement was channelled through the missions themselves which provided and managed the bulk of the primary and many of the secondary schools. Mission schools were often argued to be genuine community schools in which the local congregation provided the land and built the premises, retaining ownership of the school whilst the missions provided the teachers and the professional supervision. Practice varied widely but although local communities might not be directly involved in management, they often possessed a genuine feeling that the school was their own to a much greater extent than in the case of government schools. The desire and willingness of local communities to support their own schools with money and work has long been demonstrated in many countries in ways ranging from the efforts of the Kikuyu in Kenya in the inter-war years to sustain their independent school system to those of present-day Kenyans to develop harambee schools and have them incorporated in the national system.

Rarely, however, did this community involvement extend to matters concerning the curriculum except in so far as the emphasis on literary and theoretical knowledge and on the international language, and the widespread failure to sustain the practical and local orientations of teaching which were generally thought by educationists to be desirable, reflected community pressure. In the post-war years the rapid expansion of education was accompanied by an increasing measure of central and of government control. In more recent years this resulted in the strange situation that the growing demand for community-oriented curricula was emanating from groups of people who were themselves outside local rural communities and formulated their ideas without real reference to the perceptions of need possessed by the local communities themselves. The introduction of decentralised administration in a number of countries, although valuable for other reasons, did not significantly alter this state of affairs. Parents and members of the community remained isolated from the places where the real decisions were taken and were encouraged simply to participate in activities of a social, fund-raising or labour-providing kind such as were commonly organised by parent–teacher associations (which were usually teacher dominated). The trend over the last few years towards devolution of real managerial responsibility to local communities is, of course, part of the wider recognition of the importance of encouraging greater self reliance in these communities.

In education this devolution has taken a variety of forms. Tanzania has decided that school committees should be established in all primary schools and should be elected by the parents of the pupils. These school committees will help to determine the school curriculum at least in respect of those local orientations which are to be built around the national core curriculum and those practical production activities which are to be jointly conducted by the school and the local community. In Kenya for a number of years free rein has been given to local communities to establish their own 'harambee' schools in parallel to the government school system. Today the bulk of nursery and day care centres in the country, half the places in secondary forms I to IV, and two pioneer harambee Institutes of Technology, the forerunners of perhaps a dozen more, have been provided in this way. In addition most primary schools in rural areas are built and equipped by the local communities, though remaining under government management. In Ethiopia it is intended that parents will be directly responsible for the management of their schools, including the appointment, housing and salaries of teachers through the decentralisation of control to some 30 000 farmers' associations. In Guinea all schools are to be managed by local authorities (*Pouvoirs Revolutionnaires Locals*) which will plan building operations, organise school production, supervise instruction and maintain discipline.

There are several reasons for this trend. The first, which underlies the Ethiopian and Tanzanian approaches, is the belief that local members of the community are in a better position to guide the integration of the school with the local community than are the teachers and education administrators unaided. The second is the growing need to tap community resources to finance educational development. The harambee movement in Kenya has shown how vigorous local communities may be in providing for what they clearly see as their own needs, whilst in Ethiopia it has been found that communities using local materials and local skills have been able to build schools of good quality at a cost less by at least a quarter than comparable schools erected by the central authority in the past. The third reason is that to involve local people in the financing and management of local schools, areas of activity in which they appear to participate readily, will spread among them awareness of their own capacity to solve other problems which face them and motivate them towards self-mobilisation. But responsibility for schools is not always thought of as being separate from wider responsibilities for development or as being simply an example of community action which may stimulate other actions. The two kinds of responsibility, for schooling and for development generally, are increasingly conceived of as being mutually dependent. Communities are being asked not simply to take increased responsibility for the education of their children but also for ensuring that their children can be productively incorporated into the community when they leave school. Thereby the community is assisting in the solution of two crucial problems, making education more directly relevant to community needs and opportunities, and promoting forms of community development which will provide more and better opportunities for school leavers.

This process of handing over responsibility to local people has perhaps been taken furthest in the context of ujamaa in Tanzania and in respect of middle level practical education in Senegal, but is present, though less explicitly stated, in the educational policies of other countries. It means that policy makers at central level can avoid making over-precise decisions about what needs to be done in local situations and can concentrate upon ensuring that appropriate structures are established through which decisions can be made and with facilitating the implementation of decisions taken. It has the further implication that whilst local people may not have ready answers to the problems which have defied us for so many years, given real responsibility, they may well in the course of time find ways to deal with them which are appropriate to their own situations. Problems which may appear insurmountable when viewed globally may become more manageable when reduced to a local and personal level. Consequently there is occurring a shift of emphasis in the planning process. Whereas previously the devolution of responsibility was thought of largely as a means of gaining more efficient implementation of nationally determined policies through involving and thereby winning the support of local people, now we see the beginnings of more fundamental approaches in which devolution is seen as integral to the decision making and planning process. Inevitably there are many problems and some dangers in pursuing such a strategy. As Nyerere has pointed out:

> it will be some time before people in the villages learn to exercise power in matters relating to their area. The popular belief that people will take up power and responsibility as soon as it is offered to them is not true. People have to be educated in the democratic process.[16]

It may well be that the best way to learn to exercise power responsibly is through experience of exercising power. In the early stages, however, there is some danger that local people will find their role frustrating and come to resent what may appear to be an abdication of responsibility by their government. Moreover we cannot assume that the decisions taken will necessarily be 'enlightened' ones. Until there is a shift in the aspirational patterns of the people there may be no guarantee that they will readily pursue the development of community linked education or of work-related studies for instance. Is it not equally likely that they will wish to follow a more traditional line, encouraging patterns of schooling which are hierarchical and modern-sector oriented? Whilst it must be noted that in Kenya the harambee movement has recently extended into the field of vocational and technical education, its original momentum was derived from community demand for secondary education, and secondary education not of an innovative kind but modelled closely on the pattern of conventional state secondary schools. Admittedly this tendency was reinforced up to 1974 by the government policy of incorporating selected harambee schools into the state system, which encouraged local communities to create schools in an image which would attract a government takeover. In Tanzania, however, this factor does not apply, yet the private secondary schools which have come into being so incongruously in this planned society are deliberate in their attempts to copy the more formalistic aspects of the state schools in order that their pupils may have the maximum opportunity of transferring to state schools, which it is reported a substantial proportion succeed in doing.[17] Here the government has been forced to step in, prohibit the establishment of new secondary schools and encourage the development of post-primary technical facilities.

Studies conducted by students at the University of Dar es Salaam have shown how even in a social context which is more strongly supportive of community education approaches than would be the case in many other parts of Africa, community management of primary schools by no means necessarily implies support for innovative practice, may well create conflict between teachers and parents, and may be manipulated to serve the interests of particular groups rather than of the majority. More important still, there is a clear danger that where local communities are given freedom of action sufficient to evoke enthusiastic response, they may well follow courses of action which subvert national policy – as in Tanzania where it is clearly intended that admission to secondary education will be limited to the quite small numbers which can be absorbed by the economy and administration and that primary education shall be essentially terminal, but where private secondary schools mushroomed in the early 1970s to provide a quarter of all secondary places. This growth confirmed the tendency for primary schools to function as screening agencies rather than as terminal community schools. Since governments may well find it difficult to close down institutions established by local people with such enthusiasm and sacrifice and may, in consequence, have not merely to recognise but seek to regulate and control them, government policy may not merely be subverted but actually pre-empted and determined by community initiatives.

Equally significant, and again both the Kenyan and the Tanzanian experience is illuminating, the devolution of genuine decision-making responsibility to local communities may promote regional inequalities in that the richer and more 'progressive' communities are more likely to be able to take fuller advantage of their opportunities. The growth of private schooling in Tanzania and of harambee schooling in Kenya was greatest in those areas which were wealthiest and also, incidentally, already best provided with government schooling.

Other countries, too, have experienced problems with the growth of private profit-making institutions which too often have not merely provided highly conventional bookish education, because books are cheaper than facilities for practical activities, but have been of extremely poor quality even in conventional terms. There may well have been good reasons, as in Nigeria and Zambia, for government intervention. On the other hand, there are instances of private schooling which are indeed highly innovative and oriented to community need, under highly imaginative leadership of a quality all too rare in educational systems no matter how organised. The work of Tai Solarin at the Mayflower School at Ikenne, Nigeria, is a case in point. Dissatisfied with the secondary grammar school in which they were working, Solarin and his wife set about building a school of their own in which there would be greater freedom of thought and belief, less rigid discipline, and a strong stress on manual and practical activities. Gradually they built up a largely self-sufficient school community in which building, maintenance and food production were undertaken by the pupils, and which was both co-educational and residential. Solarin reports that concessions had to be made to public opinion – initially Latin was taught to give the school an aura of respectability – and its popularity rose as its examination results proved at least comparable to those of neighbouring schools. However governmental and church opposition to a school operating on what appeared a somewhat eccentric basis was less easy to overcome and critics have been numerous. Nevertheless, both through the school and through his outspoken participation in educational discussions, Solarin has injected a welcome dose of non-conformity and iconoclasm into the educational thinking of Nigeria.

A second example might be Asfaw Yimeru, the founder of the Asra Hawariat school in Addis Ababa, a mainly primary school of some 4000 children. Following the failure of its first school leavers to find employment, the school has stressed the importance of 'Moya' (family) education activities. The school follows the normal government pattern up to the fourth year, and has indeed been criticised for being highly conscious of the importance of examination success, but it has been argued that Moya activities place examinations in their true perspective. A sizeable minority of the enrolment still consists of the orphans for whom the school was originally founded and these continue to live in the school. In addition, however, some twenty local families live in the school's two compounds, turning them into villages in their own right. A community library has been established and evening classes for the adults are provided. Older and former pupils are encouraged to look after the younger children and to teach in the lower classes. Agriculture and craft are encouraged with the aim of turning out self-reliant producers, and much of the school building and maintenance is undertaken by the school community.

There is no doubt that it is not easy to strike an appropriate balance between promoting individual and community initiatives and maintaining central direction overall. As Weiler has pointed out, not only do we have to seek to reconcile divergent local perceptions of need and purpose with government's own conception of national purpose but we must recognise that devolution is more likely to involve decision-making through conflict than through consensus.[18] Tensions between parents, community leaders, teachers, bureaucrats and planners are inevitable in the process and may even be magnified by it. This should not however be taken to mean that the devolution of responsibility should be abandoned or that we should revert to processes of consultation which are merely a facade for central control. Devolution is clearly no complete answer but in the long run it offers some hope that schooling may be more genuinely an emanation of the community in a self-reliant society. Careful thought must be given to delineating precisely which areas of responsibility are to be devolved, to whom and through what machinery, allocating a measure of real responsibility whilst at the same time ensuring that local communities possess in sufficient measure the resources and support in the form of advice, expertise and money to make this responsibility a reality. And above all, perhaps, the development of community responsibility for schooling must not be seen as an isolated course of action but one which must be linked with other activities whereby a community may learn to take initiatives but at the same time act responsibly. This will be no speedy process and much will depend upon the extent to which central authorities sustain the genuine will that it shall succeed.

## SERVICES TO THE COMMUNITY

One of the basic characteristics of the community school as we now conceive of it is that it should contribute directly to the community in which it is situated, notably in terms of joining with other educational agencies to meet the learning needs of all members of that community. Again in much of this thinking we hear the echoes of the past. Not infrequently have schools been called upon to engage their pupils in community development activities, to send them out to assist in such matters as repairing roads and bridges, clearing drainage ditches, cleaning up market places and public spaces. Some schools have gone well beyond such activities and have been involved in important refforestation projects, piloting the production of new crops, and providing literacy classes for the adult population, whilst teachers have themselves frequently played an important role in community councils. Other schools have undertaken paid contract work in harvesting or the making or collection of building materials. For many years, too, it has been envisaged that the facilities of the school, often the most significant building in the community, should be made available to the adult community and to out-of-school youth for recreational, instructional and other purposes, and that school farms and workshops should be used by extension officers to demonstrate new techniques and crops to local farmers. Indeed sometimes, as in the Tanganyikan middle schools of the 1950s, schools were consciously designed for this purpose.

Whilst many examples may be given of such activities, in general it must be concluded that their impact was and is weak. The activities undertaken by pupils have been mainly thought of as contributions to their own education, developing their community consciousness through involvement in community action, rather than as positive service to the community. Activities tended to be sporadic, occasional responses to particular short-term local needs rather than sustained long-term programmes. To devise such programmes which would be within the capacity of school children and yet make a real contribution to the community, which would be educational and not merely menial activities exploiting the labour of the child, and which could be undertaken as a regular part of the work of the school year after year, demanded imagination and commitment from both teachers and community leaders. But both groups were inclined to believe that the real job of the school was to teach children and prepare them for their examinations. Members of the community who found an occasional visit to their workplaces by school children a welcome and diverting novelty were inclined to object if such visits became more regular and more demanding upon them, particularly when they did not either understand or necessarily accept the reasons for their being regarded as suitable objects for study. School facilities, particularly in the primary schools which were closer to their communities, were often unsuitable for adult use, and teachers, particularly at secondary level, have often been unhappy about sharing their equipment and premises with outsiders who might misuse and damage them. School farms and gardens were rarely sufficiently developed to be of value in extension work, partly because of the perennial problems of maintaining them during school holidays which were often intentionally arranged to coincide with the most important periods of the farming year to make it possible for children to assist their parents on their own family farms at these times. Many well-intentioned teachers found it difficult to overcome the psychological barrier which led local people to observe the curious goings on in the school gardens with interest but without feeling that these were of any relevance to them on their own farms. Finally the common assumption that school premises were under-utilised and should therefore be available for use by adults for substantial periods of time proved to be unsound where social demand resulted in the use of premises for double or even, as in Zambian towns, treble sessions and where the absence of electric or even of adequate oil lighting made impracticable their use in the evenings.

Efforts are now being made in a number of countries to overcome some of these problems, notably in terms of facilities. In Liberia and Tanzania the intention is to provide schools with additional facilities which will be designed for shared use, whilst in Ethiopia the aim is to provide communities with skill-training centres which will also be available to the schools. The initiative for such development stems largely from the non-formal sector of education but the logic of sharing facilities is unassailable. However, such additional facilities may be costly and one notes that in several instances the finance is being provided by international agencies. Whether model schools built in this manner will prove replicable across the whole country may be in doubt. More significantly we may perhaps ask whether the sharing of facilities really implies any fundamental change in the school. School and community may remain functionally separate even where facilities are shared.

We are again hearing the demand that teachers, in addition to their teaching roles in schools, should assume new responsibilities for the education of the community and, as one of the most important reserves of educated manpower available to local communities, provide leadership to the community. The Lagos conference considered that

> The teacher has to develop into, or make room for, a new type of educator who will be a community leader, an 'animateur' who will establish direct links with the community and various social groups, will provide career guidance and information on many aspects of modern life, will promote a scientific approach to life and to the environment and will establish with the learner a relationship based on exchange and mutual respect.[19]

Much of the quotation above relates to the qualitative improvement of schooling and it may be interpreted as regarding links with the community as contributing to this end. However the use of the word 'animateur' suggests that community leadership is understood to be part of the teachers' role and that they are not simply to be linking agents.

Some concern has been expressed in an earlier chapter about the concept of the teacher as 'superman'. Grabe has reported, for example, that in Upper Volta

> The lone teacher in the village R.E.C. (Rural Education Centre) is expected to supervise and carry out instruction, manage a profitable school farm, act as local animateur, form a liaison with the village leaders . . . In return for this variety of heavy duties he would be paid only half the salary of his counterpart in the primary school, have more limited security of job tenure, and almost certainly have inferior housing.[20]

It is not surprising that such teachers have failed to live up to highly inflated expectations and it is extremely doubtful whether the more favourably treated primary school teachers in that country would have been any more successful.

The role for the teacher which we are discussing is different from that sometimes asked of him in the past in perhaps three main ways. First, it means institutionalising teacher involvement in the community, requiring this of him as a regular part of his duties and no longer regarding it as simply an activity which an individual teacher may undertake from time to time if he wishes over and above his normal school work. Of course teachers are most likely to be invited to assist the community in matters to which their training and education is relevant – clerical work and accounting, for instance, or the interpretation of regulations or explanation of national events. But if they are to become genuine *animateurs* they must be equipped with new skills not normally thought of as being relevant to a teacher. Furthermore they must be given additional motivation for the task which may mean that credit must be given for meritorious work in the community. Again they must have genuine opportunity to do such work which may mean ensuring that their teaching duties do not take up the whole of their time and that the community accepts the situation. This is a vital point. In the long term the teacher must earn the respect of the people he is working with through demonstrating the value of what he has to offer, but in the initial stages he must be protected against allegations that he is neglecting his school pupils. The kind of teacher participation we may expect to see will differ from community to community, depending upon its needs, the availability of alternative specialist expertise and the strength of existing leadership. In the situations where the teacher is most needed there must be genuine competence and a new professionalism if he is to be more effective than his counterparts in the past, and even with appropriate training we are asking a great deal of him in terms of his adaptability and sensitivity.

Secondly, this new role is different in that the prime purpose of his community activities is to serve the needs of the community and not simply to provide experience and social training to his pupils. This implies that the role must be far more explicitly defined than in the past. Thirdly, it is no longer envisaged, as it often was in the past, that the school and its teachers will be the sole agents of education permanently located in the community, but rather that they will take their place alongside other agencies of nonformal education and of development generally working in and with the community.

A number of experiments is currently being conducted in

ways of training and deploying teachers to meet the needs of this new situation. UNESCO-assisted teacher training institutes have been established in Cameroon, Ethiopia, Ivory Coast, Sierra Leone, Liberia, Niger and Togo with the intention of training not simply classroom specialists but rural educators capable of initiating and organising a variety of community development activities. At Kakata in Liberia young primary school teachers are receiving training in techniques of adult education and on graduation will be allocated to rural schools in villages where they will be joined by agricultural development officers trained in another new centre along lines which will enable them to work co-operatively with the teachers. In its early stages Kakata faced a number of problems and for a time was forced to abandon the provision of practical experience of adult education within the programme. Only time will tell whether its young teachers, and particularly the young women among them, will have been able to make a significant impact upon the communities to which they were assigned, communities in which they might initially be strangers, unable to communicate with local people in their own language, and whether they will have been able to resist the inevitable pressure from their pupils and older colleagues that they devote all their energies to the education of the children in their schools.

In Cameroon the establishment in 1969 of the Institute of Rurally Oriented Applied Education (IPAR) was a significant development from the earlier Rurally Oriented Primary Teacher Training Institute on which it was based. IPAR would not only train a new generation of teachers but would combine this with other functions including in-service training, research and the production of prototypes, textbooks and teaching materials. There was here clear recognition of the inadequacy of merely reforming initial training given the scale of the problem and the inertial factors at work in the existing system. In effect responsibility for the radical reform of the school system was placed in the hands of a single institution. It was recognised that no matter how well trained or educated the pupil might be, his desire and capacity to promote the advancement of his community would be sapped if the community was itself not prepared for change and willing to give him the opportunity to apply his education. Consequently the teacher had of necessity to be concerned with promoting the kinds of change in the community which would enable his pupils to function as was intended. Thus his community function was not so much an extension of his role as a teacher but a fundamental part of it, and as such it would be more limited than has sometimes been advocated. His task would not be so much to train the adults to transform their community as to motivate them to welcome and co-operate with the products of the school, and this task would largely be achieved not through overt exhortation but through the influence of the school itself, remodelled to provide examples of community living which would be relevant to the wider community: 'The "school" not only presents an example of life and action conducive to a desire within the community for change; it also provides a model for the activities to be undertaken with a view to meeting that desire'.[21] When the school has succeeded in influencing the community by example, it is expected that the teacher will be invited to guide and assist the adults in transforming their own community.

In view of the psychological barrier to which we have referred above, the apparent simplicity of this model must be questioned. Without substantial transformation the school cannot provide the necessary model and, without access to similar kinds of resources, the community will be unable to follow the example offered. The school can only provide such a model if it is itself a working and producing community and in this respect some of the ideas we shall discuss below in relation to linking schooling and work may be relevant. More fundamental still is the question of whether a school is capable of providing a model for a community and whether, even if it can, the community will be able to see its relevance. How far can examples be developed and how far communicated by an institution which remains basically a school, and retains its autonomous position, physically within the community but essentially independent of it? For the school to purpot to serve as a model for the community will itself tend to set it apart from the community, to reinforce its autonomy and separate identity.

A third experimental approach has been initiated at Bunumbu in Sierra Leone. In this case a primary teacher training college has been transformed into a community teachers' college concerned with four main areas of action, the development of a new rurally oriented primary school curriculum, supporting teachers in the area through serving as a resource centre and through mobile in-service teacher education teams, the transformation of some twenty pilot schools within a twenty mile radius of the college into community centres, and the training of a new cadre of community teachers to staff these centres. In its multi-dimensional role the college is not dissimilar to IPAR but the roles projected for the teachers and the centres are very different. The new teachers, like those at Kakata, will be equipped through their training, which will include practical knowledge about agriculture, the working of agricultural co-operatives, home economics, handicrafts, farm workshop practice, environmental science and techniques of adult education and community leadership, to teach both primary school children according to the new syllabus and rural adults. Instruction for the adults will include woodwork and handicrafts, nutrition, health education and agriculture. In his role as an *animateur* within his community, the principal function of the teacher will be to teach. He will perform this function as part of a team which will include agricultural extension officers, co-operative inspectors, community development officers, and local community leaders and voluntary workers. With this clarity of role definition and with appropriate training the objectives of the experiment appear more realistic and practicable, and the efforts being made to try out the community development centre idea in a limited number of centres each in close contact with the college may well yield experience which will make the envisaged creation of a countrywide network of such centres a more feasible proposition. Since the inception of the Bunumbu experiment in 1974, the Sierra Leone Education Review, conducted in 1975 by the University of Sierra Leone in conjunction with the government, has proposed the establishment of Community Education Centres to be run independently of, but in association with, the reformed primary schools.

Although up to this point we have been mainly examining the contribution the teacher may make directly to the community, we need briefly to remind ourselves that remarkable and novel recent examples of pupil participation are not lacking. In Somalia and Ethiopia this took the form of participation in national campaigns. The national literacy campaign inaugurated in Somalia in 1973 followed the successful adoption of the

Roman alphabet for the writing of Somali and its immediate introduction as the medium of instruction in schools. A two-year campaign utilising all educated Somalis as instructors was estimated to have made 400 000 people literate and was followed by a one year campaign in which literacy was associated with teaching about health and livestock management. For this second phase all schools were closed for one year to free teachers and pupils to participate more intensively, and the outcome was that over three-quarters of a million people were able to pass the test set at the end of the campaign. In Ethiopia the *zemecha* campaign for development through co-operation was launched in 1974 and deployed some 60 000 secondary and university students together with their teachers to teach rural people the principles of the Ethiopian revolution and to assist them in local development activities, land reform, and the formation of farmers' associations. This programme was to last for five years at least in order to reach as many as seven million people. It is difficult to judge how permanent the benefits of such programmes will be and whether the cost in terms of the interruption of the schooling process will be justified. One of the purposes of such campaigns is to re-educate those participating as instructors and again it is not clear how effectively this will be achieved. Time will tell whether participation in campaigns which are not associated with structural changes in the relationship of the school system to society at large and to individual communities may not prove to be merely an interlude, interrupting the education of young people without seriously modifying it.

THE SCHOOL AS A COMMUNITY

In these various ways, through orientating the school life and curriculum towards the community, through involving the community in the life of the school and through seeking to make the school of direct service to the community, efforts are being made to link schools and their communities more closely together. Nevertheless most of the reforms envisaged in Africa still see the school as an institution which, whatever else it may do, continues to treat young people as a separate and discrete part of the community, to withdraw them into seclusion for a significant part of their time and to provide them with instruction different in kind and process from that which is available to other members of the community. There are sound administrative and pedagogical reasons for doing so and indeed it is difficult to see how else the school can operate so long as it retains its dual role. Yet the consequence may be that all the efforts to bridge the gap between the classroom and the community will remain token, ameliorative and remedial so long as the life of the school remains fundamentally different from the life of the community. It may be necessary, the argument runs, not merely to seek to modify the life of the community to make it more supportive of the kind of schooling we are trying to create, but also to change the nature of the school as a community within the wider community. Some educationists have long argued that there is something odd about preparing children for life by teaching them about the community which awaits them outside the walls of the school whilst compelling them to live in a very different manner within those walls. We teach children about processes of decision-making and prepare them for participation in these processes whilst subjecting them to authoritarian control and direction, denying them virtually all experience of making choices and decisions. We teach them about improved ways of family living whilst insisting that they live in school as part of a regimented mass consisting essentially and unnaturally of one age-range and often one sex. And even more fundamental as we shall see, we prepare them for productive roles in their communities through bringing them into communities which are themselves not production units.and in which the learning of skills may be isolated from management of production and from the realities of earning a living.

The incongruity of these proceedings was perhaps first effectively pointed out in Nyerere's *Education for Self-Reliance* in 1967. If schools were to prepare children effectively for participation in the emerging Tanzanian society, they themselves must become

> communities which practise the precept of self-reliance . . . economic as well as social and educational communities . . . This not a suggestion that a school farm or workshop should be attached to every school for training purposes. It is a suggestion that every school should be a farm; that the school community should consist of people who are both teachers and farmers and pupils and farmers . . . the farm would be an integral part of the school – and the welfare

of the pupils would depend on its output, just as the welfare of a farmer depends on the output of his land.[22]

The intention would not be realised if pupils were participating simply as labourers. They should also share responsibility for taking decisions.

A similar argument was advanced in connection with the ruralisation of education in the Cameroon. If the teacher was to be able to play a community leadership role and if the school was to be able to influence the community to seek his leadership, the teacher training institute must serve as a 'living model for the organisation of activities in the rural school, and the rural school as model for the organisation of village activities'.[23]

The Lagos Conference called for more effective integration of the school with life in this respect through the organisation of schools in such a way that they may eventually become self-managed and self-financed units and through the introduction of productive work into the curriculum. Whilst in Guinea each secondary, higher or vocational institution has a governing body composed exclusively of elected students under the chairmanship of the principal and responsible for all aspects of education and production, and for the management of property, this concept of the school community has not been taken far elsewhere. The exception to this is in respect of the interest being taken in involving schools in production, which is an important aspect of the second major theme defined by the Lagos Conference and to which we now turn.

## Linking School and Working Life

In two major senses it would be true to say that schools in Africa have for many years been concerned with links between education and working life. First they have been called upon to provide the skilled manpower required by the economy; indeed, this has been the dominant theme of recent educational planning. From the point of view of the clientele even the most academic subjects have been studied with a view to their value in eventually securing employment, and it has been argued that it is precisely because schooling has been so intimately connected with the employment market that its reform has been so difficult.

However in the contemporary context of mass education, it is clear that we are not primarily concerned with modern-sector employment as in the past but with enabling those young people whom the modern-sector will be unable to absorb to make their own way, probably as self-employed workers and to a large extent within their own local communities (thus both generating economic activity in these communities and reducing the rate of migration to the towns).

Secondly, educationists have long urged the necessity of blending theoretical with practical studies, many of which, such as woodwork, metalwork and gardening, might have vocational value in addition to educational value. But the argument for such activities has closely followed the thinking of Dewey who wrote:

> It is the business of the school to set up an environment in which play and work shall be conducted with reference to facilitating desirable mental and moral growth . . . The problem of the educator is to engage pupils in these activities in such ways that while manual skill and technical efficiency are gained and immediate satisfaction found in the work, together with preparation for later usefulness, those things shall be subordinated to education – that is, to intellectual results and the forming of a socialized disposition.[24]

Application of this concept has proved so very difficult for many teachers that practical activities have tended to become isolated from general education, and consequently have withered. Whilst much of this traditional thinking remains current and with justification, we must be quite clear that we are no longer thinking in the same terms. Practical and vocational studies are no longer thought of as subordinate to general education: in the new school, it is being argued, work and education must meet on equal terms. Nor is this merely a question of balance in the curriculum but one of school organisation. The search is on for new ways of combining theory, practice and production in an interactive and dynamic pedagogy.

It is, however, to narrow curricular considerations, and in particular to skill-training, that attention has most generally been given so far. African countries have not been unaware of the progress being made in India and, notably, Sri Lanka, in developing pre-vocational subjects in school. In Sri Lanka more than 80 such subjects had at one time been introduced into the school system, the intention being that each school should identify the specific skills needed for the occupations predominating in its locality. Farming and fishing, and animal husbandry had remained important but to them had been added local trades and crafts such as basket making, pottery, weaving, tailoring, and the like.

In Africa there has for some time been a tendency to allocate areas of general skill to specialist schools at post-primary level, as in Tanzania where secondary schools have either an agricultural, technical, commercial or domestic science orientation, or in Togo where the second stage of junior secondary education will be compulsory for all in either general secondary, technical, agricultural or arts and crafts schools. This latter model with its retention of general secondary schools is not dissimilar to what has long been the case in other countries where grammar schools, secondary modern schools, technical high schools and specialist training institutions have been operated side by side, ranged in a heirarchy of esteem reflected in selection procedures. This often strongly criticised diversification of post-primary schooling has resulted partly from belief that the physical development of primary age children is inadequate for certain kinds of skill training, that much of this training may be wasted if they leave school at an age when they are too young to take up employment immediately, and that training is better provided when an adequate basis of general education, and notably literacy, has been achieved. These considerations have led Kenya to decide to extend primary education by three years, and Tanzania to raise the age of entry into primary schooling. The process of selecting pupils for post-primary education or training on the basis of their academic attainment is therefore of long standing and the diversification of post-primary facilities is no real innovation. Although it may be accompanied by new processes of selection based upon guidance and counselling as mentioned above, the selective nature of the process remains so long as such facilities are not available to all primary school leavers, and so long as certain facilities possess greater esteem than others. Consequently some countries like Togo and Ghana intend to extend the period of open-access education to include junior secondary education. In

Nigeria it is probable that a common three-year programme with a strong emphasis on pre-vocational training will be offered but in Togo there will be selection into different schools for the final two years. Benin has adopted a new unitary concept of the educational system and it is categorically stated that 'the child who enters school will no longer leave until he is equipped with a trade; i.e. neither age nor the level at which compulsory schooling stops will be fixed dogmatically'.[25]

At the same time there has been a new interest in providing skill-training in the primary school, partly because of the cost of providing additional years of schooling and partly because it is hoped thereby to mould attitudes in such a way as to make more acceptable selection of those who will receive further formal education. In Ghana it is proposed to expose children deliberately to the techniques of various crafts from the very first level to the end of education. In the six-year primary course practical activities related to animal and crop husbandry, local crafts and vocations will be provided. This will be followed by three years free and compulsory junior secondary education in which in addition to academic subjects pupils will choose two skills from woodwork, masonry, metalwork, technical drawing, pottery, marine science, automobile practice, tailoring, beauty culture, catering and other vocations thought relevant. The following stage of secondary education will be selective, offering two-year general, technical and commercial courses. Whilst overcoming the age problem, it will be recognised that the process of selection at the end of junior secondary stage could be crucial in determining the status and effectiveness of the pre-vocational courses.

Guinea seeks to provide twelve years of compulsory schooling in three cycles each of which will dovetail with community vocational needs and will incorporate a production element. In the six-year elementary stage all pupils will be introduced to agriculture, stock rearing, fishing and handicrafts. Twenty per cent of their time will be spent on vocational studies and a further 10 per cent in production activities. At both three-year stages of secondary education, study schemes are offered which are designed to give pupils a technical education, a scientific training and a trade qualification, and each secondary school will offer one or more of five such schemes: agro-pastoral studies (taken by two-thirds of the total student body), civil engineering, mechanical engineering, nautical studies and social sciences. At both levels 30 per cent of the students' time will be spent on vocational education, and 20 per cent (rising to 30 per cent) in production. There are also *Ecoles Nationales Professionelles* which offer three-year training courses for executive grade staff either following the first or the second cycle of secondary education, entry to which is by examination. This comprehensive and potentially expensive system has been under development since 1959 in many of its major aspects and the expenditure on it of almost one-third of the national development budget is 'justified by the conviction that education is a "heavy industry" to be regarded as the sole path to the social elevation of the whole nation'.[26]

Senegal has sought a low cost solution to the problem, avoiding the necessity of a massive extension of conventional secondary provision and seeking to eliminate tensions between the general education and the vocational components of a student's programme. Only 40 per cent of the school-age population can at present attend school and of these only a fifth can go beyond primary school. The conclusion might have been drawn that therefore vocational training should be incorporated in the primary school. This solution was, however, rejected on the grounds that this would involve a harmful division between the aims of the programme and the methods used for its implementation:

> Primary school provides knowledge that is not immediately translatable into know-how; it consists of basic education following which children are directed ('guided') according to the ability they have acquired. If this pattern were followed . . . what would be achieved, at best, would be a remedial process on the educational plane without reaching the target of economic and cultural integration.[27]

Also rejected was the idea of using non-formal approaches to training on the grounds that these had been tried in that country but had failed because they had not been accompanied by measures to ensure that the community would be able to absorb the products and make use of the skills acquired. The middle-level practical education programme which was decided on was based upon handing over to communities both the responsibility for devising ways of absorbing young people usefully and for devising appropriate forms of training. Middle-level practical education was therefore to be provided at post-primary level in centres operating in parallel with the secondary schools and not as part of the school system.

Mali offers experience which also throws doubt upon the effectiveness of school-based provision. In 1962 a policy was introduced of providing mass education in 'fundamental schools' in which through manual work in the fields, in fishing, and in workshops, pupils would be prepared to be producers, following which a minority would have the opportunity of going on to general secondary education. Ten years later the policy was declared to have failed. There had been a costly explosion of provision at all levels of education without overcoming the problem of young people being psychologically alienated from their communities and insufficiently motivated to learn and apply their skills in productive life. Research is being conducted into the problem but this country is deliberately abstaining from arriving at hasty and over-optimistic solutions.

The fundamental problem is that merely to train young people in vocational skills will not of itself create employment opportunities and that unless there are employment opportunities the other benefits to be derived from the reformed curriculum will largely be lost. The maintenance of healthy attitudes towards the community based upon understanding and awareness of its problems and potential, and the creation of motivation to promote the development of that community, will be of little value if the young person finds it necessary to seek his fortune elsewhere. Many previous attempts to train rural craftsmen have come to nothing because the market for their skills was not sufficient to sustain self-employment.

Local communities, of course, need a wide variety of skills. But the building of houses, manufacture of simple tools and utensils, furniture and the like is to a considerable extent already accommodated in such communities by the existing stock of skills. The primary school leaver, like the rural craftsman before him, may be able to offer improved techniques – though this is by no means certain, particularly in so far as he may have been instructed by existing village craftsmen – but if the cost of making use of these improved techniques is high in relation to the benefits to be gained, local people may, as in the past, prefer to continue to rely on their own efforts. Where the benefit is such as to justify the cost it is likely that urban manufacturing will already be providing higher quality products at prices which the rural craftsman may find it hard to undercut, and we have already noted the tendency for traditional rural industries to die out in face of this competition. Thus we cannot be sure that the market will be capable of absorbing significant numbers of new craftsmen. Existing craftsmen whose skills may have been handed down from father to son may not only look with disfavour on possible competition from primary school leavers but may well have the resourcefulness to defeat them in a competitive situation, even where the primary school leaver is prepared to accept low profit-margins and the low standard of living associated with rural crafts.

The problem of numbers is acute. The local economy may be able to absorb some primary school leavers and possibly incorporate them in indigenous apprenticeships of a kind which are particularly common in West Africa. But the numbers leaving school year after year are such that unless rural economies are transformed, which seems unlikely in the short run, there appears little hope of self-employment for the majority in craft occupations. Even where there is a potential market for the school leavers' skills, as Boakye has pointed out for Ghana, it may not be easy for them to establish themselves in business. His longitudinal study suggests to him that without proper backing there is little or no chance for the young craftsmen to put what they have learned into practice 'thus rendering all efforts fruitless'.[28]

One alternative is, of course, for such school leavers to become farmers utilising their various craft skills for their own benefit and that of their neighbours without necessarily seeking to market their skills. This is likely to be seen by school leavers and their parents as a last resort and it is questionable how far the introduction of skill-training into primary schools will be able to transform the situation. Possession of skills and exposure to practical work alone will not transform attitudes and aspirations. Since the skills taught may well have a market value in urban areas, the policy may increase the tendency of young school leavers to try their luck in the towns. Some hopes have been expressed that many of them may be absorbed there in the informal sector of industry, in roadside production of basic essentials, but it could well be that the informal sector is already operating at capacity and that new school leavers are unlikely to possess the degree and kinds of skills or the capacity for entrepreneurial activity which will enable them to compete in what is already a highly competitive and, in some instances, organised activity.

No miracles can therefore be expected from the introduction of such skill training into school. But more positively it may be argued that given other forms of development in the rural economy, possession of such skills may assist the school leaver to seize what opportunities may exist. It may be argued that they will not be worse off than they are now when their education has provided them with no such utilisable skills.

Whilst a great deal of interest is being shown in the development of work orientated programmes in schools, African countries are approaching the issue in a variety of ways with varying degrees of commitment to the principle. Some are moving very strongly in the direction of vocational training as we have seen. Others retain a largely traditional view in which practical work complements theory as part of general education. Malawi recognised the danger that excessively detailed and 'refined translation of occupations into educational requirements is likely to inflict the education system with obsolete and irreversible programmes', and argued that schools should provide basic levels of education which could on relatively short notice be channelled to more specific occupational demands as these were revealed.[29] As we have noted, Guinea has clearly stated the amount of time to be spent on each aspect of the curriculum but in other countries this is not clear, and in any case many problems remain, both of allocation of time and of effectively integrating theory with practice in a school system still performing its dual role. The Lagos Conference was aware of this and warned that 'precautions still need to be taken in order to find the best distribution of time as between teaching theory and practice'.[30] Few countries would be inclined to follow the Togo precept of suppression of all that is not immediately practical since they believe that not only would this present a threat to the development of intellectual ability needed at all levels of the nation's life but that it would not prove an effective training for innovative and entrepreneurial craftsmen such as we may need to produce if they are to be successful.

The working document prepared for the Lagos conference noted that whilst in a number of African countries there had been concern to redress the balance in the curriculum between theoretical and practical studies, a more decisive innovation appeared to be the introduction of productive work into the curriculum:

> The rationale for productive work in the curriculum is not merely concern for the development of certain skills for employment. Productive work also has pedagogical and ethical merits; it associates the student with the vital activity of the community, basic to its development, and at the same time abolishes the dividing line which artificially separates study from manual work.[31]

The idea that the schools should become production units, that they should not only have farms and workshops but *be* farms and workshops was first effectively spelled out for Africa by Nyerere in *Education for Self-Reliance*. Since 1967 it has been taken up in varying degrees in other countries than Tanzania. The reasons for its appeal, however, are not merely the promised synthesis between study and work. In addition production by schools promised to contribute to some extent to the financing of schooling and to reduce the burden on central government. In this sense the idea has been in circulation for many years and there are many examples of schools, notably in the inter-war years, in which sale of farm produce has been encouraged to raise revenue (not surprisingly, particularly in the schools run by voluntary agencies). Without under-stressing the importance in current thinking of the financial issue, the argument for involving schools in production activities has been taken well beyond the utilitarian. In Tanzania in particular, as we have seen, the concept was that schools should not merely be community-oriented, teaching children about the community outside the school and training them in the skills they would eventually need on leaving school, but that the school should be integrated with the community, sharing in its production and development activities. These local communities, it was planned, would evolve towards self-sufficient socialist communities, a process which it was admitted would take many years. In the meantime it was believed that, whilst children would benefit from sharing in the realities of their parents' lives, at the stage of embryonic socialism the interaction between school and community through shared activities would not be enough to enable the children to grow in understanding of ujamaa sufficiently to lead the way to socialism. Consequently the school itself should become a community practising socialism and enabling children to appreciate its value through experiencing it both at home and in school. For the school to become a genuine community, work and production could not be simply peripheral activities but had to move into the centre of the child's life in the way that it was central to the life of his parents.

In Guinea every school is intended to be at one and the same time a centre for the propagation of science and technology and a modern production unit. Thirteenth-year classes have been introduced recently as an extension of the normal twelve-year programme which are, in effect, production units in which 80 per cent of the students' time is given over to production. Young people in these classes are to be grouped in production teams which are intended to form the basis of socialist communes when they leave school. These communes are to be in effect model villages which will, by example, influence surrounding villages, demonstrating socialism in action. Their strength will be that they are based upon sound school training and will include young people already 'committed to social relationships of a democratic and militant nature'.[32] Productive activities in school will prepare them for collective management of the commune and for co-operative relationships, and will commit them to socialist principles through practising socialism.

In Ethiopia it is intended that eventually the schools will become self-reliant and self-sufficient. In agricultural areas the plan is for each school to have at least ten hectares of land whilst in urban areas schools will be attached to garages, industries or other productive units. In Benin each school is to be organised as a school co-operative with its own production unit. The co-operative will be a society of students, managed by themselves in collaboration with the teachers in order to carry out patriotic and cultural activities, physical education and sports, and agricultural, craft and cultural production. The production unit, it is envisaged, will at least partially finance the schools. The plan became operational in 1975, in which year there were 764 cooperatives in 1500 basic schools and 18 in 70 middle level institutions. These were reported to be achieving outputs averaging over 10 000 CFA francs per co-operative in the basic schools and 200 000 CFA francs at middle level. The experience of a small village school at Bensekou, which after two years had an income from its own production of nearly 84 000 CFA francs and which so stimulated the local village that production rose to five times its former level, provided the experience upon which the policy was based, and broad consultations with parents, teachers and pupils were conducted before it was generally introduced.

In Zambia, by contrast, the President's Solwezi decree of July 1975 simply declared that every educational institution was a production unit from that time forth and that every pupil would engage in productive work as an integral part of his or her normal studies. Some production work affecting a minority of pupils had previously been undertaken in Young Farmers' Clubs, and Junior Engineers, Technicians and Scientists (JETS) organisations which assembled electrical instruments for eventual sale. Now, however, each school was required to set up production unit committees including teachers, pupils, parents and other members of the community to plan and run production activities. By the end of the following year 80 per cent of educational institutions were reported to have established some production project and substantial quantities of maize, vegetables, cotton, tobacco, sunflower seeds and poultry were being produced by rural schools. In the non-agricultural areas, with rather more ingenuity, the manufacture of such items as blackboard dusters, school uniforms, reflective number plates and warning triangles for vehicles was being attempted. Services were offered by some schools including hair plaiting and mini-bus transport. Initial enthusiasm was cooled somewhat by problems of water supply, land and tools, and by scepticism as to the real value of many of these activities. The declared intention of the programme was to re-establish the dignity of labour and to develop the creative instincts of the community. Whilst initially schools were instructed that production activities should take place without disturbing the formal subject curriculum, a committee has recommended fuller integration of production, with academic studies to constitute 50 per cent, practical activities 30 per cent and cultural activities 20 per cent of the timetable.

It is not easy to measure the degree of success being achieved in these various approaches at this early stage. That it will not be easy to translate theory into practice is attested by early Tanzanian experience. In 1974 having noted the continuing adherence to 'international standards', Nyerere went on to refer to a second problem, 'our apparent inability or unwillingness to really integrate education and life, and education and production'. Some progress had been made but

> Parents, politicians, and workers, as well as educators, are suspicious of, or hostile to, the educational innovations required. But the total result is that few of our schools are really an integral part of the village life, except in the sense that they occupy village children for so many hours a day. And what is true in the villages is even more true of the towns. Further, few schools – if any – can really claim that their production makes any large contribution even to their own upkeep, much less to the society in general.[33]

Once again we have to point out the necessity for consistent political will if the reforms are to be given the opportunity of proving their value and warn that even processes of consultation are no safeguard against popular opposition to a policy which, whilst not fulfilling traditional aspirations, does not speedily demonstrate that it can be beneficial.

There are in addition a number of general considerations regarding the place of production activities in schools which must be noted here. The nature of the production activity will depend upon the potential in the environment and the available market for produce. The example quoted of Bensekou school in north-east Benin involved the production of cotton in a region in which this was the principal product. Here the school merely had to replicate existing production practice and utilise existing marketing procedures. Not all schools will find themselves so favourably placed, able to produce a crop for which a large market exists, which does not involve competition with local production and which can support greatly increased production stimulated by the school in the locality. Not all teachers will have the necessary skill and, although no great degree of skill or knowledge is needed for some kinds of agricultural or other production or to increase or diversify production in some instances, where schools are situated on marginal land (often because the local community has already taken up the most productive land) something more than the knowledge and skill possessed by the local farmer may be needed.

Moreover, whilst production may be achieved, the linking of production with education and training is a far more difficult thing. If the aim is to make money, then a favourably placed school may well find it expedient to concentrate upon one form of production, say of a single crop. But this may involve pupils in a high degree of repetitive work, since much production is necessarily repetitive, with repetition continuing even after the skill has been learned, whilst the range of skill-training or educational activity based upon or associated with the production function may be limited unless the teacher is a person of considerable ingenuity. Moreover if the crop chosen is cultivated locally and if techniques of production normally used in the area are to be employed, the pupil may indeed learn no skill which his experience at home has not already taught him.

If the work of the school is to contribute significantly to the development of the local area it may involve more than merely demonstrating that money can be made by increasing existing production. It may involve demonstrating the value of new crops or products, and of improved techniques of production, storage or marketing. Substantial retraining of serving teachers may consequently be essential. It is probable also that a school seeking to promote innovation in its community should not seek to move too far ahead of that community or to utilise techniques which that community is not in a position to take up. But to confine pupils to the production practices appropriate to their particular local community may restrict the development of skills of wider applicability.

If the main purpose of production activities is to provide a realistic framework within which pupils may learn skills and acquire other knowledge and understanding, then what may well be required is the development of a range of production activities within a single school. Thereby a variety of skills may be learned which will stand the school leaver in better stead than possession of only one, which will afford a wider range of opportunities for links to be made with theoretical studies, and will broaden his basis of awareness, which may be one of the more important things he will carry with him into the community on leaving school. However if a school did seek to develop a range of skills and production activities not only would the demands upon the teaching staff be increased but the effectiveness of the production as a money earner might well be reduced overall.

It is therefore important to be clear about the purpose of the introduction of production activities, and whilst it is commonly intended that several purposes be served, rarely in policy statements is the priority between them made clear. The outcome could all too easily require the teacher to reconcile the irreconcilable and to seek to achieve all these aims, with the likelihood that he will fail to achieve any of them. The policy adopted must be realistic in terms both of the environment of individual schools, the capacity of serving teachers, and the availability of support services of information, materials and training.

## Strengthening the African Cultural Identity

The third theme for the reform of education advanced at the Lagos Conference was cultural authenticity in schooling, and education generally, as a means whereby it might serve the needs of national development more effectively. The conference declared that:

> Authenticity and modernity in education are an effective combination for rejecting, at the level of institutions and at the level of content, imported patterns and ready-made formulae. The receptivity of educational systems and individual experience towards the universal heritage of knowledge as well as the harmonizing of educational institutions with the other national institutions on which development and progress depend are contingent thereon.[34]

It is perhaps significant that the ministers should have felt impelled to make this declaration at this time. As we have noted, despite much concern in the past that school systems should not merely be copies of foreign models but be adapted to the nature and needs of African society, the pressures for expansion in the years immediately before and after independence, and the priority given to the production of high and intermediate level educated manpower had in fact resulted in the adoption of internationally conventional models. But even when it became recognised that such school systems did not appear to be capable of achieving the goals set for them, much of the reform initiated was of a relatively superficial kind, again reflecting progressive international practice.

This new call for authenticity was not simply the long-standing call for 'relevance' which had widely been used as an argument for the adoption of reforms touching the content and methodology of schooling, but which did not alter its basic nature and function. Nor was it simply the equally old call for a return to traditional educational practices such as has frequently been expressed by educationists holding an idealised view of pre-colonial African society. As Amadou-Mahtar M'Bow stated at Lagos:

> the renewed esteem for African cultural values and traditions, in all their richness and abundance as a way of relating with others and with the whole world, must avoid the temptation to become backward-looking. On the contrary it should appear as one of the elements of a novel synthesis in which the most useful contributions of the past are mingled with the knowledge, values and attitudes needed for an understanding of today's world and control over an often harsh environment.[35]

In the declaration quoted above, authenticity and modernity march hand in hand, and in this respect the declaration represents a positive step forward. But is it merely a new catch phrase, full of satisfying emotional appeal, or does it genuinely offer practical guidance as to how schooling may be reformed?

A number of ideas were expressed at the Lagos conference. M'Bow stressed the curricular implications of the principle – a much greater stress on basic training in the sciences but also the provision of knowledge of the machinery of national, regional and international relations to enable people to play a greater part in changing their own societies and constructing a more just international order. Emphasis should be placed on practical and first-hand experience to free pupils from 'the feeling of unreality occasioned by the conflict between a bookish, imported culture and the exigencies of a daily life in which productive activities loom so large'. African tradition, he argued, made no harmful distinction between learning and everyday life. He also argued, but more vaguely, that the methods and the spirit of education should be adapted to the realities of Africa, and that this would involve preparing teachers for their new roles and reforming examinations.

The conference was clearly looking well beyond the old idea of introducing cultural activities, dance and song for instance, into the life of the school. The tendency of such activities to become semi-recreational and peripheral is well known. Although they may have some value, as practised in the past they can be regarded neither as truly educational nor as a deep cultural experience. More fundamental changes were sought at Lagos and the second commission of the conference, dealing with basic education, saw in the new relationships between the educational system and the environment which were being discussed not merely a powerful means of development but an instrument for authentic liberation – political, intellectual and psychological, cultural, scientific and technological. These relationships involved the integration of schooling with other non-formal educational processes in the framework of lifelong education.

The conference therefore saw authenticity and modernity largely in terms of the new structures for integrating the school with the community, the development of the school as a productive community, and the introduction of a curriculum rooted in the environment rather than simply in the disciplines of knowledge. These measures would not merely make schooling more relevant but be important means whereby more authentically African systems and styles of education might evolve.

The second main thrust of the conference recommendations in this respect was in the area of language. There was a need to ensure intellectual and scientific independence, to protect against alienation and subjugation and to facilitate dialogue on a universal scale in the spirit of the new international order which must, it was declared:

> be satisfied by the full and complete restoration of the national languages as languages of instruction. Whilst they correspond to the profound aspirations of the general public, and ensure for the present and the future the reconciliation that the African needs with his environment and his integration into society at large, they place the educational effort in a new dialectical relationship which ensures the dissemination of culture and knowledge in society and the intellectual emancipation of the community by the elimination of any elite status. An approach of this kind should lead to the revival of the national languages as vehicles of scientific and technical progress; it will enable our societies, freed from all the effects of foreign domination, to contribute in their own unique way to the fruitful dialogue upon which the full development of various civilizations depends.[36]

The emotional appeal of this statement is immense. The practical problems it poses are great and need little recapitulation here. For many years, of course, it has been argued by educationists that young children should begin their education in the language of their homes in order that they may better master the basic skills upon which their later education will be based. Colonial policies of the inter-war years preached the use of the vernacular as a medium of instruction as part of the process of adaptation described earlier. In practice however African refusal to be 'imprisoned in their own vernaculars' and the severe practical difficulties of preparing materials and teachers linguistically competent to use them impeded the implementation of this policy beyond the very earliest stages of schooling. Whether we are concerned simply with the use of the multiplicity of mother tongues in education or with the more practicable but politically difficult choice of a limited number of dominant vernaculars or even of a single vernacular, the difficulties of reproducing the existing stock of knowledge in vernacular form and of introducing it into the schools cannot be understated. Yet we may recall that Malaysia has made substantial progress in its Bahasa

Malaysia policy in a multiple language situation. Within Africa we may note the progress made by Tanzania in respect of the use of Swahili, and of Somalia in a much shorter time in replacing Italian and English with Somali, a language which remained unwritten until as late as 1972. In these two instances the political problems of choice of language were a great deal easier than face many other countries. Progress, for example, has been much slower in Kenya which, in spite of the adoption of Swahili as an official language, faced problems from the presence of large groups of people who speak a non-Bantu language and the more limited extent to which Swahili was already diffused among the population. Kenya adopted its New Primary Approach involving active learning through the use of English some years ago and sought to promote the policy through quite elaborate programmes of curriculum development, teacher education and materials production. In spite of widespread popular support, the cost and difficulty of extending the approach into the rural areas proved too great a burden and the principle of English-medium instruction is now questioned. In general terms much will depend upon the determination of the political authorities to make the vernacular language policy work, which implies the allocation of very considerable resources to the enterprise, and upon the acceptability of the language policy to the people, particularly where schooling has traditionally been associated with access to international languages as languages of opportunity. Clearly the question of choice of language of instruction cannot be divorced from decisions and practice regarding the language used for government, business and commerce. Where an international language remains the language of opportunity in these fields, it will confirm the tendency for secondary education to be in that language and encourage policies of introducing the language as early as possible in the primary programme. These problems are well recognised in Zambia where a balance between pedagogical principles, public acceptability and practicability has been sought in its choice of the medium of instruction. Following the national debate of 1976–7 the revised proposals for educational reform confirmed the older approach by which English has been the medium of instruction from Grade I, but emphasised the need for children to be linked with their cultural heritage through the teaching of Zambian languages as subjects. Parents

were reminded that they themselves retain an important responsibility for teaching their children the proper use of the mother
tongue. Guinea, which intends that all subjects should be taught
in local vernaculars for the first five years of education, has
admitted similar problems whilst Togo and Benin have been
compelled to retain French for the time being as the medium of
instruction.

However there are deeper questions to be asked than those
relating to practical issues. Will the use in education of a national
language ensure the retention by the African student of his
cultural identity and his integration into his community and
society? By itself it probably cannot ensure these things although
in conjunction with other reforms of the curriculum and of the
structure of the school system it may well contribute towards
them. But language and educational policy alone will not affect
those factors which at present tend to alienate people from their
traditional environment, which they do not see as possessing the
potential to realise their aspirations for a better life. The drift to
the towns, the pursuit of material goals and the worship of
mammon, the conflict between groups identified other than by
language – these are characteristic not only of nations which do
not possess their own national language and which educate their
children through languages other than their mother tongues –
and the roots of these phenomena will not necessarily be affected
by language policy. Using national languages as the medium of
instruction in schools will not alter the function which schools
currently serve, though it may make them in some ways more
efficient in serving that function, and it could possibly thereby
strengthen them against other fundamental reform.

Similarly, we may well feel that the adoption of a single
national language in education will promote national integration
and increase the degree of equality of opportunity which we offer.
However we would recognise that the selection of a single
vernacular language of instruction will necessarily confer upon
some children the advantage of learning in their mother tongue
which would run counter to these goals. The alternative might be
to promote as far as possible the use of mother tongues rather than
common national languages in education. This would reduce the
extent of the differentiation problem without fully removing it,
but would have the added advantage that, as educationists have

long argued and as the Yoruba language project at the University of Ife appears to show, children will learn more effectively in their own language and develop qualities of originality in their work which are often absent where children are learning in an alien language.

Once again, however, this will not necessarily do more than increase the efficiency of the school in contributing to the alienation of children from their immediate communities and facilitating and encouraging their moving into the modern sector. It may also be argued that in terms of national integration and the efficient operation of the modern sector, a policy of encouraging many vernacular language groups may be counter-productive. This may be compensated for by ensuring that in addition all pupils have the opportunity of learning a second language which may be the national language – indeed the conference of African ministers argued that 'This promotion of African national languages does not preclude, but on the contrary lends itself to a pragmatic and functional use of foreign languages for the purpose of fruitful exchanges on a basis of equality'.[37] But in so far as such second languages, whether African or 'foreign', are the languages of the national and modern sectors, they may well retain such importance in terms of the natural aspirations of the pupils that they will continue to dominate the curriculum. If, however, we seek to retain the second language merely as a subject, how far will this generate genuine and sufficient competence for its use? How can we avoid overloading the curriculum with linguistic studies at a time when the necessity for practical, pre-vocational and cultural studies is being so strongly urged?

More significant, however, is the question of how far education in the vernacular will serve to encourage the majority of children who do not secure selection for further education and for eventual modern-sector employment, to return to and integrate satisfactorily with their own local communities. The assumption here is that an important reason for the alienation of young people from their own communities is the fact that they have been educated in a language not that of the community. How far is this true? If they fail to gain selection will they not continue to feel themselves to be failures as before, will they not continue to find it difficult to adjust their level of aspirations to that which the community can satisfy? These are questions which cannot easily be answered. We do not really know how far a child who is educated in, for example, English, loses his capacity to communicate effectively in his mother tongue. We may suggest, however, that the child who finds it difficult to fit back into his local community does so more because of natural frustration and rejection; in so far as he may have lost touch with the culture of his home, he may well have done so for reasons other than the different cultural values implanted by a second language.

We must not forget, however, that for the African ministers of education the main argument was that a national language policy was essential if intellectual independence was to be achieved. There is little doubt that the continued use of international languages, quite apart from the fact that it facilitates the use of foreign teachers, textbooks and teaching materials, thereby encouraging dependence and the transmission of alien cultural ideas, must inevitably confirm the already close cultural and intellectual links with the former colonial powers. There is a tendency, upon which we have already remarked, for the best international practice or current major trends in educational and other thinking to be far too readily absorbed into African education systems and educational debates. There has also been a parallel tendency for study and research to be captured by the methodologies and objectives in vogue overseas with a consequent diversion of intellectual energy away from local problems into the more abstruse common ground of international scholarship. Of course, African scholars and educationists should not seek to cut themselves off from the rest of the world; indeed the Lagos conference makes it clear that what is sought are improved relationships based upon equality and genuine dialogue. In this respect it may be argued that for these desirable changes to take place at the level of high scholarship, it is not so much the language of discourse which is significant but the spirit in which the dialogue is approached. Independence is a quality of mind born of confidence based upon achievement as well as commitment, and cannot be achieved simply. International intellectual life will, in any case, continue in the major international languages and it seems unlikely that the promotion of national languages will directly affect the operation of such conferences as the Lagos conference itself which achieve interaction and consensus through the use of international languages.

We must, however, distinguish between the kind of intellectual independence we are seeking at international level and domestically. In so far as the use of local national languages in education may, by removing cultural obstacles and diversions, facilitate the learning processes of young people and enable them to contribute more effectively to their countries' banks of relevant knowledge, there is sufficient reason for pursuing the policy in spite of the kinds of problems suggested and in spite of the many questions which must be posed as regards its value for other purposes. Indeed we shall only learn the answers to these questions through the evaluation of experience and there will be much interest both in the Yoruba Language project at Ife and in the experience of those countries which are extending the role of indigenous languages in their education systems.

## References

1. International Bureau of Education and Network of Educational Innovation for Development in Africa, *Educational Reforms and Innovations in Africa* (Paris: UNESCO, 1978) Reform in Basic Education in Mali, p. 20.
2. Conference of Ministers of Education of African Member States, Lagos, 27 January–4 February 1976, *Final Report*, (Paris: UNESCO, 1976) General Report, p. 14.
3. *Ibid.*, Report of Commission I, p. 21.
4. *Ibid.*, p. 22.
5. G. Guilavogui, 'The Basis of the Educational Reform in the Republic of Guinea', *Prospects*, vol. v no. 4 (1975) p. 436.
6. K. King, 'The Community School, Rich World, Poor World', in K. King (ed.), *Education and Community in Africa* (University of Edinburgh, 1976) p. 12.
7. S. Kay, 'Curriculum Innovations and a Traditional Culture, a Case History of Kenya', *Comparative Education*, vol. ii no. 3 (October 1975).
8. H. W. R. Hawes, 'Curriculum and Reality in African Primary Schools', (London: Longman, 1979) p. 59.
9. K. F. Hirji, 'School Education and Underdevelopment in Tanzania', *Maji Maji*, 12 Sept 1973, p. 21.
10. *Educational Reforms and Innovations in Africa*, Reform of the Education System in Togo, p. 43.
11. Conference of Ministers of Education, *Final Report*, Address by Mr Amadou-Mahtar M'Bow, p. 60.
12. Republic of Zambia, *Education for Development, Draft Statement on Educational Reform*, (Lusaka: Ministry of Education, 1976) p. 67.

13. Conference of Ministers of Education, *Final Report*, Report of Commission I, p. 23.
14. Hawes, 'Curriculum and Reality', pp. 98–9.
15. D. Court and K. Kinyanjui, *Development Policy and Educational Opportunity: The Experience of Kenya and Tanzania* (Paris: IIEP/UNESCO, 1978) pp. 72–3.
16. J. K. Nyerere, Interview with Altaf Gauhar, *The Guardian*, 8 January 1979.
17. M. Mbilinyi, 'The Study of Education and "the Community"', in King, *Education and Community in Africa*, p. 85.
18. H. N. Weiler, 'Education and Development: From the Age of Innocence to the Age of Scepticism', *Comparative Education*, vol. 14 no. 3 (October 1978) p. 191.
19. Conference of Ministers of Education, *Final Report*, General Report p. 15.
20. S. Grabe, quoted by the editors, in M. Ahmed and P. H. Coombs, *Education for Rural Development, Case Studies for Planners* (New York: Praeger, 1975) p. 344.
21. R. Lallez, *An Experiment in the Ruralisation of Education, IPAR and the Cameroonian Reform* (Paris: UNESCO, 1974) p. 83.
22. J. K. Nyerere, *Education for Self-Reliance*, (Dar es Salaam: Government Printer, 1967).
23. Lallez, *An Experiment in the Ruralisation of Education*, p. 80.
24. J. Dewey, *Democracy and Education* (The Free Press, 1921) pp. 196–7.
25. *Educational Reforms and Innovations in Africa*, The Fundamental Reform of Education in Benin, p. 32.
26. Guilavogui, 'The Basis of the Educational Reform', p. 435.
27. *Educational Reforms and Innovations in Africa*, Middle Level Practical Education in Senegal, p. 14.
28. J. K. A. Boakye, 'The Trends of Change in African Education: the Ghana Case', paper presented to conference on the Trends of Change in African Education, Institute of Development Studies, University of Sussex, 16 May 1977, p. 9.
29. Malawi, *Education Plan of Malawi 1973–1980*, Ministry of Education, 1973, p. 13.
30. Conference of Ministers of Education, *Final Report*, Report of Commission I, p. 23.
31. *Ibid.*, General Report, p. 15.
32. Guilavogui, 'The Basis of the Educational Reform', p. 440.
33. J. K. Nyerere, Speech to the Dag Hammarskjold Seminar on Education and Training and Alternatives in Education in African Countries, Dar es Salaam, 20 May 1974.
34. Conference of Ministers of Education, *Final Report*, Declaration 2.4.iii, p.31.
35. *Ibid.*, Address by Mr Amadou-Mahtar M'Bow, p. 60.
36. *Ibid.*, Declaration 2.5, p. 31.
37. *Ibid.*

# Linking Formal and Non-formal Education

Underlying the trends of educational innovation in both the formal and non-formal fields which we have been discussing is a concept perhaps best stated in the Bell report to the World Bank which described

> our vision of the need of every country, industrialised or developing, for a flexible, comprehensive network of provisions and opportunities for education and training. Ideally such a network should be diverse enough to be responsive to many needs and kinds of learners but sufficiently unitary to avoid shunting any group, such as rural children and youth, girls and young women, or those from poorer homes, into dead-end educational channels or inferior learning options.[1]

This statement reflects a significant change from earlier thinking such as that of the World Bank's own working paper of 1974 which envisaged alternative and parallel systems of formal and non-formal education as being a means of providing at least some education to underprivileged groups. Some educationists felt that there was positive advantage in keeping the two systems separate since non-formal education did not appear to encourage and legitimate unrealistic demands for social mobility, as did the school, but instead might be expected to generate lower and more realistic aspirations by offering genuine hope that these could be met. At the same time such a system would not constitute a challenge to the supremacy of formal schooling and possibly, by preserving the separate identity of schools, would confirm the legitimacy of allocating privilege and prestige to those who had received schooling. This dual concept was not without its appeal as an immediately practicable possibility. But it was discredited very quickly, partly because analysis of experience such as that of Upper Volta with its efforts over twenty years to provide a separate system of rural education centres in parallel to primary schooling showed that such a system would be unacceptable to local people as soon as they became aware that the two systems would in fact not be equal, and partly because the ideal of genuine social justice and equity was itself being strongly asserted. Consequently the search began for ways of relating formal and non-formal education within non-discriminatory networks.

As we have seen, African countries have generally accepted that the school has a fundamental role to play in such a network. But there is also growing consciousness of the value of non-formal education and training as part of the network. The problem we now face is how and how far to articulate these diverse forms of provision together within a 'sufficiently unitary' network. Certain kinds of non-formal education, as we have seen, have been regarded as supplementary to formal schooling, in that through providing literacy classes and second-chance opportunities through correspondence and other means, they have sought to provide the same kind of education as formal schools to those whom the formal school has failed to reach. These supplementary opportunities may include access to examinations and certification normally the preserve of the formal school, and also opportunities thereby to enter or re-enter at a late stage the formal school system itself. We have noted the danger that such non-formal provision may come to be regarded as an inferior second class route to formal education, and that in tying itself to patterns of instruction, syllabuses and examinations designed for the formal school and subject to much criticism, it may lose the advantages of cheapness, flexibility and practical relevance often claimed for it.

We have also seen non-formal education regarded as complementary to formal schooling, providing what formal schooling does not and perhaps cannot provide, that is training and education tailor-made to fit the needs and circumstances of specific groups and communities. The Lagos conference recommended that this should be the way in which the two should be viewed, 'as . . . complementary elements in an overall national effort to ensure each member of the society equal educational opportunities'.[2] But herein lies the problem. If the two forms of provision are separate, meeting different needs of different clienteles through different means, they may well be considered complementary but can they be regarded as affording equal educational opportunities?

The problems involved in linking formal and non-formal education in a nationwide, lifelong learning system may be illustrated by examining some patterns of educational provision in Africa which may be regarded as linkage models. The first and simplest model is perhaps the community school itself, a school which in addition to educating young people seeks also to provide appropriate education for adult members of its community, so linking the two elements of education within a single institution and a single system. An example at institutional level would be the community school at Kwamsisi in Tanzania which was developed by Korogwe College of National Education working with teachers and members of the community. Other colleges are currently seeking to develop schools on this pattern which involves the primary school serving as a community education centre by developing two wings of operation. The primary school wing has pioneered the reform of the primary school curriculum along community-centred lines including study in the four areas of functional literacy and numeracy, citizenship and political education, self-help and cultural activities, and community studies. These studies were linked to development projects in the village. The adult education wing sought to provide functional education and training, making full use of the school facilities. With UNICEF and UNESCO help additional facilities including a community assembly hall, a co-operative centre, agricultural storage facilities, workshops, a dispensary and day care centre were developed. A study of the project conducted in 1974 noted that the primary school wing was still very much concerned with preparing children for the primary school leaving examination and for secondary school entrance and that the development of the community orientation was being impeded by the insistence of teachers and parents that the children should not lose their opportunities for further education because of their participation in an experiment.

However the two-wing approach raises further issues of

principle. In so far as they are separate elements serving different clienteles and different purposes, the wings may indeed be regarded as complementary but how far can they be regarded as providing equal educational opportunities. The African Ministers of Education recognised the inherent danger that individuals receiving non-formal education might find themselves trapped within it and denied the kind of benefits which the formal school offers to its own clientele. We shall return to this point. A second consideration is that whilst a community school may indeed provide useful service to the adult community, there is some considerable danger that it will remain essentially a school and in face of aspirational pressures tend to allocate only secondary and possibly declining importance to its community role. This danger would exist even where teachers receive appropriate training so long as they are required to play two roles. If on the other hand the adult wings of such community schools are provided with their own professional staff, the administrative and functional separation of the two wings may result in their being associated simply as a matter of convenience – in order to share facilities perhaps. How far would such an approach really differ from situations where formal and non-formal education programmes are separately run?

In Ethiopia, for example, it is proposed to construct 500 community skill-training centres to be run by farmers associations or co-operative societies of town dwellers in parallel with schools, but offering facilities to be used alike by adults, youth and children through appropriate time-tabling. Here the facilities are primarily intended for adults but may be used by schools. Such centres may well provide a useful service and offer the cost savings and convenience of shared facilities. They may have an additional advantage over the community school in that they are perhaps less likely to give excessive priority to the education of children. But again such an arrangement may be criticised as not clearly offering equal educational opportunities to its various clienteles.

A third pattern may be that of the community centre at Kibaha in Tanzania initiated with Scandinavian help in 1964. The centre is designed to improve a wide range of aspects of local village life and includes a number of associated sections. It has a health training centre, a farmers' training centre, a rural development unit and a mobile library service. Incorporated in these sections are smaller specialised units such as a dairy farm, a poultry unit, and nutrition and home economics units. All of these provide courses of various durations to local people and, as described so far, the centre does not differ greatly from other multi-purpose, non-formal education centres referred to earlier. However there is an important difference in that Kibaha also includes a primary and a secondary school and seeks to associate non-formal with formal education in the task of raising the quality of life in the area. A single overall management agency would theoretically offer a greater degree of co-ordination and linking of activities than a series of independent units, whilst at the same time developing a wide range of specialised activities under expert leadership.

However it is not clear how far the formal schools will function within the overall framework or merely remain adjuncts to it. As they develop their community orientation along the lines favoured in Tanzania they will be greatly aided by the ready availability of resource units and staff, particularly if the latter are required to accept responsibility for assisting the schools. In such a pattern schooling may well benefit. The secondary school which has developed an agricultural bias has, however, been required, like other Tanzanian secondary schools, to select its entrants from the whole country, an arrangement which seems bound to reduce its local impact. The question remains, in what ways will the adult clienteles of the non-formal sections benefit from the association? Will they not have been shunted into an inferior learning system?

One answer to this question is that equality of educational opportunity does not necessarily mean that all should receive the same education. It may be argued that different groups of people have different learning needs which may be met by different means and that the real problem is to ensure a sufficient quantity and diversity of educational opportunities. To provide a common pattern of education for all would not equally meet the needs of all. The key issue, therefore, may be the extent to which people, having benefited from one kind of provision, should be allowed access to another, and not only because they may need it but because they want it. The African ministers saw this issue clearly and recommended that complementary forms of formal and nonformal education should be so structured within a nationwide learning system that mobility between the two would be possible. Essentially this means that whilst a diversity of provision should be created, bridges should be built between them over which individuals may pass.

There is no real problem in terms of mobility between different forms of non-formal education or between early formal and later non-formal education. Programmes for school leavers are found in many countries, for example in the *Centres à Orientation Pratique* in Mali, the village polytechnics in Kenya, or the Caritas Agricultural Training Centre in Nianing, Senegal. Their relationship to the formal system is essentially a one-way relationship. The centres pick up young people at an age when they will be sufficiently mature to learn manual skills of production, when they will possess sufficient general education to facilitate the training process and when, having been rejected by the formal system, they may be reconciled to their lot and more strongly motivated to take advantage of the training opportunity. Such facilities appear to be an essential though limited part of the network we are seeking.

The major problem is in respect of opportunities for mobility from non-formal to formal education. If these opportunities were to be confined to the few most talented individuals, they would not put excessive strain on the capacity of the formal system and perhaps more significantly would leave the non-formal section free to pursue its distinctive and essentially practical and specific purposes. To deliberately restrict such opportunities might well constitute a denial of equal opportunities, however. Yet to open up access, particularly to those levels of the formal system which are as yet not universal, to the large numbers who may be expected to want to move from non-formal to formal education, even assuming that the school places can be made available, might well have an undesirable backwash effect upon the non-formal sector. Clientele pressure might well distort important areas of non-formal education and change their valuable complementary function into a possibly less valuable supplementary function. Once the door is opened non-formal education which fails to prepare adequately for entry into the formal sector might well be rejected by its clientele.

If bridging of this kind is to be effective, much will depend upon the reforms contemplated in the formal school sector. Where schools are concerned with equipping young people for productive lives in their local communities, they are likely to have much in common with non-formal education and transition from one to the other will be much facilitated. At the same time there might be little value in withdrawing people from non-formal education and passing them through a more expensive formal programme if at the end they join the throng of frustrated and unemployed school leavers. But the attraction of the formal school rests upon the fact that it provides opportunities of access to the higher levels of the employment structure and it is possible that to extend second-chance and late-entry opportunities to groups so attracted will tend to hinder the efforts of re-schoolers to divert the middle level of the school away from its strong modern-sector orientation. We must also note the possible implications of developing comprehensive nationwide frameworks of non-formal education in the interests of equity as well as for development purposes. In discussing non-formal education we questioned whether current models of non-formal education were genuinely capable of wide extension – whether the resources would be available not merely for the educational provision but for promoting the kind of development which would enable communities to absorb the products productively and to make effective use of the instruction given – and we also asked whether the extension of non-formal education might not result in bureaucratic rigidities which might seriously reduce its effectiveness. If non-formal education is to be part of a universal lifelong education network, and if it is to be functionally interrelated with the formal education system, does this not involve the systematisation of non-formal education itself? If non-formal provision is to provide equality of opportunity, does this not mean that it must be far more widely available than at present and to a considerable extent follow a common pattern offering the same range of educational opportunity to all? If such an extension is to be achieved does this not mean that its growth and direction must be controlled and co-ordinated in order to avoid the pressure upon limited resources and the diversity of provision which might well result from leaving its development largely to community initiatives? And if this is the case, can non-formal education retain its responsiveness to particular local needs and situations – can it be geared practically to local development projects, for example?

There are many questions here and as yet we are not in a position to answer them except to suggest that it will require both strong political commitment and extremely sensitive management to build such a basic education network which will avoid the pitfalls whilst retaining the vigour and relevance of which it is potentially capable.

An example of a comprehensive and carefully worked out scheme for linking formal and non-formal education on a national basis, and one which will clearly encounter these problems, is to be found in the proposals for Community Education Centres in the Sierra Leone Education Review of 1976. The Review begins by stressing the need to see the education system as a whole consisting of interrelated and interdependent parts. Basic education, which for some time at least will be terminal for very many, will be provided both in formal primary schools and in new Community Education Centres (CECs). There will be common goals, embracing literacy, numeracy, rational understanding of environment, occupational skills, and positive attitudes and character traits. The CECs will be run in close liaison with primary schools and there will be sharing of facilities, but nevertheless 'the CECs should not be regarded as stepchildren within the existing formal system, nor should they be thought of merely as an "alternative" for a different age group.'[3] Initially they will serve adolescents and adults who have never been to school, and also school leavers who will eventually, as primary education expands, be the main target group. Thus in the early stages of development the CECs will form both part of the base and also part of the superstructure of the education system. They will provide supplementary and complementary programmes at both levels. Eventually they will merge with primary schools and become unified community schools, but the distinction between the two elements, it would seem, will remain, since at that stage each will deal with a different age range and the programmes for older entrants will be flexibly structured in the non-formal tradition rather than consist of whole-time extended periods of general education.

These centres will, however, differ from some other forms of supplementary or complementary non-formal provision in that they will be built into a single education system with clear bridges over which students may pass either into junior secondary schools or more advanced vocational or trades centres. Many of our questions are thereby raised. In the early stages many entrants to CECs will not have been to school, yet when the possibility is provided for them to move on to secondary schools at the end of their course, will not the CECs take on the appearance of a second-class primary school? In the later stages, when the bulk of the entrants are primary school leavers rejected for secondary education, will not the CECs be dominated by their concern to win a second chance of secondary entrance and so become a form of intermediate preparatory school? The Review itself recognises the problem and asks 'How are the primary schools to be related to the community education centres so as to ensure that they develop in such a way as to complement each other?'[4] It does not answer this question other than to note the need to resist the tendency for technical secondary education to be disassociated from other strands of secondary schooling, and to recommend close and continuing consultation between all the agencies involved.

It must be concluded that none of the models described, no matter what their other virtues (which may be considerable), is capable of achieving a perfect reconciliation between the demands of development and those of equity. Perhaps, then, we should be realistic and admit the necessity of adopting compromises which fall well short of the ideal.

For some time to come in many countries of Africa basic education will have to be provided both in school and out of school and it seems inevitable that the latter will not merely appear to be, but will in fact be, inferior to the former in terms of opening up possibilities of personal advancement, although it may well be superior in terms of promoting local community progress. In the longer term it appears likely that the pattern of linkage between formal and non-formal education will follow the later-stage model envisaged in Sierra Leone. Universal schooling of limited duration, possibly commencing at a later age and of a reformed kind, will provide the education base and thereafter a diversity of formal and non-formal provision will be made available to as many people as possible. Bridges will be built between only some kinds of non-formal education and the later stages of formal schooling, and the attempt will be made to encourage a recurrent pattern of education and training in which periods of study and training will alternate with periods of work.

By this means greater equality of opportunity will exist, if only in respect of opportunity to compete for those forms of post-basic education which are most in demand. Parallelism of provision will in this pattern be avoided at the basic education stage, but will inevitably continue to exist at post-basic levels since few African countries are likely in the foreseeable future to be able to offer universal secondary schooling. However at the post-basic stage, it may be argued, the diversification of educational opportunities is likely to be both more viable and more acceptable to clienteles for a number of reasons.

It is anticipated that basic education will develop in young people patterns of aspiration and behaviour which, coupled with appropriate skills, will enable them to take advantage of later training opportunities and thereby to improve their life chances and to take whatever opportunities may exist around them. Those who are fortunate enough to continue formal schooling to higher levels immediately will have been selected by aptitude and character and not merely according to formal academic ability, and will carry with them a better understanding of the community they will be called upon to serve. They will be joined by others who have followed a recurrent route, and together they will form a leadership group which, whilst it will inevitably be an elite of sorts, will not be quite so characterised by elitist feelings and perceptions.

It should not be assumed, however, that the fundamental shift in attitudes which is envisaged will be caused simply through the reform of basic schooling. It has been argued that the school, whatever its form, is unlikely to bring about such changes so long as it remains a selection instrument and so long as opportunities beyond basic schooling remain unequal. In the model we are considering both of these elements remain, although in ameliorated form. For the basic school to play its part harmoni-ously in the new framework and for the other components, both formal and non-formal, of post-basic education to be effective, the major attitudinal shift must be among the members of the community outside the school. To provide more equal oppor-tunities of competing for the more favoured forms of post-basic education will not necessarily satisfy them or reconcile those who must follow the non-formal route to their lot. The broad attitudinal changes which are the essential underpinnings of the reform must result from two factors. The first and least significant of these is the growing realism about the prospects offered in the modern sector which should encourage acceptance of alternative if less glittering forms of training and life chances. It must be recognised that by itself such a realisation may involve frustration and some degree of demoralisation. Consequently the second factor is crucial: it is growing awareness of the real potential which exists for improvement in people's own lives and circumstances and for this to exist there must be real achievement in the development of disadvantaged rural and urban communities.

Such real achievement will depend, it has been argued, on effective investment in these communities, investment which will increase the capacity of members of these communities to help themselves and which will include an appropriate educational component. This educational component may well take the form of non-formal training in occupational skills, home and community improvement techniques, linked to local development projects and serving highly specific and immediate purposes. These are precisely the kinds of educational investment which can least easily be fitted into a nationwide system such as we have been examining. The contention, therefore, may be that we should draw a distinction between those kinds of non-formal education which must be based upon previous formal education (which may be more appropriately termed 'further' education) and those for which no such previous education is necessary (even though it may be helpful). It then becomes possible to see how further education provision may be systematised and articulated with formal schooling whilst for a transitional period, which may last for some considerable time, a good deal of effort may be applied to promoting other forms of non-formal education which may make a positive contribution to people's lives without our having to concern ourselves with systematising it and relating it to other kinds of educational provision. Thereby much of the flexibility, cheapness, and immediate relevancy of non-formal education and training may be preserved.

This implies that we abandon the vain search for ways in which many different kinds of educational provision, each with its own value and contribution to make, may be so systematised that they offer equality of opportunity – or at least that we do so until such time as the basic plus further education structure can be completed and real development at community level has created an attitudinal climate which will make it possible for the structure to work as intended. It is then conceivable that if project-related non-formal education has proved its value, the people who are benefiting from it will wish it to continue and it will be unnecessary to seek to impose a system upon it.

## References

1. D. E. Bell, (Chairman), *Report of the External Advisory Panel on Education to the World Bank, 31 October 1978* (Washington, DC: The World Bank, 1978) p. 15.
2. Conference of Ministers of Education of African Member States, Lagos, 27 January–4 February 1976, *Final Report*, (Paris: UNESCO, 1976) p. 44.
3. University of Sierra Leone, *All our Future, Report of the Education Review 1973–4*, (Freetown: Government Printer, 1976) p. 9.
4. *Ibid.*, p. 81.

# Conclusion

In the first part of this book we asked what kinds of social change were taking place in our countries, what development might mean for our people, how educational patterns are affected by social change and in what general ways we have tried to use education to promote desired kinds of development. We were concerned to place educational systems firmly in their societal context and to establish the necessity of viewing them not in isolation but as a set of social institutions acting upon but at the same time being acted upon by other features of our societies.

In Part II we examined in more detail some basic issues relating to education and a number of specific aspects of development, noting some of the ways in which thinking about the role of education has evolved but challenging in the light of many years of experience some views of this role which have become very widely accepted and are all too rarely questioned. We noted how ideas about development strategy appear to be changing and how in the light of these we need to rethink the part which education may be able to play. It was suggested that many current criticisms of schooling may be ill-founded, that many of its apparent failings may be attributed to factors beyond the control of the educationist and to our failure to allocate realistic goals to school systems. The problem may lie as much in our enormous expectations as in the performance of the school.

We then turned, in Part III, to the problems of reforming education systems so that they may meet development needs more precisely and efficiently. We noted the limitations of planning techniques as so far developed in achieving a more accurate match between the two and commented upon what we have learned from experience about the difficulty of reforming school systems in particular, and the techniques which we may need to use if we are to achieve greater success in the future. School systems, it was suggested, are not easily manipulated to meet changing needs and goals, and the inertial forces we may encounter in seeking to improve their quality are very powerful and are not necessarily all discreditable.

In Part IV we examined trends in current thinking about the roles which education systems should play in development and the patterns of provision which may be most appropriate for this purpose, and noted some examples of efforts being made to apply this thinking in practice. We sought to identify some of the potential benefits and some of the problems associated with the use of non-formal educational approaches and with some patterns of re-schooling. Finally we asked how far and in what ways formal and non-formal approaches might be combined to provide an effective nationwide structure to meet all the various learning needs of our peoples. In this survey of new ideas and innovative practice we were not concerned with approving some and rejecting others, with arguing that one particular policy was right and another wrong. Our purpose was to survey the field and to raise some of the questions which educationists and others must ask when they come to judge the appropriateness of certain policies and practices for application in their own particular situation. These questions were derived from the broader discussion of development aims and strategies and of the function of education in the earlier sections of the book.

It has been suggested that in spite of our firm belief that education has a vital part to play in promoting various kinds of development, we educationists have not been sufficiently well equipped to undertake this task. Too few of us have known enough about the nature and processes of social change and of development to be able to contribute effectively to discussion of what education should be doing and of what it can and cannot achieve in given circumstances. In our own uncertainty we have often been unwilling to challenge the easy and often erroneous assumptions which others have made about the nature and capacity of education. One consequence has been that in spite of all the talk about integrated development planning and about education as a national investment, education systems have grown up largely in isolation, with only the most tenuous relationships to other developmental activity. Occasionally, to be sure, we glance over our shoulders at statements of national goals and educational policy but we easily find some justification there for continuing to do what we are already doing and little enough reason to re-examine our consciences. In a vague and in-articulate way some of us perhaps felt that education should assert the importance of developing individual minds and bodies in face of all the pressures of the mass society, that it was not our job to thrust our pupils into the planners' moulds. And many of us were more conscious of the pressures we were experiencing from the demands of parents and pupils than of those of more remote planning bodies.

But the result has been a possibly widening disjunction between what school systems were being expected to do and what they actually were doing, resulting in constant criticism from on high and a loss of confidence among those actually engaged in education. This process cannot continue without further under-mining the value of what we do and our own professional capacity to raise its quality. This enterprise to which we devote such a large proportion of our national resources has tended to operate like a primitive sailing ship responding sluggishly to contending winds and tides. Surely it must develop its own internal capacity to select and pursue its course. This is not to argue that educationists alone have the right to decide what needs to be done, as our earlier discussion should have made clear, but that the selection of the right course and the most efficient maintenance of that course must depend very largely upon the crew who man the ship, upon their seamanship and their self-confidence.

The implication of this for us is that as responsible education-ists we need constantly to re-examine what we are trying to do, to re-define and keep clearly in mind our fundamental purposes, and to clarify the real nature of the problems we face. We should beware of over-simplistic analyses and guard against emotional rhetoric. We owe it to ourselves, our pupils and our people to examine new ideas and proposals with a critical, not to say suspicious eye, and to avoid the common temptation to leap onto passing bandwagons and to applaud too readily that which claims to be new, authentic or revolutionary. Many new ideas turn out to be old ideas in new clothing and that which is genuinely new is not necessarily better than that which is old. The virtues of authenticity should not blind us to the value of that which is universal, nor should we too readily assume that older practice cannot be authentic. Some innovations which claim to be revolutionary may not in fact attack the roots of our problems and will not therefore be capable of bringing about revolutionary change, and in some cases we may have better hope of success from evolutionary processes. But we cannot stand still. Either we will go ahead or we will slide back. No single educational pattern will retain forever its relevance and efficiency in rapidly changing societies. There may be much of value in the new ideas, just as we may feel there is much of value in the old which we would wish to preserve, and we do ourselves no good service if we either seize too quickly upon the new or refuse too resolutely to discard the old.

It has not been the purpose of this book to propose solutions or to formulate proposals – indeed there may be many readers who at this point are feeling somewhat frustrated that no concrete prescriptions for success have been arrived at, or who find that many issues on which they were fairly clear at the outset are now clouded with questions. But at the beginning it was pointed out that the purpose of the book was to assist the reader to set out in search of a fuller understanding of his own country, of its development and of the place of education in that process – not to take him to the end of that journey. Partly this is because our situations differ so considerably, and partly because in any case none of us can be sure where the journey will end – certainly there are no quick and easy solutions and we do ourselves a disservice if we suppose that there are. It has also been pointed out that at this time there are major gaps in our knowledge about some very fundamental matters which may need to be filled before we can be confident in our pronouncements, and that to a considerable extent we may have to proceed by trial and error in order to learn from experience. Even so, our children are not guinea pigs to be experimented on with impunity and we must subject ideas to very critical scrutiny before we try them out in practice. Certainly we must make the fullest use of the experience which we and other countries already possess and monitor very carefully any future developments. Failures are not to be swept under the carpet but dissected for the lessons they may teach us. Similarly, apparent successes must be carefully analysed to provide us and others with fuller understanding of why they succeeded and whether they may succeed again under somewhat different circumstances.

Of course certain general propositions have been advanced in this book, and indeed in this conclusion. It has been suggested that our unreformed educational systems have in the past achieved a greater measure of success than they have sometimes been given credit for, that much criticism of school systems has been unjustified, that reform of school systems to meet changing needs must proceed hand-in-hand with other changes in society outside the school, that the transformation of school systems will be a slow and difficult task dependent in large measure upon the professional capacity of educationists, and that it may well be desirable to explore the potential of complementary patterns of education to free the school to do better those things which it can do well. These propositions too must be critically examined in the light of national and local purposes and circumstances.

The suggestions for further study and enquiry which follow are intended to assist the reader to continue further along the road upon which he has set out, to help him find out the facts of his own situation in order to begin to answer some of the questions raised, and to encourage him to formulate further questions and pursue further enquiries. The road will be hard but rewarding.

# Suggestions for Further Study

The suggestions which follow do not claim to be comprehensive but to indicate certain lines of enquiry which will help the reader to understand better his own situation and to perceive more clearly the relevance of the many considerations advanced in this book to his situation. They will of necessity demand enquiries to be made among colleagues, parents, teachers, students and other members of the community. The suggestions should be modified and extended as appropriate.

(1) Select a particular major change which has taken place in your community in recent years. Using the diagram on page 17 as a model, try to map out the various causes of this change and the consequences to which it appears to be leading. Compare your conclusions with those of others investigating this particular change by this method.

(2) In consultation with a group of people sharing a common culture, find out:

   (a) what they believe to be the essential and distinctive features of that culture;
   (b) what are the principal changes taking place in that culture at present;
   (c) what the major sources of change are;
   (d) how far they welcome change and what specific features of their culture they would hope to preserve.

(3) In consultation with a group of local people, investigate the process of informal education as it currently exists in their community. Define the principal characteristics of the process in terms of the following questions:

   (a) Whose responsibility is it?
   (b) What are its various aims – social, moral, religious, civic and economic – in order of importance?

(c) What rewards, punishments, and sanctions are in use as means of motivating or disciplining young people?

(d) How is instruction given? How far is it first-hand, how far vicarious, how far directed to the intellect?

(e) How far is the content clearly prescribed? How far is it future/present oriented?

(f) How far is the process different for different individuals or groups according to age, sex, status, etc.?

(g) How adequate is the process in preparing the child for life in this community, and for preparing him for life in his national community?

(4) Examine statements of national goals for education as set out by policy-makers in your country. Are priorities defined? Which of the stated goals may be categorised as 'conservative', 'innovative' or 'liberative' as defined on pages 30–1? What potential for conflict between goals exists in these statements? Compare the statements of the policy makers with the views of parents and children.

(5) In consultation with a group of people drawn from different cultural groups within your country consider the extent and causes of disunity within the country. How far do they believe that through education these problems may be remedied?

(6) In consultation with a group of experienced primary school teachers consider the existing primary school curriculum in your country:

(a) Is it equally well suited to the background and needs of children in different parts of the country?

(b) In what ways do children from different home backgrounds respond differently to the demands of the curriculum and what different problems do they face?

(c) What are teachers currently doing to meet any such problems?

(7) In considering the economic role of education, the first task is to collect a certain amount of basic data, and the second is to analyse this data in the light of the questions and consider-

ations raised in chapter 4. It is suggested that you might begin with the kinds of data listed below, much of which will be found in the latest edition of the UNESCO Statistical Yearbook, in your current development plan, in national surveys conducted by the World Bank or by other bodies, and in national statistical reports, etc. The data may not always be up to date but you should try to use what is available.

| *Population Data* | *Number* | *Rate of Growth* |
|---|---|---|
| Total | | |
| School age | | |
| Urban | | |
| Rural | | |
| Major ethnic or tribal groups | | |
| Major religious groups | | |

ECONOMIC DATA

Current GNP, current GNP per capita, rates of growth in recent years.

Contribution to GNP of major sectors of the economy (e.g. agriculture, manufacturing, service industries, etc.) and rates of growth in these contributions.

Annual recurrent revenue, amounts of aid received, rates of growth in recent years.

Financial allocations to the various major sectors of the economy in the current development plan.

Major occupational groups in the population, for example:

Professional (doctor, lawyer, senior civil servant, graduate teacher, etc.);

Managerial (leading businessmen in commerce, manufacturing, construction, etc.);

Executive (junior civil servants, clerical occupation, supervisors in industry, etc.);

Technicians or tradesmen (mechanic, electrician, shopkeeper, etc.);

Commercial farmers;

Manual (subsistence farmers, other semi- and unskilled workers).

Average income per annum of members of these groups.
Rate of increase in wage employment.

EDUCATIONAL DATA

Current enrolment at each level of the school system, and percentage of age group.
Current recurrent expenditure on each level of education and average cost per pupil per annum.
Number of school leavers from each level of the school system entering the employment market in the current year.
Percentage of illiterates in the total population.

(8) Design and conduct a survey of students in teacher training colleges. Among the many questions you may wish to ask include the following:

(a) What were their reasons for entering teacher education?
(b) What are their hopes and what their expectations of their career in education?
What other aspirations have they for their personal futures?
(c) What courses are they studying, what relative importance do they ascribe to these courses and how much time do they allocate to each?
(d) What changes in their programmes of study would they most welcome?

(9) Design and conduct a survey of experienced serving teachers either in primary or secondary schools. Construct career profiles showing the following:

(a) In how many schools have they taught and for how long in each? What patterns of movement are revealed, for example from rural to urban schools, from lower to higher classes?
(b) At what stage did they receive promotion and what other form of recognition do they feel they have received?
(c) What opportunities for further education and for further professional training have they received, of what kind and with what consequences?

(d) What contact do they have with inspectors, teacher training colleges, resource centres, other schools and other teachers, etc?

Also collate their views of:

(a) Their career opportunities.
(b) The relevance and value of any training they may have received.
(c) The kinds of further training and education they would prefer.
(d) The kinds of educational change they would most/least prefer.
(e) The extent to which they would welcome responsibility for introducing changes into their schools.

(10) Assume that you have been given responsibility for introducing a new syllabus in your subject into your school system. List the various kinds of action which will be necessary including design, materials production, dissemination of materials, teacher training, provision of buildings/ equipment, development of new examinations, etc. Then enter these kinds of action on a grid constructed as below:

*Time scale in years and months*

| *Action necessary* | *First year* | | | | | | | | | | | | *Second year* | | | | | | | | | | | |
|---|---|---|---|---|---|---|---|---|---|---|---|---|---|---|---|---|---|---|---|---|---|---|---|---|
| | 1 | 2 | 3 | 4 | 5 | 6 | 7 | 8 | 9 | 10 | 11 | 12 | 1 | 2 | 3 | 4 | 5 | 6 | 7 | 8 | 9 | 10 | 11 | 12 |
| 1. | | | | | | | | | | | | | | | | | | | | | | | | |
| 2. | | | | | | | | | | | | | | | | | | | | | | | | |
| 3. | | | | | | | | | | | | | | | | | | | | | | | | |
| 4. | | | | | | | | | | | | | | | | | | | | | | | | |
| etc. | | | | | | | | | | | | | | | | | | | | | | | | |

Finally on the grid enter up the dates of the various stages of implementation, for example the beginning of the design phase, the initiation and completion of materials production, etc., ensuring that the various actions are in phase with each other (for example, that the syllabus does not have to be taught before the materials are available or the teachers trained). The growing size and complexity of your grid, which should be a large one, will illustrate the problems and cost in effort, money and time of even apparently straightforward innovations.

(11) In consultation with a suitable group of parents consider:

  (a) What do they expect schooling to do for their children, what do they dislike about existing schooling, in what ways do they encourage and help their children?

  (b) Using a categorisation of learning need and clientele such as that of Coombs and Ahmed (pages 216–17) define what they believe to be their own principal learning needs in order of importance, and how they think these might be met.

  (c) What part does literacy play in their daily lives and what literature is available to them? What use do they make of radio programmes? What contact do they have with extension and similar community development officers?

  (d) How far do they feel that they can positively contribute to the improvement of their own lives and how far are they prepared to learn from each other rather than from an outside expert?

(12) In consultation with a group of teachers consider:

  (a) How far and in what ways they see themselves and their pupils as being able to serve as community *animateurs*, what problems would they anticipate, what training and resources would they require?

  (b) In their schools what specific kinds of decision-making responsibility might be allocated to teachers and/or parents and/or pupils?

  (c) What local production activities might they introduce into the schools, who might teach them, how much time might be allocated to them, what purposes would be served, and how would these be related to 'classroom teaching'? What resources, etc., would be needed?

  (d) What programmes of study structured around community problems would be possible in their schools, what kinds of activities could pupils realistically undertake, what outcomes would they anticipate and what problems would they expect to encounter?

# Select Bibliography

A comprehensive bibliography for each country has not been attempted. A number of titles referring to particular countries have been included, however, as being of general significance.

Abdurrahman, M. and Canham, P., *The Ink of the Scholar – The Islamic Tradition of Education in Nigeria* (London: Macmillan, 1978).

Abernethy, D. B., *The Political Dilemma of Popular Education: an African Case* (Stanford University Press, 1969).

Acheampong, I. K., 'Guide to the Study of the Charter of the National Redemption Council', (February, 1972).

Adamalekun, L., *Sékou Touré's Guinea* (London: Methuen, 1977).

Adams, D. (ed.), *Education in National Development* (London: Routledge & Kegan Paul, 1971).

Ahmed, M., *The Economics of Nonformal Education* (New York: Praeger, 1975).

Akinpelu, J. A., 'The Educative Processes in Non-literate Societies: An Essay in the Anthropological Foundations of Education', *West African Journal of Education*, vol. XVIII, no. 3 (October 1974).

Altbach, P. G. and Kelly, D. H., *Higher Education in Developing Nations – a Selected Bibliography* (New York: Praeger, 1975).

Anderson, C. A. and Bowman M. J. (eds.), *Education and Economic Development* (Chicago: Aldine, 1965).

Anderson, C. A., *The Social Context of Educational Planning*, Fundamentals of Educational Planning, no. 5 (Paris: UNESCO IIEP, 1967).

Anderson, J., *The Struggle for the School* (London: Longman, 1970).

Andreski, S., *The African Predicament: A Study in the Pathology of Modernization* (London: Joseph, 1968).

Bamgbose, A. (ed.), *Mother Tongue Education: The West African Experience* (London: Hodder & Stoughton, 1976).

Barkan, J. B., *An African Dilemma – University Students, Development and Politics in Ghana, Tanzania and Uganda* (Nairobi: OUP, 1975).

Battle, V. and Lyons, C. H. (eds.), *Essays in the History of African Education* (New York: Teachers College Press, 1970).

Becket, P. and O'Connell, J., *Education and Power in Nigeria: A Study of University Students* (London: Hodder & Stoughton, 1977).

Beeby, C. E., *Planning and the Educational Administrator*, Fundamentals of Educational Planning no. 4 (Paris: UNESCO IIEP, 1967).

Beeby, C. E., *The Quality of Education in Developing Countries* (Cambridge, Mass: Harvard University Press, 1968).

Beeby, C. E. (ed.), *Qualitative Aspects of Educational Planning* (Paris: UNESCO IIEP, 1969).

Bell, D. E. (Chairman), *Report of the External Advisory Panel on Education to the World Bank, 31 October 1978* (Washington, DC: World Bank, 1978).

Bennis, W. G., Benne, K. D., Chin, R. and Corey, K. E. (eds), *The Planning of Change* (3rd edition) (New York: Holt Rinehart & Winston, 1976).

Bereday, G. Z. F., and Lauwerys, J. A. (eds), *Educational Planning* (London: Evans World Yearbook of Education, 1967).

Berman, E. G. (ed.), *African Reactions to Missionary Education* (New York, London: Teachers College Press, 1975).

Bernard Van Leer Foundation, *Relevant Technology – A New Strategy for Development and Education in Rural Areas* (The Hague, 1977).

Bernstein, H. (ed.), *Under-development and Development: the Third World Today: Selected Readings* (Harmondsworth: Penguin, 1973).

Blaug, M., 'Literacy and Economic Development', *The School Review*, Winter 1966.

Blaug, M. (ed.), *Economics of Education: Selected Readings* (two vols.) (Harmondsworth: Penguin, 1968 and 1969).

Blaug, M., *Education and the Employment Problem in Developing Countries* (Geneva: ILO, 1973).

Blaug, M., *Economics of Education: A Selected Annotated Bibliography* (third edition) (Oxford: Pergamon, 1978).

Blaug, M. and Mace, J., 'Recurrent Education: The New Jerusalem', *Higher Education*, vol. 6, (1977).

Boateng, E. A., *A Political Geography of Africa* (Cambridge University Press, 1979).

Bonanni, C., 'Fundamental and Basic Education: Some Differences', *Literacy Work*, vol. 7 no. 1, (Spring 1978).

Bown, L. and Tomori, S. H. O. (eds), *Handbook of Adult Education for West Africa* (London: Hutchinson, 1979).

Brembeck, C. S. and Thompson, T. J. (eds), *New Strategies for Educational Development: The Cross-Cultural Search for Nonformal Alternatives* (London, Lexington and Toronto: Lexington Books, 1973).

Brookfield, H. C., *Inter-dependent Development* (London: Methuen, 1975).

Brown, G. and Hiskett, M. (eds), *Conflict and Harmony in Education in Tropical Africa* (London: Allen & Unwin, 1975).

Cairncross, A. and Puri, M. (eds), *Employment, Income Distribution and Development Strategy Problems of the Developing Countries, Essays in Honour of Hans Singer.* (London: Macmillan, 1976).

Caldwell, J. C. (ed.), *Population Growth and Socio-Economic Change in West Africa* (Columbia University Press, 1976).

Callaway, A. and Bettenhausen, K., *Approaches to Employment Problems in Africa and Asia* (London: Commonwealth Secretariat, 1973).

Callaway, A., *Educational Planning and Unemployed Youth*, Fundamentals of Educational Planning no. 14 (Paris: UNESCO/IIEP, 1971).

Case, H. L. and Niehoff, R. O., *Educational Alternatives in National Development: Suggestions for Policy Makers* (East Lansing: Michigan State University Institute for International Studies in Education, 1976).

Castle, E. B., *Growing up in East Africa* (London, Nairobi, Ibadan: Oxford University Press, 1966).

Castle, E. B., *Education for Self Help: New Strategies for Developing Countries* (London, Nairobi, Delhi: Oxford University Press, 1972).

Centre for the Study of Education in Changing Societies (CESO), *Primary Education in Sukumaland, Tanzania* (Groningen: Wolters-Noordhoff, 1969).

CESO, *Educational Problems in Developing Countries* (Groningen: Wolters-Noordhoff, 1969).

Chambers, R. and Belshawe, D., 'Managing Rural Development: Lessons and Methods from Eastern Africa', Discussion Paper No. 15, University of Sussex Institute of Development Studies, June 1973.

Chambers, R., *Managing Rural Development: Ideas and Experience from East Africa* (Almquist & Wiksell International, 1974).

Christian Council of Kenya, *After School, What? Further Education, Training and Employment of Primary School Leavers.* (Nairobi: CCK and Christian Churches Educational Association, 1966).

Colclough, C. and Hallak, J., 'Some issues in Rural Education – Equity, Efficiency and Employment', Discussion Paper No. 89, Sussex University Institute of Development Studies, 1976.

Coleman, J. S. (ed.), *Education and Political Development* (Princeton University Press, 1965).

Coles, E. K. T., *Adult Education in Developing Countries* (2nd Edition), (Oxford: Pergamon, 1977).

Commonwealth Secretariat, *Youth and Development in Africa* (London: Commonwealth Secretariat, 1969).

Commonwealth Secretariat, *Education in Rural Areas*, Report of the Commonwealth Conference on Education in Rural Areas, Ghana 1970 (London: Commonwealth Secretariat, 1970).

Commonwealth Secretariat, *The Role of Teachers' Organizations in National Development*, Report of the Commonwealth Conference of Teachers' Organizations, Cambridge 1972 (London: Commonwealth Secretariat, 1972).

Commonwealth Secretariat, *A Handbook of Educational Administration and Supervision*, Preliminary Report of the Commonwealth African Regional Seminar on Administration and Supervision in Education, Freetown, Sierra Leone, May 1973 (Freetown, 1973).

Commonwealth Secretariat, *Teaacher Education in a Changing Society – Commonwealth Conference on Teacher Education, Nairobi, Kenya 1973* (London, 1974).

Commonwealth Secretariat, *Approaches to Employment Problems in Africa and Asia* (London: Commonwealth Secretariat, 1973).

Commonwealth Secretariat, *Report of the Sixth Commonwealth Education Conference, Jamaica 1974* (London: Commonwealth Secretariat, 1974).

Coombs, P. H., *The World Educational Crisis, a Systems Analysis* (New York: OUP, 1968).

Coombs, P. H., *What is Educational Planning?*, Fundamentals of Educational Planning Series no. 1 (Paris: UNESCO/IIEP, 1970).

Coombs, P. H. and Hallak, J. (eds), *Educational Cost Analysis in Action: Case Studies for Planners* (3 vols) (Paris: UNESCO/IIEP, 1972).

Coombs, P. H. with Prosser, R. and Ahmed, M., *New Paths to Learning for Rural Children and Youth* (Essex, Conn., USA: International Council for Educational Development, 1973).

Coombs, P. H. with Ahmed, M., *Attacking Rural Poverty, How Nonformal Education Can Help*, (Baltimore: Johns Hopkins University Press, 1974).

Coombs, P. H., 'Nonformal Education in Rural Development', *Educational Development International*, vol. 2 no. 4 (October 1974).

Couch, M., 'A Select Bibliography on Educational Trends in Developing Countries', *International Review of Education*, vol. XVII (1971/2) (special no.).

Court, D. and Ghai, D. P. (eds), *Education, Society and Development: New Perspectives from Kenya* (Nairobi: OUP, 1974).

Court, D., 'The Education System as a response to inequality in Tanzania and Kenya', *Journal of Modern African Studies*, vol. 14 no. 4 (1976).

Court, D. and Kinyanjui, K., *Development Policy and Educational Opportunity: The Experience of Kenya and Tanzania* (Paris: IIEP/UNESCO, 1978).

Coverdale, G. M., *Planning Education in Relation to Rural Development*, Fundamentals of Educational Planning Series no. 21 (Paris: IIEP/UNESCO, 1974).

Cowan, L. G., O'Connell, J. and Scanlon, D. G. (eds), *Education and Nationbuilding in Africa* (New York, Washington, London: Praeger, 1965).

Curle, A., *Educational Strategy for Developing Societies, a Study of Educational and Social Factors in Relation to Economic Growth* (London: Tavistock, 1963).

Curle, A., *Educational Problems of Developing Societies, with Case Studies of Ghana and Pakistan* (New York, London: Praeger, 1969).

Curle, A., *Education for Liberation* (London: Tavistock, 1973).

D'Aeth, R. H., *Education and Development in the Third World* (Farnborough: Saxon House, 1975).

Dalin, P., *Limits to Educational Change* (London: Macmillan (with IMTEC), 1978).

Damachi, U. G. *et al.* (eds), *Development Paths in Africa and China* (London: Macmillan, 1976).

Debeauvais, M., 'The Popularity of the Idea of Innovation: A Tentative Interpretation of the Texts', *Innotech Journal*, vol. 1 no. 2 (July 1977).

De Vries, E., *Man in Rapid Social Change* (London: SCM Press, 1961).

Dewey, J., 'Educational and Social Change', *Social Frontier*, vol. 3 (May 1937).

Dewey, J., *Democracy and Education* (reprint of 1916 edition) (New York: Macmillan, 1948).

Dodd, W. A., *Primary School Inspection in New Countries* (London, Nairobi, Ibadan: OUP, 1968).

Dore, R., 'De-school? Try using Schools for Education First: The Educational Impasse in the Developing World', Discussion Paper 6, Institute for Development Studies, Sussex University (January 1974).

Dore, R., *The Diploma Disease: Education, Qualification and Development* (London: Allen and Unwin, 1976).

Dubbeldam L. F. B., *The Primary School and the Community in Mwanza District, Tanzania* (Groningen: Wolters-Noordhoff, 1970).

Emmerson, D. K. (ed.), *Students and Politics in Developing Nations* (London: Pall Mall, 1968).

Evans, D. R., 'Technology in Nonformal Education, a Critical Appraisal', *Comparative Education Review*, no. 20 (1976).

Evans, J. L., *Children in Africa, a Review of Psychological Research* (New York: Teachers College Press, 1970).

Fafunwa, A. B. and Adaralegbe, A. (eds), *Education in Nigeria – Towards Better Administration and Supervision of Instruction*, proceedings of first seminar on

School Administration and Supervision (Institute of Education, University of Ife, 1971).

Fafunwa, A. B., 'Education in the Mother Tongue – a Nigerian experiment, the Six Year (Yoruba Medium) Primary Education Project at the University of Ife, Nigeria', *West African Journal of Education*, vol. xix no. 2 (1975).

Faure, E. *et al.*, *Learning To Be, the World of Education Today and Tomorrow* (Paris: UNESCO, 1972).

Federal Ministry of Education, Nigeria, *Investment in Education*, the report of the Commission on Post-School Certificate and Higher Education in Nigeria (The 'Ashby Report') (Lagos: Federal Government Printer, 1960).

Federal Republic of Nigeria, *Second National Development Plan 1970–74* (Lagos: Ministry of Information, 1970).

Federal Republic of Nigeria, *National Policy on Education* (Lagos: Ministry of Information, 1977).

Foster, P. J., 'Ethnicity and the Schools in Ghana', *Comparative Education Review*, October 1962.

Foster, P. J., *Education and Social Change in Ghana* (London: Routledge, 1965).

Foster, P. J. and Clignet, R., *The Fortunate Few – A Study of Secondary Schools and Students in the Ivory Coast* (Illinois: Northwestern University Press, 1966).

Foster, P. J. and Sheffield, J. R. (eds), *Education and Rural Development*, World Yearbook of Education (London: Evans, 1974).

Freire, P., *Pedagogy of the Oppressed* (Harmondsworth: Penguin, 1972).

Freire, P., *Education for Critical Consciousness* (London: Sheed & Ward, 1974).

The Gambia, *Education Policy 1974/5–1984/5*, Third draft (n.d.)

Gardner, R. (ed.), *Teacher Education in Developing Countries, Prospects for the Eighties* (University of London Institute of Education, 1979).

Gay, J. H. and Cole, M., *The Cultural Context of Learning and Thinking* (London: Methuen, 1971).

Gay, J. H. and Cole, M., *The New Mathematics and an Old Culture: A Study of Learning among the Kpelle of Liberia* (New York: Holt, Rinehart & Winston, 1967).

Geertz, C. (ed.), *The Quest for Modernity in Asia and Africa* (Free Press, 1963).

Goldthorpe, J. E., *The Sociology of the Third World: Disparity and Involvement* (Cambridge University Press, 1975).

Grandstaff, M., *Alternatives in Education – A Summary View of Research and Analysis on the Concept of Nonformal Education* (East Lansing, Mich: Michigan State University Institute for International Studies in Education, 1974).

Great Britain, *Education Policy in British Tropical Africa*, Cmd. 2374 (London HMSO, 1925).

Great Britain, *Memorandum on the Education of African Communities*, Col. No. 103 (London: HMSO, 1935).

Great Britain, *Statement on Colonial Development and Welfare*, Cmd 6175 (London: HMSO, 1940).

Griffiths, V. L., *The Problems of Rural Education* (Paris: UNESCO/IIEP, 1968).

Gugler, J. and Flanagan, W. G., *Urbanization and Social Change in West Africa* (Cambridge University Press, 1978).

Guilavogui, G., 'The Basis of the Educational Reform in the Republic of Guinea', *Prospects*, vol. v no. 4 (1975).

Gutkind, P. C. W. and Wallerstein, I., *The Political Economy of Contemporary Africa* (London: Sage, 1976).

Hall, B. L., 'The Structure of Adult Education and Rural Development in Tanzania', Discussion paper no. 67, Sussex University Institute of Development Studies (1975).

Hancock, A., *Planning for Educational Mass Media* (London: Longman, 1977).

Hanson, J. W., *Imagination and Hallucination in African Education* (East Lansing, Mich: Michigan State University, Institute for International Studies in Education, 1965).

Hanson, J. W., and Brembeck, C. S. (eds), *Education and the Development of Nations* (New York: Holt, Rinehart & Winston, 1966).

Hanson, J. W., *Report on the Supply of Secondary Level Teachers in English-speaking Africa* (Reports prepared on 15 African countries together with a summary volume) (East Lansing, Mich: Michigan State University for the Overseas Liaison Committee of the American Council on Education, 1969–74).

Harbison, F. H. and Myers, C. A., *Education, Manpower and Economic Growth: Strategies of Human Resource Development* (New York, London: McGraw-Hill, 1964).

Harbison, F. H. and Myers, C. A. (eds), *Manpower and Education: Country Studies in Economic Development* (New York: McGraw-Hill, 1965).

Harbison, F. H., *A Human Resource Approach to the Development of African Nations* (Washington: American Council on Education, Overseas Liaison Committee, n.d.).

Hauser, P. M., 'Cultural Obstacles to Economic Development in Less Developed Areas', *Human Organisation*, vol. 18 no. 2 (1959).

Havelock, R. G. and Huberman, A. M., *Solving Educational Problems, the Theory and Reality of Innovation in Developing Countries* (Paris: International Bureau of Education, UNESCO, 1977).

Hawes, H. W. R., *Lifelong Education, Schools and Curricula in Developing Countries*, report of an international seminar, Hamburg 1974, (Hamburg: UNESCO Institute for Education, 1975).

Hawes, H. W. R., *et al.*, *Curriculum and Reality in African Primary Schools* (Harlow: Longman, 1979).

Hennessy, P., 'Manpower Plans are Wild Guesses', *Times Higher Education Supplement*, 19 January 1973.

Heyneman, S. P., 'Why Impoverished Children Do Well in Ugandan Schools', *Comparative Education*, vol. 15 no. 2 (June 1979).

Hill, P., *Studies in Rural Capitalism in West Africa* (London: Cambridge University Press, 1970).

Hirji, K. F., 'School Education and Underdevelopment in Tanzania', *Maji Maji*, September 1973.

Hoogvelt, A. M. M., *The Sociology of Developing Societies* (London: Macmillan, 1976).

Hopcraft, P., 'Does Education Increase Farm Productivity', Working Paper no. 279, Institute for Development Studies, Nairobi University, 1976.

Houghton, H. and Tregear, P., *Community Schools in Developing Countries* (Hamburg: UNESCO Institute for Education, 1969).

Huberman, A. M., *Reflections on the Democratisation of Secondary and Higher Education* (Paris: UNESCO, 1970).

Huberman, A. M., *Understanding Change in Education: An Introduction* (Paris: International Bureau of Education, UNESCO, 1973).

Hufner, K. and Naumann, J. (eds), *Economics of Education in Transition* (Stuttgart: Ernst Klett Verlag, 1969).

Hughes, M. (ed.), *Administering Education: International Challenge* (London: Athlone Press, 1975).

Hunter, G., *Modernizing Peasant Societies: a Comparative Study in Asia and Africa* (London: Oxford University Press, 1969).

Hunter, G., Bunting, A. H. and Bottrall, A. (eds), *Policy and Practice in Rural Development*, proceedings of the Second International Seminar on Change in Agriculture, Reading, 1974. (London: Croom Helm, 1976).

Husen, T., *Social Background and Educational Career: Research Perspectives on Equality of Educational Opportunity* (Paris: OECD, 1972).

International Bureau of Education, 'Education for Rural Life', *Bulletin of the International Bureau of Education*, no. 183 (1972).

International Bureau of Education and Network of Educational Innovation for Development in Africa, *Educational Reforms and Innovations in Africa* (Paris: UNESCO, 1978).

International Institute for Adult Literacy Methods, *Rural Education: A Select Bibliography* (Paris: UNESCO International Institute for Educational Planning, 1975).

International Labour Office, *Employment in Africa, Some Critical Issues* (Geneva: ILO, 1973).

International Labour Office Mission, *Interim Report on Education in a Rural Area of Western Nigeria* (Ibadan: Ministry of Economic Planning and Social Development, 1967).

Irvine, S. H. and Sanders, J. L. (eds), *Cultural Adaptation within Modern Africa* (New York: Teachers College Press, 1972).

Jolly, R. and Coleclough, C., 'African Manpower Plans: An Evaluation', *International Labour Review*, vol. 106 no. 2–3 (1972).

Jolly, R., De Kadt E., Singer, H. and Wilson, F. (eds), *Third World Employment – Problems and Strategy: Selected Readings* (Harmondsworth: Penguin, 1973).

Jolly, R. (ed.), *Education in Africa: Research and Action* (Nairobi: East African Publishing House, 1969).

Kabwasa, A. and Kaunda, M. (eds), *Correspondence Education in Africa* (London: Routledge, 1973).

Kajubi, S. (ed.), *Reform of the Professional Education of Teachers in Africa*, report of the Conference of the Association for Teacher Education in Africa, Makerere 1973 (ATEA, 1973).

Kamarck, A. M., *The Economics of African Development* (New York: Praeger, 1967).

Kaunda, K., *Humanism in Zambia* (Lusaka: Zambia Information Services, n.d.).

Kay, S., 'Curriculum Innovations and a Traditional Culture, a Case History of Kenya', *Comparative Education*, vol. 11 no. 3 (1975).

Kenyatta, J., *Facing Mount Kenya* (London: Mercury Books, 1961).

Killick, T., *The Economics of East Africa: A Bibliography 1963–75* (Boston, Mass: G. K. Hall, 1976).

King, K., 'Productive Labour and the School System: Contradictions in the Training of Artisans in Kenya', *Comparative Education*, vol. 10 no. 3 (October 1974).

King, K., *Education and Community in Africa, proceedings of a seminar held in the Centre of African Studies* (University of Edinburgh, 1976).

King, K., *The African Artisan: Education and the Informal Sector in Kenya* (London: Heinemann, 1977).

Klinberg, O. and Zavalloni, M., *Nationalism and Tribalism among African students* (Brussels: Mouton et Cie, 1969).

Klingelhofer, E. L., *A Bibliography of Psychological Research and Writings on Africa* (Uppsala: The Scandinavian Institute of African Studies, 1967).

Kreinen, I., *Israel and Africa* (New York: Praeger, 1964).

La Belle, T. J., Coombs, P. H. *et al.*, 'Nonformal Education: A Symposium', *Comparative Education Review*, vol. 20 (1976).

Lallez, R., *An Experiment in the Ruralisation of Education, IPAR and the Cameroonian Reform* (Paris: UNESCO, 1974).

Laye, C., *The African Child* (London: Fontana, 1959).

Lewis, L. J., *Educational Policy and Practice in British Tropical Areas* (London: Nelson, 1954).

Lewis, L. J., *The Phelps-Stokes Reports on Education in Africa* (London: OUP, 1962).

Lewis, W. A., 'Education and Economic Development', *International Social Science Journal*, vol. xiv no. 4 (1962).

Lloyd, P. C. (ed.), *The New Elites of Tropical Africa* (London: OUP, 1966).

Lloyd, P. C., *Africa in Social Change, Changing Traditional Societies in the Modern World* (Harmondsworth: Penguin, 1967).

Lloyd, P. C., *Classes, Crises and Coups* (London: Paladin, 1973).

Lockheed, M. E., Jamison, D. T. and Lau, L. J., *Farmer Education and Farm Efficiency: A Review of the Literature* (World Bank Development Economics Department, 1978).

Long, N., *An introduction to the Sociology of Rural Development*, (London: Tavistock, 1977).

Lowe, J. (ed.), *Adult Education and Nation Building: A Symposium on Adult Education in Developing Countries* (Edinburgh University Press, 1970).

Lowe, J., Grant, N. and Williams, T. D., *Education and Nation Building in the Third World* (Edinburgh: Scottish Academic Press, 1971).

Lowe, J., *The Education of Adults — a World Perspective* (UNESCO/Ontario Institute for Studies in Education, 1975).

Lyons, R. F., *Administrative Support for Educational Reform* (Paris: IIEP, 1977).

Mair, L., *New Nations* (London: Weidenfeld and Nicolson, 1963).

Mair, L., *African Societies* (London: Cambridge University Press, 1974).

Malassis, L., *The Rural World, Education and Development* (London: Croom Helm, 1976).

Markowitz, I. L. (ed.), *African Politics and Society: Basic Issues and Problems of Government and Development* (New York: Collier–Macmillan, 1970).

Middleton, J. (ed.), *From Child to Adult* (New York: Natural History Press, 1970).

Minogue, M. and Molloy, J. (eds), *African Aims and Attitudes – Selected Documents* (London: Cambridge University Press, 1974).

Montgomery, J. D., *Alternatives and Decisions in Educational Planning*, Fundamentals of Educational Planning Series no. 22, (Paris: UNESCO/IIEP, 1977).

Morrison, D. R., *Education and Politics in Africa – The Tanzanian Case* (London: Hurst, 1976).

Moumouni, A., *Education in Africa* (London: Deutsch, 1968).

Musgrove, F., 'Education and the Culture Concept' *Africa*, vol. XXIII (1953).

Myrdal, G., *Asian Drama, an Enquiry into the Poverty of Nations* (three volumes) (Harmondsworth: Penguin, 1968).

Network of Educational Innovation for Development in Africa (NEIDA), *Inventory of Educational Innovations in Africa* (Dakar: UNESCO, 1978).

Niehoff, R. O. and Neff, K. L. (eds), *Nonformal Education and the Rural Poor* (East Lansing, Mich: Michigan State University, 1977).

Nuffield Foundation and Colonial Office, *African Education, a Study of Educational Policy and Practice in British Tropical Africa* (Oxford University Press, 1953)

Nyerere, J. K., *Freedom and Unity* (Dar es Salaam: OUP, 1967).

Nyerere, J. K., *Education for Self Reliance* (Dar es Salaam: Government printer, 1967).

Nyerere, J. K., *Ujamaa: Essays on Socialism* (Dar es Salaam: OUP, 1968).

Nyerere, J. K., *Freedom and Development* (Dar es Salaam: OUP, 1973).

Nyerere, J. K., *Man and Development* (Dar es Salaam: OUP, 1974).

Onuoha, N. K., 'The Role of Education in Nation-Building: A Case Study of Nigeria', *West African Journal of Education*, vol. XIX no. 3 (October 1975).

Paulston, R. G., *Nonformal Education: An Annotated International Bibliography of the Non-School Sector* (New York: Praeger, 1977).

Petch, G. A., *Economic Development and Modern West Africa* (University of London Press, 1966).

Phillips, H. M., *Literacy and Development* (Paris: UNESCO, 1970).

Phillips, H. M., *Basic Education – A World Challenge, Measures and Innovations for Children and Youth in Developing Countries* (London, New York: Wiley, 1975).

Piper, D. C. and Cole, T., *Post-primary Education and Political and Economic Development* (Durham, NC: Duke University Commonwealth Studies Centre, 1964).

Ponsioen, J. A. (ed.), *Educational Innovations in Africa: Policies and Administration* (The Hague: Institute of Social Studies, 1972).

Raju, B, M., *Education in Kenya – Problems and Perspectives in Educational Planning and Administration* (Heinemann Educational Books, East Africa, 1974).

Ranger, T., 'African Attempts to Control Education in East and Central Africa 1900–1939', *Past and Present*, no. 32 (December 1965).

Republic of Kenya, Ministry of of Education, *A Study of Curriculum Development in Kenya* (Chairman, G. S. Bessey) (Nairobi, 1972).

Republic of Kenya, *Development Plan, 1974–8* (Nairobi: Government Printer, 1974).

Resnick, I. (ed.), *Tanzania: Revolution by Education* (Arusha: Longmans of Tanzania, 1968).

Ronen, D., 'Alternative Patterns of Integration in African States', *Journal of Modern African Studies*, vol. 14 no. 4 (1976).

Rostow, W. W., *The Stages of Economic Growth: A Non-communist Manifesto* (London: Cambridge University Press, 1960).

Rowley, I. D., *The Politics of Educational Planning in Developing Countries* (Paris: UNESCO/IIEP, 1971).

Ruscoe, G. O., *The Conditions for Success in Educational Planning*, Fundamentals of Educational Planning Series no. 12, (Paris: UNESCO/IIEP, 1969).

Scanlon, D. G., *Traditions of African Education* (New York: Teachers College Press, 1964).

Schapera, I., *Tribal Innovators: Tswana Chiefs and Social Change 1795–1940* (London University Press, 1970).

Schiman, D. A., 'Selection for Secondary School in Ghana', *West African Journal of Education*, vol. xv no. 3 (October 1971).

Schramm, W., *Big Media, Little Media* (Washington, DC: Academy for Educational Development, 1973).

Schumacher, E. F., *Small is Beautiful: A Study of Economics as if People Mattered* (reprint of 1973 edn) (London: Blond and Briggs, 1976).

Sheffield, J. R. (ed.), *Education, Employment and Rural Development*, the proceedings of a conference held at Kericho, Kenya, September 1966 (Nairobi: East African Publishing House, 1967).

Sheffield, J. R. (ed.), *Road to the Village: Case Studies in African Community Development* (New York: African–American Institute, 1974).

Sheffield, J. R. and Diejomaoh, V. P., *Nonformal Education in African Development* (New York: African–American Institute, 1972).

Sheffield, J. R., Moris, J. R. and Hermans, J., *Agriculture in African Secondary Schools, Case Studies from Botswana, Kenya and Tanzania* (New York: African–American Institute, 1976).

Sierra Leone, *National Development Plan, 1974/5–1978/9* (Freetown: Ministry of Development and Economic Planning, 1974).

Sifuna, D. N., *Vocational Education in Schools – A Historical Survey of Kenya and Tanzania* (East African Literature Bureau, 1976).

Simkins, T., *Nonformal Education and Development*, Manchester University Monograph no. 8, 1977.

Singer, H. W., *The Strategy of International Development: Essays in the Economics of Backwardness* (London: Macmillan, 1975).

Solarin, T., *Mayflower: Story of a School* (Lagos: John Wise Publications, n.d.).

Spaulding, S., *Teacher Education: What Next?* (Paris: International Education Year Special Unit, UNESCO, 1970).

Spaulding, S., 'Educational Planning: Who Does What to Whom and with What Effect?', *Comparative Education*, vol. 13 no. 1 (March 1977).

Taylor, A. (ed.), *Educational and Occupational Selection in West Africa* (London: OUP, 1962).

Todaro, M. P., *Economic Development in the Third World* (London: Longman, 1977).

Trevaskis, G. A., *Inservice Teacher Training in English-Speaking Africa* (New York: Afro – Anglo – American Programme, 1969).

Tuquan, M. I., *Education, Society and Development in Under-developed Countries* (The Hague: Centre for the Study of Education in Changing Societies, 1975).

Twum-Barima, K., *Development of Agricultural Education* (Ghana Publishing Corp., 1978).

UN Economic Commission for Africa, *Development Education: Rural Development through Mass Media* (New York, 1974).

UN Economic Commission for Africa, *African agricultural development: Reflections on the Major Lines of Advance and the Barriers to Progress* (New York, 1966).

UN Economic Commission for Africa, *The Present Situation and Future Prospects* (New York, 1977).

UNESCO and UN Economic Commission for Africa, *Final Report*, Conference of African States on the Development of Education in Africa, Addis Ababa 15–25 May, 1961 (Paris: UNESCO, 1961).

UNESCO, *Economic and Social Aspects of Educational Planning* (Paris: UNESCO, 1964).

UNESCO, *Readings in the Economics of Education* (Paris: UNESCO, 1968).

UNESCO/UNICEF Co-operation Programme, *Basic Education in Eastern Africa*, Report on a seminar, Nairobi, Kenya, 1974 (Nairobi: UNESCO, 1974).

UNESCO, *Education in a Rural Environment* (Paris: UNESCO, 1974).

UNESCO, *International Standard Classification of Education* (abridged edition) (Paris: UNESCO, July 1975).

UNESCO, *The Experimental World Literacy Programme: A Critical Assessment* (Paris: UNESCO and UNDP, 1976).

UNESCO, *Final Report*, Conference of Ministers of Education of African Member States, Lagos, 27th January–4th February, 1976 (Paris: UNESCO, 1976).

UNESCO, *The Economics of New Educational Media: Present Status of Research and Trends* (Paris: UNESCO, 1977).

UNESCO, *Final Report*, International Conference on Education, Geneva, August–September 1977 (Paris: International Bureau of Education, UNESCO, 1977).

UNESCO, *Educational Reforms and Innovations in Africa* (Paris: UNESCO, 1978).

UNESCO/IIEP, *Fundamentals of Educational Planning*, a series of more than twenty booklets only some of which appear separately in this bibliography.

UNESCO Regional Office for Education in Africa, *Population, Education and Development in Africa South of the Sahara – a Selective Annotated Bibliography* (Dakar: UNESCO, 1978).

United National Independence Party, *Syllabuses on Political Education in Zambia* (Lusaka: Office of the Secretary-General of the Party, 1975).

Universities of Eastern Africa, *Strategies for Educational Change*, report of the Conference of the Universities of Eastern Africa on Teacher Education, Dar es Salaam, 1972 (Institute of Education, University of Dar es Salaam, 1972).

University of Sierra Leone, *All Our Future: Report of the Educational Review 1973–4* (Freetown: Government Printer, 1976).

Vaizey, J., *The Economics of Education* (London: Faber, 1962).

Van den Berghe, P. L. (ed.), *Africa, Social Problems of Change and Conflict* (San Francisco: Chandler Publishing Co., 1965).

Van Rensburg, P., *Education and Development in an Emerging Country* (Uppsala, 1967).

Van Rensburg, P., *Report from Swaneng Hill: Education and Employment in an African Country* (Stockholm: Almqvist and Wiksell, 1974).

Van Rensburg, P., *The Serowe Brigades – Alternative Education in Botswana* (London: Macmillan, 1979).

Vivian, S., *A Handbook on Inservice Teacher Training in Developing Countries of the Commonwealth* (London: Commonwealth Secretariat, 1977).

Wallerstein, I. (ed.), *Education and Social Change in the Colonial Situation* (Wiley and Sons, 1966).

Wandira, A., *The African University in Development* ( Johannesburg: Ravan Press, 1977).

Watkins, R. (ed.), *Inservice Training: Structure and Content* (London: Ward Lock, 1973).

Weiler, H. N. (ed.), *Education and Politics in Nigeria* (Freiburg: Verlag Romberg, 1964).

Weiler, H. N., 'New Directions in Educational Planning: Implications for Training', Supplement to *IIEP Bulletin*, December 1976.

Weiler, H. N., 'Education and Development: From the Age of Innocence to the Age of Scepticism', *Comparative Education*, vol. 14 no. 3 (October 1978).

West African Council for Teacher Education, *Report of the Second Conference on Primary Teacher Education and Rural Transformation, 1970* (University of Lagos, 1971).

Wheeler, A. C. R., *The Organisation of Educational Planning in Nigeria*, African Research Monographs no. 13 (Paris: UNESCO/IIEP, 1968).

Williams, P. (ed.), *The School Leaver in Developing Countries* (London University Institute of Education, 1976).

Williams, P. (ed.), *Prescription for Progress? A Commentary on the Education Policy of the World Bank* (London University Institute of Education, 1976).

Wood, A. W., *Informal Education and Development in Africa* (The Hague: Mouton, 1974).

World Bank, *The Problems of Urban Growth in Developing Countries*, World Bank Sector Working Paper (Paris).

World Bank, *Education: Sector Working Papers*, September 1971 and December 1974 (Washington, DC).

World Bank, *Rural Development: Sector Policy Paper* (Washington, DC, 1975).

World Bank, *The Assault on World Poverty* (Baltimore: Johns Hopkins University Press, 1975).

World Bank, *World Development Report 1979* (Washington, DC, 1979).

World Bank, *Rural Enterprise and Non-farm Employment.* (Washington, DC, 1978).

World Confederation of Organizations of the Teaching Profession, *Teacher Organizations and National Development*, Report of the Southern African WCOTP Regional Conference, Swaziland, 1972 (Washington: WCOTP, 1972).

# Index